The Economy of Salvation
According to the Early Church

A Biblical, Patristic, Liturgical, and Canonical Study

Revised and Extended Edition

HIS GRACE BISHOP RAPHAEL

The Economy of Salvation According to the Early Church:
A Biblical, Patristic, Liturgical, and Canonical Study

Translation from Arabic by St. Mary & St. Moses Abbey.

Designed & Published by:
St. Mary & St. Moses Abbey Press
101 S Vista Dr, Sandia, TX 78383
stmabbeypress.com

Dedication

I dedicate this work to the one I love, the Coptic Orthodox Church, at the doorsteps of whose love I was raised. I have loved its tunes, rites, asceticism and wounds suffered for the sake of Christ, its Bridegroom. And I have realized the beauty, precision, and authenticity of every teaching I have received from it since my infancy.

I, along with many, am a debtor to this Church which has endured from the hardness of its children more than what it has tasted from the bitterness of its enemies.

May you remain, my Church, strong and high among the churches unto the coming of your Bridegroom in His Second Coming.

Bishop Raphael

Contents

Foreword

His Grace Abba Raphael's Master's thesis, which is on the Economy of Salvation According to the Early Church from a Biblical, Patristic, liturgical and canonical standpoint, came at a time in which erroneous teachings are circulating; [teachings] which are foreign to our mother Church; teachings which are at odds with Holy Scriptures, the saintly Early Fathers, and all who have taught us throughout history. His Grace began responding to some of these erroneous teachings, which are strange to our Coptic Orthodox Church, and expounded at length the topic of "Economy of Salvation." His Grace made clear the following [points]:

1. The one catholic[1] apostolic Church had one doctrine on the understanding of the economy of salvation, from the descent of the Holy Spirit to the Council of Chalcedon in AD 451.
2. The Church believes that the entire human race (from the [immediate] sons of Adam to the end of the ages) inherited Adam's Original Sin, and in light of this truth, the economy of salvation was implemented.
3. The Coptic Orthodox Church preserved this faith and teaching, and has taught it to our present time.
4. The new notions, which snuck in from the Byzantine Church since the mid-past century, are considered contrary to what our Church, the glorious Coptic Orthodox Church, has received from the first catholic Church.
5. Therefore, His Grace will recount, with recourse to Holy Scriptures and the sayings of the Fathers, the story of creation from the beginning, the inheritance of the ancestral Original Sin of our father Adam and our mother Eve, and he will respond to the claims and erroneous

[1] i.e., universal.

> teachings concerning them, confirming that they are erroneous [indeed]...

For we have received this faith from:

1. The Fathers who studied and searched the Holy Scriptures with high aptitude.
2. [Those who] recorded the sayings of the saintly Early Fathers: Athanasius, Cyril, Dioscorus, etc.
3. Also the fathers of our time: Pope Kyrillos IV, Pope Kyrillos V, Pope Kyrillos VI, and Pope Shenouda III.
4. The recent holy councils and the sayings of the saintly Fathers.

Congratulations to His Grace Bishop Raphael for [completing] the Master's [degree], though he deserves a Doctorate [instead], and thanks to this concentrated effort. I am joyful about the project of publishing his thesis as a book, that it may be a precious reference for the [coming] generations.

May the Lord bless these pages for the readers, and may He reward His Grace Bishop Raphael for his fruitful effort in teaching, preserving the Orthodox faith, and responding to the claims and strange erroneous teachings.

Through the prayers of our beloved shepherd, His Holiness Pope Tawadros II, and the honorable metropolitans and bishops of the Church, may the grace of the Lord be upon us all,

Bishop Moussa

General Bishop of the Youth

Preface

By the grace of our Lord Jesus Christ, this thesis was submitted to Holy Sophia University, to receive a Master's degree in Theology. And because of the much clamor which is taking place as a result of this research, I have decided to offer it to the entire Coptic Orthodox Church, beginning with the clergy, servants, all who face the work of teaching in the Church, and ending by all the people, old and young.

The goal behind publishing this work is that it may be in the hands of every person that they may judge by themselves: Is this the author's personal opinion and personal understanding, or is it the understanding of the Early Church, which is recorded in the Holy Scriptures, the interpretations of the esteemed Fathers, and what we pray with in liturgical services?[2]

It will also become a referential document in the hands of the stewards of Church servants, in all ecclesiastical ranks, so that they may be, first [themselves], at ease about the integrity of what they have received, and that they may answer, with meekness, wisdom, and the fear of God, whoever is waging war against the Church, and accusing it of deviating from the mind[3] of the Fathers.

I offer this work as a gift to His Holiness Pope Tawadros II, all the honorable metropolitans and bishops of the holy Church, all the priests in Egypt and abroad,[4] all the devout servants, and all the people, hoping that the Lord of glory may preserve His holy Church without stumbling, till His coming, awaited with fervent longing.

Raphael, General Bishop

---

[2] Literally: in the liturgies.
[3] Or: understanding.
[4] Literally: the land of immigration.

Thanks and Appreciation

With my whole heart, I thank my good God for all the gifts He has granted us.

I thank my Church, the great, the witness of the sufferings of Christ, which has never refrained from offering pure teachings to its children.

I would like to thank those who have contributed to forming who I am and my directions in life: my father in the flesh, the late Deacon Erian Hakeim, and my spiritual father who has guided all the steps in my life, His Grace Bishop Moussa—may God protect him. I would also like to thank the late Pope Shenouda III who instilled in us from our infancy, the ardent love of, passion for, and loyalty to the Coptic Orthodox Church.

I would like to thank His Grace Bishop David, the representative of the president of Holy Sophia University, who encouraged me to complete and submit this research.

I would also like to offer a special thanks to Hegumen Abraham Azmi, the dean of Holy Sophia University, for all his effort, labor, and late night reviews of this thesis, word for word, with the addition of notes and ideas. I would also like to thank him for adjusting the academic side of the writing and for helping with all his academic experience.

Thanks to all who have contributed to collecting the texts of the Fathers, due to my lack of time as a consequence of bishopric responsibilities. They have provided the references and quotes, without however wishing to be acknowledged.

May all be blessed, through the intercessions of the Mother of God and all the saints, especially those who have preserved the faith, pure and upright: Pope Athanasius the Apostolic, St.

Cyril the Great, St. Severus, St. [John] Chrysostom, the great Cappadocian Fathers, St. Ambrose, St. Augustine, and all the fathers, especially my father, the pride of the Church, His Holiness Pope Tawadros II—may God preserve him.

Abstract

By the phrase "economy of salvation" is meant what God has done for humanity, from creation to eternal life.

The holy, catholic Church had, from the beginning, a holy and true understanding of this economy, and rejected any interpretation that was not in harmony with the true Faith.

Our Coptic Orthodox Church has preserved this upright Faith, from the time of the pure Apostles up to our present-day, using the same expressions of the Early Fathers, and their vocabulary, whether in explaining, teaching, or prayer in the liturgical services.

There is currently a trend spreading in Christendom, explaining the economy of salvation in a way contrary to what was settled upon in our Coptic Orthodox Church. And some believe that this trend of interpretation represents the true thought of the Early Fathers, and that what exists in our Coptic Orthodox Church is a flawed theology belonging to Western interpretations and the theology of the Middle Ages.

Therefore, going back to the primary sources of the Early Fathers' thought was necessary, with texts from Holy Scripture, liturgical prayers, and the canons of local and ecumenical Councils which are recognized by the Church—so that we may know the truth of what we have received from these other explanations.

Through research, the Coptic Orthodox Church was found to have preserved what it had received from the Fathers, of the divine truth and its interpretation, using the same expressions, terms and concepts, from the beginning and even to this day.

This explanation may be summarized by the following truths of the Faith:

The human being is the rational living being who is loved by God, and is the image of God, in intellect, holiness, freedom, will, and dominion. The human being is also the image of God in oneness with multiplicity.

When Adam sinned, all human beings contracted his sin, because he is the head of humanity and its root, and because of the principle of the oneness of the human race; therefore, human beings contracted sin, death and corruption. In this vein, the Fathers use expressions that denote our relationship with Adam's sin, like: "For that we sinned in Adam first, and trampled underfoot the Divine commandment;"[5] "We became partakers of Adam's offense, and because of his sins we were punished;"[6] "We offended him long ago both because of the transgression in Adam, and after that because of our own sin that tyrannizes us;"[7] "For the whole nature of man became guilty in the person of him who was first formed [Adam];"[8] "Pleasures and impurities rushed into the nature of the flesh, and a savage law sprang up in our members. So our nature contracted sin 'through the disobedience of the one man' (that is, Adam). That is how 'the many were made sinners'[9]—not because they transgressed along with Adam (since they did not yet exist), but because they were of his nature, which had fallen

---

[5] Cyril of Alexandria, *Commentary on the Gospel according to S. John* 2. (London, ENG: Walter Smith, 1885), 585.

[6] Cyril the Great, *Al-Sojoud Wa Al-Ibada Bi-Al Rouh Wa Al-Hak* [Worshipping and Serving in Spirit and in Truth], G.A. Ibrahim, trans. (Egypt: The Orthodox Center for Patristic Studies, 2017), 461. [Translated from Arabic text].

[7] Cyril of Alexandria, *Commentaries on Romans, 1-2 Corinthians, and Hebrews*, J.C. Elowsky, G.L. Bray, M. Glerup, and T.C. Oden, eds.; D.R. Maxwell, trans. (Downers Grove, IL: IVP Academic, 2022), 113.

[8] Cyril of Alexandria, *A Commentary upon the Gospel According to S. Luke* 1, R.P. Smith, trans. (Oxford, ENG: Oxford Press, 1859), 171.

[9] Romans 5:19.

under the law of sin."[10] Therefore, the entire human race was heading towards perdition and loss.

The good God, out of His love for humankind,[11] devised the economy of salvation. And this economy was [accomplished] by way of the incarnation of the only-begotten Son, the Logos, uniting with human nature [taken] from the Virgin St. Mary; becoming like us in everything, [yet He] alone was without sin. So He had His own body, which He used as an instrument for our salvation, in that:

1. He united His divinity with His humanity, so it [His humanity] became stronger than death. And it was befitting of Him to be a substitute and replacement for all of humankind; for He is above all. And He became the new Adam, in place of the first Adam, and a new Head for the new humankind [which is] in Him.
2. He taught humankind about the Father, taught us the way of godliness, and worked righteousness, so that we may receive in Him and through Him, righteousness, after we had contracted Adam's sin.
3. He tasted death in place of all, being a Firstborn, Head, Chief, New Root for humankind in Adam's place. And by this, He paid the debt which was owed by all, that is, death.
4. He defeated death and rose from the dead, so He healed us of death, and corruption of [our] nature which we contracted[12] in Adam.
5. He granted that we unite with Him, by faith, Baptism, and the Eucharist, so that we may receive in this unity

[10] Cyril of Alexandria, *Commentaries on Romans, 1-2 Corinthians, and Hebrews*, J.C. Elowsky, G.L. Bray, M. Glerup, and T.C. Oden, eds.; D.R. Maxwell, trans. (Downers Grove, IL: IVP Academic, 2022), 6–7.
[11] Literally: human beings or men.
[12] Or: suffered.

adoption by[13] God the Father, and receive in Christ what we lost in Adam, in that:

6. He made His [own] life flow into us, so we received in Him and through Him, life, righteousness, restoration of the divine image, the promise of the resurrection from the dead, and incorruptibility at His Second Coming.

Key Words or Phrases

The economy of salvation, ancestral sin, original sin, Adam's sin, the mind of the fathers, healing, redemption, the oneness of the human race, deification.

[13] Literally: to.

CHAPTER ONE

Introduction

Several theological, interpretational problems were stirred up in the Church, preoccupying many of the youth and [church] servants and leading to a sort of discord, skepticism and finger-pointing. Many have requested the declaration of the Church's opinion on these nuanced theological issues.

Because I consider myself a friend of many on both sides of the ideological conflict, and have had ample discussions with both sides, I have discovered common points in understanding on some of the raised issues. Therefore, I have taken it upon myself to attempt the role of ideological reconciliation. The fruit was this humble study, which I place in the hands of the mighty God and before the beloved Coptic Orthodox Church, that it may help the priests and the servants of the word in understanding these issues.

Some church servants and youth have been preoccupied with some doctrinal discussions on social media. And some have adopted new ideas about the explanation of the economy of salvation, based on certain studies, research, and scientific articles, which were done by some of the educated, irrespective of whether these were of the children of the Coptic Orthodox Church or other churches. They accuse the Church of wallowing in—of having adopted—Western theology and the theology of the Middle Ages in Europe, and that we, in the Coptic Orthodox Church, currently follow the teaching of Anselm,[14] the Archbishop of Canterbury in the Middle Ages.

Yet others forcefully adhere to what we have received from our saintly Fathers, being certain of the validity, soundness, and orthodoxy of the teachings of the Church from the era of the Apostles and Saint Mark the Evangelist to the era of His Holiness Pope Tawadros, passing by, of course, the teacher of generations, His Holiness Pope Shenouda III.

As some have tried to sow doubts about the teachings of the Fathers which were handed down to the Church, this places upon all the responsibility of searching in the treasures of the Early Fathers, in a faithful and pure spirit, unaffected by the thoughts of others; that the Church may be filled with the richness of the Fathers' interpretations, in light of the Holy Scriptures, the Coptic liturgies, the Fathers who are considered pillars, and the canons of the ecumenical and local Councils which are affirmed by the one catholic Church.

The topics of the contention are many and branched. You could easily, however, discover the beginning of the thread, because an error necessarily leads to an error, and so the chain of errors continues, linked and connected. Had it been left like this, the whole of the Christian faith would have deviated into extremely strange currents, away from the mind of our Lord Jesus Christ.

---

[14] Anselm, Bishop of Canterbury (AD 1033–1109) was a theologian and philosopher, of French origin. He had an important influence on subsequent thinkers, including Thomas Aquinas and William of Ockham, and on the subsequent doctrine of the Roman Catholic Church in various aspects. Anselm passed away in Canterbury in AD 1109 and was buried in the Cathedral there.

The Purpose of the Research

This research addresses the following hypotheses:

- ❖ That the one catholic Church in the first centuries, in the period from Pentecost on the fiftieth day to the time before the schism of AD 451 in Chalcedon, the Church had one specific doctrine regarding the understanding of the economy of salvation which was accomplished by the Lord Christ.
- ❖ That the first catholic Church taught that the human race had inherited Adam's Original Sin without partaking in the act.
- ❖ That the implementation of the economy of salvation cannot be understood except in light of understanding the truth of the inheritance of Adam's sin by all of the human race. "Therefore, as through one man's offense judgement came to all men, resulting in condemnation, even so through one Man's righteous act the free gift came to all men, resulting in justification of life."[15]
- ❖ That the Coptic Orthodox Church has preserved through the ages what it has received from the first catholic Church regarding the doctrine of salvation. There is a direct and clear connection between what the first catholic Church taught and what the Coptic Church currently teaches, which has not changed through the ages.
- ❖ The new notions concerning the doctrine of salvation, which have infiltrated into the Coptic Orthodox Church from some theologians in the Byzantine Church since the middle of the past century, are considered

[15] Romans 5:18.

contrary to what the Coptic Orthodox Church has received from the first catholic Church.

Therefore, the aforementioned hypotheses will be studied to arrive at the conclusion of whether they are valid or invalid, entirely or partially. The purpose is to confirm whether the Coptic Church has preserved until today what the one catholic Church taught from its outset after the resurrection of Christ to the time before the Council of Chalcedon.

The Question of the Research

The principal question of the research is the [following]:

> Has the Coptic Orthodox Church preserved until today what it received from the one catholic Church, from the establishment of the Church by the descent of the Holy Spirit on Pentecost to the time before the schism of AD 451 in Chalcedon?

This principal question is accompanied by the following sub-questions:

- Did we inherit Adam's sin or only its consequences, that is, death and corruption?
- What is the difference between the Eastern and Western theology, and when did the disagreement emerge? Also, how were the East (Constantinople) and the West (Rome) in communion together until the 11th century (AD 1054)?
- Was death, which befell Adam and his seed, a result or a punishment from God? Does God really punish the wicked? Did He create Hades and Hell or are they merely a psychological state as a consequence of the separation from God and His glory?

- Had Adam not sinned, would the only-begotten Son have become incarnate?
- Is it wrong to say, "Christ died on our behalf," and use instead, "died for our sake"? What is the difference? Is the idea that Christ died "on our behalf," "instead of us," and "in our place," a Western idea, which is not accepted by the Fathers of the East? And is penal substitution the last of the Arian and Nestorian strongholds, as they say?
- Subsequently, what is the meaning of "the Redeemer"? And "the ransom"? And what was the price paid off to purchase us? To whom was the price paid off? What is the debt we owed? How did the Lord Christ pay it off by His cross? What is the meaning of, "who through the eternal Spirit offered Himself without spot to God?"[16]
- Has the West truly adopted the judicial theory in explaining the economy of salvation? Did the Fathers of the East reject it? Did the word "justice" not appear at all in the writings of the Eastern Fathers, as they claim? Are the writings of the Western Fathers devoid of the healing aspect of the cross of Christ and His precious salvation?
- Were all human beings crucified with Christ on Golgotha? What is the meaning of, "the death of all was completed in the lordly body?"[17,18] What is the meaning of, "I have trodden the winepress alone, and from the peoples no one was with Me?"[19]
- Did all human beings rise with Him? Did they ascend with Him, and sit with Him at the right hand of the Father? Including the unbelievers, atheists, and the

---

[16] Hebrews 9:14.
[17] In Arabic text: in the body of the Lord.
[18] Saint Athanasius, *On the Incarnation*, J. Behr, trans. (Yonkers, NY: SVS Press, 2011), 71.
[19] Isaiah 63:3.

ungodly [human beings]? Did we all ascend with Him, or did He carry up our first-fruits to heaven?

- What do the Fathers mean by their emphasis on the expression, "His own body, His own temple, and His instrument"?
- What does "our unity in Christ" mean? Do we become God, gods exactly like Him, deified or what?
- What is meant by "gathering all in Christ"?
- What is the value of the Old Testament sacrifices? Do they have a connection with the sacrifice of the Lord Christ on the cross?
- What does "and without shedding of blood there is no remission"[20] mean? Why shedding of blood? And why death, to begin with, as a means for forgiveness?

These inquiries, and others, are answered by those influenced by the new theology (neo-patristics, liberal theology, and others) in a way that is at odds with the way of those who adhere to the traditional interpretation stored in the conscience of the Church. The more serious problem is that those with new ideas have adopted a movement to sow doubt in the firmness of the Church, and its faithfulness to Christ, the Holy Scriptures, and the sound orthodox faith. Therefore, I am making a painstaking effort in this research, by the grace of our Lord Jesus Christ, as much as possible, to quote texts from Scripture, the interpretations of the Fathers, and the liturgical texts, with no partiality; so that we may realize, together, what the upright faith is, concerning some of these inquiries that are related to the explanation of the economy of salvation. The current purpose of this research is to prove that there are multiple ways to explain the salvific economy, which are complementary ways,

[20] Hebrews 9:22.

and not at odds nor conflicting. I specifically mean: the healing and ontological aspect along with the penal and judicial aspect.

The Scope of the Research

- ❖ This research studies the doctrine of the economy of salvation that was taught by the first catholic Church, only in the period from its establishment on Pentecost in the Church's first year, up to the schism of the Council of Chalcedon in AD 451.
- ❖ This research studies what the first catholic Church taught through Biblical texts, the interpretations of the Fathers, who are considered pillars in the catholic Church before the schism, liturgical texts and the canons of the ecumenical and local Councils.
- ❖ This research does not study any views of any specific church, even if it is a sister church of the Coptic Church, after the schism which took place in AD 451.
- ❖ This research does not deal with comparisons between what the Coptic Church teaches and what other churches teach, except for the Byzantine Church, for I hypothesize that some of its theologians have recently introduced teachings contrary to the doctrine of the first catholic Church.
- ❖ This research does not address other theological studies related to the doctrine of Baptism, or the Eucharist, or the role of grace and works, or the role of the Holy Spirit in the economy of salvation.

As **St. Athanasius the Apostolic** said:

> And, in short, the achievements of the Savior, effected by his incarnation, are of such a kind and number that if anyone should wish to expound them he would be like

> those who gaze at the expanse of the sea and wish to count its waves. For as one cannot take in all the waves with one's eyes, for those coming on elude the perception of one who tries, so also one who would comprehend all the achievements of Christ in the body is unable to take in the whole, even by reckoning them up, for those that elude his thought are more than he thinks he has grasped.[21]

Therefore, it was necessary that the domains of the research be limited to [the following]:

1. Who is man[22] and what is his nature? Also, what is meant by his "being the image of God"?
2. What is the effect of Adam's sin on humankind?
3. How did the Lord Christ, in His holy incarnation, treat this problem?

These domains will be studied by comparing what the Coptic Orthodox Church has preserved with the new heresies that have emerged in the Byzantine Church by some of its neo-theologians. Some [people] are trying to subtly introduce these heretical ideas into the Coptic Orthodox Church.

Summary

- I have not addressed the details of the theology of Baptism, nor the Eucharist, nor the importance of works for salvation, nor the role of the Holy Spirit in our salvation, nor many other aspects which are not the subject of this research.
- I have limited the explanation to texts from Holy Scripture, the interpretations of the Fathers, who are

---

[21] Saint Athanasius, *On the Incarnation*, J. Behr, trans. (Yonkers, NY: SVS Press, 2011), 107.

[22] Also: the human being.

considered pillars in the catholic Church up to the era before Chalcedon, the Coptic Divine Liturgy and daily Psalmody, and the canons of the ecumenical and local Councils addressing the domain of this research.

- Because the economy of salvation cannot be understood apart from the study of the inheritance of Adam's sin, as can be inferred from the Scriptures, the sayings of the Early Fathers, and the liturgies, it was necessary that the research on the economy of salvation include a section on the inheritance of Adam's sin. It is understood, to begin, that the inheritance of Original Sin, that is, our first father Adam's sin, does ***not*** mean that we partook with him in the eating, for we did not yet exist. We were, however, in him, that is, in his loins, for we are his seed. The inheritance of sin does not mean that sin is a substance which is mixed with human nature, but in the simplicity of the Fathers' expression, that human nature sinned, all of it, in the person of Adam who sinned.
- The work of redemption by the cross of our Lord Jesus Christ is a very great work, which is multifaceted and can accommodate many kinds of complementary explanations. What has been presented of explanations throughout history, in the East and West, may be grasped in a complementary way, rather than a conflictive way, except for the deviant ways of explaining which the catholic Church rejected from the beginning.

Illustrative Background

The Historical Sequence of Christian Thought

In preparing for this study, a research of the Biblical, Patristic, liturgical and canonical basis of the economy of salvation which the Lord, Redeemer and Savior Jesus accomplished, it was necessary, in the beginning, to review the historical sequence of Christian thought in the following respect:[23]

1. The Fathers of the first centuries explained the economy of salvation as a great mystery, the understanding of whose aspects is limitless. In the course of their exegesis came all the terms of healing, renewal, restoring the human being to his first rank, paying off the debt, suffering punishment instead of men, the fulfillment of the judgment in Christ on the cross in place of all, restoring the divine image in man, restoring our adoption by God the Father, restoring life, and the promise of eternity and incorruptibility to those who unite with Christ...
2. The Church in the first five centuries, that is before Chalcedon, was only one catholic Church; the faith and its explanation were shared between the East and West. What is meant by the one catholic Church is that it was *the* Church spread abroad throughout the entire world, bearing the same one faith. In the beginning, it had five great apostolic centers, that is, the churches of Jerusalem, Antioch, Alexandria, Rome, and then Constantinople.
3. In the Council of Chalcedon, [the Churches of] Alexandria and Antioch were separated [from the rest of the Churches], through the unwarranted excommunication and exile of St. Dioscorus. The Churches which did not accept Chalcedon were persecuted. This persecution is clearly seen in the biographies of Severus of Antioch and Jacob Baradaeus, for example.
4. After the departure of the Coptic Church in Chalcedon, the non-Chalcedonian Churches gave attention to

[23] "Orthodox Church History," *Las Vegas Orthodox*, 30 Dec. 2016, https://lasvegasorthodox.com/orthodox-library/orthodox-church-history/.

shepherding their people and keeping them steadfast in the holy faith which was handed down to them by the saints Athanasius, Cyril, Dioscorus, Severus of Antioch and other Fathers of the catholic Church from before the Schism. They adopted the view of preserving the faith without adding to, removing from, or innovating it.

5. After the Council of Chalcedon, there appeared in the East (Constantinople, Greece, and the churches affiliated with them) theologians who innovated and added to the explanation of the theological basis of salvation, with the addition of their own opinions, theologians like Gregory Palamas, John of Damascus, Simeon the New Theologian, and others.
6. There also appeared in the West (Rome and the churches affiliated with it) other theologians who had their own opinions on the theological explanation [of salvation], like Thomas Aquinas, Anselm of Canterbury and others.
7. A gap in interpretation occurred between the East (the Byzantines and their followers) and the West (the Latins and their followers), which eventually led to the Great Schism between the East and West in AD 1054 (eleventh century).
8. In the five centuries after the schism that occurred between the [Roman] Catholics and the Greeks, and until the Protestant reformation[24] movement, that is, from the eleventh century to the sixteenth century, the [Roman] Catholic Church inclined in its interpretation of the economy of salvation to focusing on the judicial aspect, perhaps because of the intertwining of the kings' politics and the management of conflicts and wars with the church. This implanted in the general Christian consciousness the idea of the angry God who is difficult

[24] Literally: protestation.

to appease, and it presented to the Christian world the Sacraments and the Priesthood as mediators to grant the appeasement of God to sinners. The healing aspect became very indistinct in their explanation.

9. Martin Luther, John Calvin, and those after them came and adopted this same theological vision of the angry God whose wrath cannot be stopped. Luther, however, found in "the righteousness of Christ by faith" the escape to break out of the oppressive authority of the clergy (in his view). And hereby was born "the erroneous interpretations of the penal substitution."
10. With the Bolshevik Revolution (AD 1917), some Russian theologians and an Eastern congregation migrated to [the United States of] America, and there they found these "erroneous interpretations of the penal substitution," which annul the meaning of the Church, the Mysteries, and the Priesthood, presenting God as an angry [Person] who is difficult to appease and does not find repose except by seeing the blood of His Son shed on the cross. The principal problem is the conflict between justice and mercy in God, that the Son, the Logos, was incarnate to resolve God's problem, and that after the cross, there is no need for anything except faith alone in the blood of Christ; so there is no need for Baptism except as a symbol, nor for the Eucharist except as a mere memorial. The reaction of these [Eastern] theologians was to forcefully focus on the healing and restorative aspect of the Mystery of the economy of salvation. They considered the judicial aspect in the interpretation of the economy of salvation a Western deviation, of which the theology of the East must be purified. They called the period prior to their exegetical theological intervention "the Period of Babylonian

Captivity," and founded a new ideological synthesis which they called "Neopatristic Synthesis."[25]

One of the founders of this movement was Georges Florovsky, a Russian who became the dean of Saint Vladimir's Seminary. Also of the notable members of the movement are John Meyendorff and John Romanides.[26] The goal of this ideological movement was to go back to the thought[27] of the Early Fathers. However, what happened in reality, unfortunately, was the synthesis of new ideas and new answers to theological issues, often centering around [the view] that God is good and does not punish, and consequently, there is no Hell nor Hades in a literal sense, that there is no punishment befalling Adam, there is no inheritance of Ancestral Sin, and the death of Christ was not instead of man's death but merely out of love alone, and that the economy of salvation, in their view, is only the restoration of the divine image in the human being and the deification of the human being (in a radical ideology asserting that, truly, we become gods).

Going back, in an unbiased spirit, is necessary, to search in the writings of the Early Fathers of the catholic Church before the Schism, with no predetermined ideas, to learn whether what the new theologians teach truly is what the Early Fathers taught; and whether our Coptic Church has also entered into "Babylonian captivity".

Therefore, with all scientific faithfulness, I wished to discuss these issues, so that there may be in the hands of every priest and every faithful servant the truth of the

[25] Horujy, S.S., "The Concept of Neopatristic Synthesis at a New Stage," *Russian Studies in Philosophy*, 57.1 (2019): 17–39.

[26] "History of Eastern Orthodox Theology in the 20th Century," https://en.wikipedia.org/wiki/History_of_Eastern_Orthodox_theology_in_the_20th_century. Accessed in June 2022.

[27] Also: ideology, mind.

faith which we received from our faithful Church, corroborated with Biblical, Patristic, and liturgical texts, and the canons of the ecumenical and local Councils.

The Immovable Faith of the Church

This research has no intention of rediscovering the faith of the Coptic Orthodox Church, nor is it to recommend the holding of councils to put in place new definitions[28] of the faith. For the matter of the faith is immovable "and was once for all delivered to the saints."[29] The Coptic Orthodox Church has preserved the faith it received from the Lord, which Saint Mark the Evangelist preached and the fathers preserved, in godliness, spirituality, and the fear of God, throughout the generations.

Saint Athanasius the Apostolic says:

> Let us also examine the tradition, teaching, and faith of the catholic Church from the beginning, which is nothing other than what the Lord gave, and the Apostles preached, and the Fathers preserved. On this the Church is founded, and whoever falls away from it can no longer be nor be called a Christian.[30]

The Existence of More than One Explanation

The passage of Christianity through twenty-one centuries, naturally led to the accumulation of many theological experiences in interpretation on the level of the churches of the whole world. Many theories appeared in history explaining the

---

[28] Also: specifications.

[29] Jude 1:3.

[30] Athanasius the Great and Didymus the Blind, *Works on the Spirit*, DelCogliano, A. Radde-Gallwitz, and L. Ayres, trans. (Yonkers, NY: SVS Press, 2011), 96.

Christian faith, and the matter became very complicated, which is of interest to no one except the specialized scholar who analyzes every idea and is able to follow its author and the evolution of the idea and its impact on the Christian thought in general. The schools of thought have become interwoven, and you find yourself standing before a whirlpool of ideas[31] whose origin you do not know nor to whom they belong. There are some ideas belonging to Protestant interpretations, and other ideas belonging to the Western theological vision; others are adopted by the school of liberal theology, others express the view of the Neopatristic school, and other ideas of yet other schools of thought. Each idea has its own luster, philosophy, proofs, defenders and supporters. And it may be an idea that is sound in relation to the faith, amidst many erroneous ideas; or, on the contrary, there may be one erroneous, deviant idea amidst many sound ideas; or it may have some truth. [All of this] makes the person incapable of distinguishing between what is true and false. Therefore, it is necessary that we go back to the simplicity of the faith declared in the Scriptures, which was explained by the Early Fathers, in purity and unanimity. And what is more important is that they prayed with it in the liturgical services.[32] We must, foremost, adhere to that with which the Church speaks to God, in the liturgical prayers, regardless of the teachings and writings of the scholars[33] and the prudent.

The Interpretations of the Early Fathers

Each of the early Christian writers, and the Church Fathers of old even up to this time, expressed, in his particular explanation and personal vision, an aspect of the redemptive work of Christ on the cross. Each of them reflected, explaining what he

[31] Also: thoughts.
[32] "Liturgical services" is literally "liturgies."
[33] Also: scientists.

experienced, tasted and encountered in the work of Christ, without ignoring or despising the interpretations and explanations of the other Fathers who are considered pillars.

The Fathers Considered Pillars in the Coptic Orthodox Church

1. The Apostolic Fathers:[34] Clement of Rome, Polycarp of Smyrna, Ignatius of Antioch, Papias.
2. Ante-Nicene Fathers: Irenaeus, Justin Martyr, Clement of Alexandria, St. Peter the Seal of the Martyrs, Pope Dionysius of Alexandria, St. Didymus the Blind, Cyprian of Carthage.
3. Nicene Fathers: Athanasius the Apostolic, Pope Alexander [I of Alexandria].
4. Post-Nicene Fathers: St. Theophilus of Alexandria, St. Cyril the Great, St. Gregory of Nazianzus, St. Basil of Caesarea, St. Augustine of Hippo, St. John Chrysostom, St. Jerome, St. Ambrose of Milan, St. Severus of Antioch, St. Dioscorus, St. Gregory of Nyssa, St. Gregory the Armenian.

The Fathers respected the writings of those before them, benefited from them, built upon their foundation, but they of course excluded what did not agree with the teaching of the catholic Church.

St. Cyril the Great says:

> I think that those who are engaged with the Holy Scriptures need to approach all writings that

---

[34] The Apostolic Fathers are the second generation after the era of the Apostles which ended by the departure of Saint John the Apostle in AD 100. They were the writers of the first and second centuries, and are considered the early teachers after the Apostles.

> might be good, noble and free from harm. In this way, by gathering what many people have observed from various points of view about the same thing, and by bringing them all to bear on one point, they will climb to a good measure of knowledge. They will imitate the bee, a wise worker, and build the sweet honeycomb of the Spirit.[35]

The great **St. Athanasius the Apostolic** says:

> I wrote this brief explanation according to what I have learned. As for you, I hope that you accept this explanation, not as a teaching exhaustive and complete in itself, but as a beginning which you need to complete relying on texts from the Scriptures and the Psalms.[36]

St. Cyril the Great also says: "A man must interpret the Holy Scriptures though others have done so already."[37]

The Fathers took pride in their own Fathers who raised them and whose disciples they were. In this [respect] **St. Cyril the Great** says: "Through the grace of our Savior I always was orthodox and I was reared also by an orthodox father."[38]

The personal experience of these Fathers does not dissociate nor part from the collective experience of the Church

---

[35] Cyril of Alexandria, *Commentary on John* 1, J.C. Elowsky, T.C. Oden, and G.L. Bray, eds.; D.R. Maxwell, trans. (Downers Grove, IL: IVP Academic, 2015), 5.
[36] Athanasius the Apostolic, *Al-Rasa'il Aan Al-Rouh Al-Kudos* [Letters on the Holy Spirit], M. Tawadros and N. Abdel Shaheed, trans. (Egypt: The Orthodox Center for Patristic Studies, 2018), 179. [Translated from Arabic text].
[37] Cyril of Alexandria, *Commentary of Isaiah*. In *Patrologia graeca* 71.12A, J.-P. Migne, ed. (Paris, 1857–1886) (henceforth cited as PG) [Translated from Arabic text]. Cf. Cyril of Alexandria, *Commentary on Isaiah* 1, R.C. Hill, trans. (Brookline, MA: Holy Cross Orthodox Press, 2008), 17.
[38] St. Cyril of Alexandria, *Letters 1-50*, J.I. McEnerney, trans. (Washington, D.C.: The Catholic University of America Press, 1987), 132.

throughout the ages, in coming in contact with the cross and in understanding the salvific work of Christ. Therefore, the catholic orthodox Church did not accept, from the beginning, any view that was not unanimously agreed upon,[39] and it understood the interpretations of the Fathers in a complementary rather than conflicting way. The understanding of the great divine work must emerge from the faith of the Church and its experiential life, which is tasted in the liturgies and the life of the Fathers and their spiritual experience, in harmony with the divine revelations contained in the Holy Scriptures.

The Holy Scriptures were the foundational reference for the Fathers' explanation of the whole faith which we received from the saints.

St. Irenaeus says:

> [We] being most properly assured that the Scriptures are indeed perfect, since they were spoken by the Word of God and His Spirit; but we, inasmuch as we are inferior to, and later in existence than, the Word of God and His Spirit, are on that very account destitute of the knowledge of His mysteries.[40]

---

[39] "For it seemed good to the Holy Spirit, and to us" (Acts 15:28).
"And the things that you have heard from me among many witnesses, commit these to faithful men who will be able to teach others also" (2 Timothy 2:2).
"Or did the word of God come originally from you? Or was it you only that it reached?" (1 Corinthians 14:36).

[40] Irenaeus *Against Heresies*. In *Ante-Nicene Fathers* 1, P. Schaff, ed. (Peabody, MA: Hendrickson Publishers, 2012), 399.

St. Athanasius the Apostolic also says: "For the tokens of truth are more exact as drawn from Scripture, than from other sources."[41]

St. John Chrysostom says: "In the holy Scriptures it is impossible without loss to pass by one jot or one tittle, we must search into all. For they all are uttered by the Holy Spirit, and nothing useless is written in them."[42]

Therefore, it is a gross error that the salvific work of Christ be viewed from a single aspect and a single point of view, apart from the collective experience of the Church and the extensive interpretational insights of the Early Fathers. There are many aspects revealed to us by these. For the road to approach this mystery, and to try to understand it, is not singular, but is a road that has many entries, or, rather, [there are] various roads through all of which we could approach, with reverence, the understanding and realization of the mystery of Christ.

It is worthy of noting that when **St. Athanasius the Apostolic** wished to explain the mystery of the incarnation, he wrote a 57-chapter-long book, concluding it with the following indicative words, that it is impossible to explain in totality the mystery of the incarnation, its end is impossible to reach, and its explanation cannot be limited to a single aspect:

> And, in short, the achievements of the Savior, effected by his incarnation, are of such a kind and number that if anyone should wish to expound them he would be like those who gaze at the expanse of the sea and wish to count its waves. For as one cannot take in all the waves with one's eyes,

---

[41] Athanasius *Defense of the Nicene Definition*. In *Nicene and Post-Nicene Fathers: Second Series* 4, P. Schaff, ed. (Peabody, MA: Hendrickson Publishers, 2012), 172 (henceforth cited as NPNF²).

[42] John Chrysostom *Homilies on St. John* 36.1 (NPNF¹ 14:125).

> for those coming on elude the perception of one who tries, so also one who would comprehend all the achievements of Christ in the body is unable to take in the whole, even by reckoning them up, for those that elude his thought are more than he thinks he has grasped. Therefore it is better not to seek to speak of the whole, of which one cannot even speak of a part, but rather to recall one thing, and leave the whole for you to marvel at. For all are equally marvelous, and wherever one looks, seeing there the divinity of the Word, one is struck with exceeding awe.[43]

In addition, understanding the divine work requires a pure soul, an undefiled spirit, and a humble heart, as **St. Athanasius the Apostolic** said:

> But in addition to the study and true knowledge of the Scriptures, there is needed a good life and a pure soul and the virtue which is according to Christ, so that the mind, guided by it, may be able to attain and comprehend what it desires, as far as it is possible for human nature to learn about the God Word. Without a pure mind and a life modeled on the saints, no one can comprehend the words of the saints. For just as, if someone would wish to see the light of the sun, he would certainly wipe and clean his eyes, purifying himself to be almost like that which he desires, so that as the eye thus becomes light it may see the light of the sun; or just as if someone would wish to see a city or a country, he would certainly go to that

[43] Saint Athanasius, *On the Incarnation*, J. Behr, trans. (Yonkers, NY: SVS Press, 2011), 107.

> place for the sight; in the same way, one wishing to comprehend the mind of the theologians must first wash and cleanse his soul by his manner of life, and approach the saints themselves by the imitation of their works, so that being with them in the conduct of a common life, he may understand also the things revealed to them, and thenceforth, as joined to them, may escape the peril of the sinners and their fire on the day of judgement, but may receive what has been laid up for the saints in the kingdom of heaven, "which eye has not seen, nor ear heard, nor have they entered into the heart of man,"[44] whatsoever things have been prepared for those who live a virtuous life and love the God and Father, in Christ Jesus our Lord, through whom and with whom, to the Father with the Son himself in the Holy Spirit, be honor and power and glory to the ages of ages. Amen[45]

Faith is a Mystery Uncontainable

Throughout the history of the Christian thought, the Christian theologians tried to explain the mystery of salvation, through many of the various exegetical methods, having as their goal the interpretation of this great Mystery, which is incomprehensible in its entirety. The catholic orthodox Church accepted most of their explanations, but some of them were not acceptable.

In this framework, we may consider that any interpretational insight could not be without truth, as long as it

---

[44] 1 Corinthians 2:9.

[45] Saint Athanasius, *On the Incarnation*, J. Behr, trans. (Yonkers, NY: SVS Press, 2011), 110.

is in harmony with the divine revelation of the Holy Scriptures, what is handed down by the Fathers, our liturgical prayers, the Creed, and the canons of the local and ecumenical Councils accepted by our Church. This is especially [the case] because the salvific work of our Lord Jesus Christ is transcendent, being impossible to grasp and understand in its entirety. In truth it is a mystery,[46] and the mystery is unsearchable, but a special grace is needed in order to comprehend even a part of its entirety.

"That you, being rooted and grounded in love, may be able to comprehend with all the saints what is the width and length and depth and height—to know the love of Christ which passes knowledge; that you may be filled with all the fullness of God. Now to Him who is able to do exceedingly abundantly above all that we ask or think, according to the power that works in us."[47]

"For who has known the mind of the LORD? Or who has become His counselor?"[48]

"Oh, the depth of the riches both of the wisdom and knowledge of God! How unsearchable are His judgements and His ways past finding out!"[49]

Therefore, no single explanation can encompass it [the salvific work of our Lord Jesus Christ] completely nor any one person, whoever one may be. The Mystery of the incarnation and of redemption, the human being will never finish understanding. But to try to understand is like getting close to the bush whose branches were burning with fire; getting close is prohibited unless we take off the sandals of human

---

[46] It is said of the deacons: "Holding the mystery of the faith with a pure conscience" (1 Timothy 3:9).
[47] Ephesians 3:17–20.
[48] Romans 11:34.
[49] Romans 11:33.

understanding.[50] It is like getting close to the dark cloud,[51] trying to see the invisible, containing the infinite, putting a beginning for the One without beginning, comprehending the incomprehensible, searching the unsearchable, and putting limits to the immeasurable. This is impossible, of course; we could, however, enter into this knowledge through a special grace from God, which is given to the pure of heart[52] and the humble.[53]

The Holy Scriptures have revealed to us a limited amount of this knowledge, appropriate for our human capacity, and though God revealed Himself to us in the Person of His only-begotten Son, our Lord Jesus Christ,[54] He, nevertheless, remains, while known, unknowable in His perfection; as the blessed Paul the Apostle said, "Oh, the depth of the riches both of the wisdom and knowledge of God! How unsearchable are His judgements and His ways past finding out! 'For who has known the mind of the Lord? Or who has become His counselor?'"[55]

Or as Zophar the Naamathite inquired, "Can you search out the deep things of God? Can you find out the limits of the

---

[50] See Exodus 3:5.
[51] "Then Solomon spoke: 'The LORD said he would dwell in the dark cloud'" (1 Kings 8:12).
[52] "Blessed are the pure in heart, for they shall see God" (Matthew 5:8). "The secret of the LORD is with those who fear Him, and He will show them His covenant" (Psalm 25:14).
[53] "At that time Jesus answered and said, 'I thank You, Father, Lord of heaven and earth, that You have hidden these things from the wise and prudent and have revealed them to babes'" (Matthew 11:25).
[54] "God, who at various times and in various ways spoke in time past to the fathers by the prophets, has in these last days spoken to us by His Son" (Hebrews 1:1–2). "And in the last days You manifested Yourself to us, who were sitting in darkness and the shadow of death, through Your only-begotten Son, our Lord, God, and Savior Jesus Christ" (The Divine Liturgy According to St. Basil – Liturgy of the Faithful).
[55] Romans 11:33–34.

Almighty? They are higher than heaven—what can you do? Deeper than Sheol—what can you know?"[56]

We, as it were, see in a mirror now; we have *some* understanding, but not *all* understanding. "For now we see in a mirror, dimly, but then face to face. Now I know in part, but then I shall know just as I also am known."[57]

St. Cyril the Great says:

> Is not therefore the mystery profound? Must we not own that the dispensation is more than language can describe? What doubt can there be of this? Let us therefore, as we offer Him our praise, repeat that which was sung by the Psalmist's harp; "How great are Your works, O Lord! in wisdom You have made them all."[58,59]

The Conceptual Framework of the Research

The Fathers were accustomed, when explaining the economy of salvation, to begin with Creation's existence out of nothing. The same course is adopted by the Coptic Divine Liturgy:

- "O God, the Great, the Eternal, who formed man in incorruption."[60]
- "Who formed us, created us, and placed us in the Paradise of joy."[61]

---

[56] Job 11:7–8.
[57] 1 Corinthians 13:12.
[58] Psalm 104:24.
[59] Cyril of Alexandria, *A Commentary upon the Gospel According to S. Luke* 2, R.P. Smith, trans. (Oxford, ENG: At the University Press, 1859), 718.
[60] The Divine Liturgy According to St. Basil – Prayer of Reconciliation.
[61] The Divine Liturgy According to St. Basil – Agios (Holy).

- "Who for the sake of goodness only brought man into existence out of nonexistence, and put him in the Paradise of joy."[62]
- "You, as a Lover of Mankind, have created me, as man.... Because of the multitude of Your tender mercies, You have brought me into existence when I was not."[63]
- "You are He who has created the heavens and that which is in the heavens, the earth and everything that is therein: the seas, the rivers, the springs, the lakes, and that which is in all of them. You are He who created man according to Your own image and after Your likeness. And You have created everything through Your Wisdom—Your true Light, Your only-begotten Son, our Lord, God, Savior, and King of us all, Jesus Christ."[64]

Creation Out of Nothing

God made all of creation out of nothing; then He made the human being distinct from all the irrational creation,[65] that he may have dominion over this creation,[66] to employ it for His service,[67] for the human being is the only rational creature among all the corporeal creation.

---

[62] The Divine Liturgy According to St. Gregory – Prayer of Reconciliation.

[63] The Divine Liturgy According to St. Gregory – Agios (Holy).

[64] The Divine Liturgy According to St. Cyril – Anaphora.

[65] "I will praise You, for **I am fearfully and wonderfully made**; marvelous are Your works, and that my soul knows very well" (Psalm 139:14).

[66] "He who formed everything by His Word, and by Your Wisdom You made man, that he may be chief over the creatures You Yourself made, and that he may manage the world in holiness and righteousness" (The Coptic Divine Liturgy According to St. Basil – Prayer of Veil). [Translated from Arabic text].

[67] "You have raised heaven as a roof for me, and established the earth for me to walk upon. For my sake, You have bound the sea. For my sake, You have manifested the nature of animals. You have subjected all things under my feet. You have not left me in need of any of the works of Your honor" The Divine Liturgy According to St. Gregory – Agios (Holy).

The mystery of this great grace, and this wonderful distinction, is that the human being is made in the image of God and according to His likeness.[68] Therefore, the value of the human being to God is like the value and love [you have] for your son in your heart as compared with the value and esteem [you have] for your luxury car, your house or all your possessions.

Who is the Human Being?

To understand the dimensions, depths and greatness of what God did for us, in His only-begotten Son, our Lord Jesus Christ, through the Holy Spirit, in the economy of our salvation, a person must first understand:

- Who is man?[69] And what is his place with God?
- Then we comprehend the effect of sin in human nature.
- Consequently, we may come to understand aspects of the salvific divine work done to restore man to his first place.[70]

This is the tactic the Fathers adopted to understand the economy of salvation, beginning with knowing who the human being is, relying on Holy Scriptures, and then expressing this in the Divine Liturgy:

---

[68] "Then God said, 'Let Us make man in Our image, according to Our likeness; let them have dominion over the fish of the sea, over the birds of the air, and over the cattle, over all the earth and over every creeping thing that creeps on the earth.' So God created man in His own image; in the image of God He created him; male and female He created them" (Genesis 1: 26–27).

[69] Or: the human being.

[70] "You desired to renew him and to restore him to his first estate" (The Divine Liturgy According to St. Gregory – Prayer of Reconciliation).
"He opened the gate of Paradise and restored Adam to his authority" (Sunday Theotokia, part 15).
"Through His cross and His holy Resurrection, He restored man once again to the Paradise" (Gospel Response of Feast of the Cross).

- "The Word of God, then, united to himself the entire nature of a human being in order to save the whole person."[71]
- "Inasmuch then as the children have partaken of flesh and blood, He Himself likewise shared in the same, that through death He might destroy him who had the power of death, that is, the devil."[72]
- "She gave all the form of humanity, with perfection to the Lord, the Creator, the Word of the Father."[73]

St. Athanasius the Apostolic explains this truth by saying:

> For God is good, or rather the source of all goodness, and one who is good grudges nothing, so that grudging nothing its existence, he made all things through his own Word, our Lord Jesus Christ. Among these things, of all things upon earth he had mercy upon the human race, and seeing that by the principle of its own coming into being it would not be able to endure eternally, he granted them a further gift, creating human beings not simply like all the irrational animals upon the earth but making them according to his own image, giving them a share of the power of his own Word, so that having as it were shadows of the Word and being made rational, they might be

---

[71] Cyril of Alexandria, *Commentary on John* 2, J.C. Elowsky, T.C. Oden, and G.L. Bray, eds.; D.R. Maxwell, trans. (Downers Grove, IL: IVP Academic, 2015), 106.
[72] Hebrews 2:14.
[73] Midnight Praises – Thursday Theotokia, Part 15. This speaks about the Virgin [St. Mary] and the mystery of incarnation of her. By "all the form of humanity" is meant that the Lord took from her complete humanity, perfectly equal to us: a body and human spirit and a rational soul.

> able to abide in blessedness, living the true life which is really that of the holy ones in paradise.[74]

And this is exactly what the Holy Scriptures declare:

ὅτι ὁ θεὸς ἔκτισεν τὸν ἄνθρωπον ἐπ' ἀφθαρσίᾳ καὶ εἰκόνα τῆς ἰδίας ἀϊδιότητος ἐποίησεν αὐτόν,[75]

"For God created man for immortality and made him an image of His own eternity"[76]

What is the meaning of the truth that we are made in the image of God? What is this image in us?

The image of God imprinted in us is the intellect, wisdom, holiness, freedom, righteousness, benevolence, goodness, mercy, inclination to virtue, knowledge, friendship with God, sonship to God, life, authority, creative thinking, everlasting immortality[77]...etc.

St. Cyril the Great says:

> The fact that man was made according to the image of God[78] has other meanings and significations. Man, alone among all the living creatures on the earth, is rational, compassionate, has a tendency toward every virtue, and has assigned to him rule over all things upon the earth, in "the image and likeness" of God. Accordingly, as man is a rational, living being, and insofar as he loves virtue, and has power over the things on

---

[74] Saint Athanasius, *On the Incarnation*, J. Behr, trans. (Yonkers, NY: SVS Press, 2011), 52.

[75] *Septuagint with Morphology*. (Stuttgart: Deutsche Bibelgesellschaft, 1979). https://www.academic-bible.com/en/online-bibles/septuagint-lxx/.

[76] Wisdom of Solomon 2:23 LXX from The Orthodox Study Bible.

[77] "Who formed man in incorruption" (The Divine Liturgy According to St. Basil – Prayer of Reconciliation).

[78] Cf. Genesis 1:26.

> earth, it is stated that he has been made in the image of God.[79]

Therefore we pray in the Divine Liturgy, saying, "And [You] inscribed in me the image of Your authority."[80]

The Psalm says: "What is man that You are mindful of him, and the son of man[81] that You visit him? For You have made him a little lower than the angels, and You have crowned him with glory and honor. You have made him to have dominion over the works of Your hands; You have put all things under his feet, all sheep and oxen—even the beasts of the field, the birds of the air, and the fish of the sea that pass through the paths of the seas."[82]

The Oneness of the Human Race

There is a foundational doctrine that explains the rest of the concepts of the Christian faith, regarding the economy of salvation specifically. This doctrine is called "the oneness of the human race." Based on this doctrine we can understand our relationship with Adam's sin, easily and clearly.

The faith of the Coptic Orthodox Church is summarized in the following:

> Humankind entirely was in Adam when he was created; so we were created in him. When Adam sinned, then, we became sinners in him. And we also died in him, and we became corrupted in him. When the Word of God was incarnate, He

[79] St. Cyril of Alexandria, *Letters 51–110*, J.I. McEnerney, trans. (Washington, D.C.: The Catholic University of America Press, 1987), 109.
[80] The Divine Liturgy According to St. Gregory – Agios (Holy)
[81] In Arabic it reads: the son of Adam.
[82] Psalm 8:4–8.

> became a new Adam; so in Him we are made a new creation, and in Him we are justified, and in Him we live and we receive incorruptibility and eternal life.

St. Athanasius the Apostolic explains this truth of the faith in his timeless book *Against the Arians*: "Thus too has the race made after God's image come to be, namely men; for though Adam only was formed out of earth, yet in him was involved the succession of the whole race."[83]

Here **St. Athanasius the Apostolic** considered that all human beings were created in Adam, and the same teaching he mentioned in *On the Incarnation*:

> Thus, then, God created the human being and willed that he should abide in incorruptibility; **but when humans[84] despised and overturned the comprehension of God, devising and contriving evil for themselves, as was said in the first work, then they received the previously threatened condemnation of death**, and hereafter no longer remained as they had been created, but were corrupted as they had contrived; and, seizing them, death reigned.[85]

It is noted in this quote that St. Athanasius explains that the human being in general was created in Adam, in incorruptibility, and that the human being, that is, the entire

---

[83] Athanasius *Four Discourses Against the Arians* 2.19.48 (NPNF^2 4:374–375).
[84] Noteworthy is that St. Athanasius, instead of using "Adam," uses "humans," which is an expression that indicates not a single human, but all humans, thereby confirming the oneness of the human race. (This footnote is by Dr. Joseph Faltas, the translator of On the Incarnation into Arabic).
[85] Saint Athanasius, *On the Incarnation*, J. Behr, trans. (Yonkers, NY: SVS Press, 2011), 53.

humankind in general, sinned in Adam, and was condemned to death in Adam.

"**For these reasons**, then, with death holding greater sway and corruption remaining fast against human beings, **the race of humans was perishing.**"[86]

It is noted here that death reigned[87] and corruption prevailed[88] against all humans, and not Adam alone. And, of course, St. Athanasius constructs his teaching based on the holy texts from Holy Scriptures, and on what he received from the Fathers before him.

St. Gregory of Nyssa says:

> What is it then which we understand concerning these matters? In saying that "God created man" the text indicates, by the indefinite character of the term, all mankind; for was not Adam here named together with the creation, as the history tells us in what follows? **Yet the name given to the man created is not the particular, but the general name: thus we are led by the employment of the general name of our nature** to some such view as this—**that in the Divine foreknowledge and power all humanity is included in the first creation**; for it is fitting for God not to regard any of the things made by Him as indeterminate, but that each existing thing should have some limit and measure prescribed by the wisdom of its Maker.

---

[86] Ibid., 55.
[87] Or: held sway.
[88] Or: remained fast.

> Now just as any particular man is limited by his bodily dimensions, and the peculiar size which is conjoined with the superficies of his body is the measure of his separate existence, **so I think that the entire plenitude of humanity was included by the God of all, by His power of foreknowledge, as it were in one body**, and that this is what the text teaches us which says, "God created man, in the image of God created He him." **For the image is not in part of our nature, nor is the grace in any one of the things found in that nature, but this power extends equally to all the race**: and a sign of this is that mind is implanted alike in all: for all have the power of understanding and deliberating, and of all else whereby the Divine nature finds its image in that which was made according to it: the man that was manifested at the first creation of the world, and he that shall be after the consummation of all, are alike: they equally bear in themselves the Divine image.
>
> **For this reason the whole race was spoken of as one man...**[89]

We find that the idea of all humankind being in Adam, pervades the thought of the catholic Church Fathers. For **St. Macarius the Great** says in his eleventh homily:

> Take the example of a king who has goods and servants under him ministering to him. However, it happens that he is taken captive by enemies. When he is captured and led out of his country, his servants and ministers must want to follow

[89] Gregory of Nyssa *On the Making of Man* 16.16–18 (NPNF[2] 5:406).

> after him. So also Adam was created pure by God for his service. All these creatures were given to him to serve him. He was destined to be the lord and king of all creatures. But when the evil word came to him and conversed with him, he first received it through an external hearing. **Then it penetrated into his heart and took charge of his whole being. When he was thus captured, creation, which ministered and served him, was captured with him. Through him death gained power over every soul and completely destroyed the image of Adam because of his disobedience so that as a result men were sidetracked and fell to worshipping demons.**[90]

And **St. Basil the Great** teaches us, saying:

> For since we **fell away from the true** delight that was in paradise, **we invented adulterated delicacies for ourselves.** And since **we no longer see the tree of life**, nor do we pride ourselves in that beauty, there have been given to us for our enjoyment cooks and bakers, and various pastries and aromas, and **such things console us in our banishment from there.**[91]

St. Basil considers here that Adam's fall and his being away from the paradisiacal delight, is our fall, all of us.

> Yet, one may also ask, for what reason was the tree in paradise, **through which the devil's attack on us was** about to take place? For if he had not had

---

[90] *Pseudo-Macarius: The Fifty Homilies and the Great Letter*, G.A. Maloney, trans. (Mahwah, NJ: Paulist Press, 1992), 92.

[91] Saint Basil the Great, *On the Human Condition*, J. Behr and A. Casiday, eds.; N.V. Harrison, trans. (Yonkers, NY: SVS Press, 2005), 54.

> the bait for his deceit, **how would he have led us on through the disobedience into death?** Because there **needed to be a commandment to test our obedience.**[92]

Note how St. Basil expresses the truth that the devil's attack against Adam in paradise was considered an attack on us all in Adam. The same teaching we find in the following texts:

> Why does he **fight against us?** Because, being a receptacle of all evils, he also accepted the disease of malice and envied our honor. **For he could not bear our life** free from pain in paradise.[93]
>
> ***
>
> Accordingly, the devil has remained as our opponent because of **the fall that came upon us** due to his abuse long ago.[94]
>
> ***
>
> For not one wrestling or contest will remain for us on high, nor will anyone be set against us and turn us aside from the blessed life. But we will have an uninterrupted existence without pain and **enjoy the tree of life, from which we were prevented from partaking since the beginning through the plot of the serpent.**[95]

St. Cyril also teaches us, [saying]:

> It is as though he were to say, **We have been condemned to death by the transgression of**

---

[92] Ibid., 77.
[93] Ibid., 76.
[94] Ibid., 78.
[95] Ibid., 80.

> **Adam, since the entire nature of humanity experienced this in him. Indeed, he was the firstfruits of our race. In Christ, however, we blossomed once more into life.**[96]

"Human nature has experienced a turning away from God's face in Adam because of his transgression."[97]

"For in Adam, as I said, we have fallen away from grace. The statement 'increase and multiply' and 'subdue the earth'[98] was addressed to the first man representing human nature as a whole."[99]

> Then Paul shows that **we are stripped of the glory that was given to us long ago.** That is why he says, "We do not yet see everything in subjection to him."[100] Now we who choose to think rightly certainly do not imagine that he says these things about one man. **Rather, he represents all of humanity in one person** and says that he regained participation in the glory that was given in ancient times. Now we must describe the construction of the entire passage and the outcome of its skillful composition. **He shows that man has lost the glory because of the transgression of Adam** in order to explain how to get it back, **just as one might show the poverty of the human race in order then to point out**

---

[96] Cyril of Alexandria, *Commentaries on Romans, 1-2 Corinthians, and Hebrews*, J.C. Elowsky, G.L. Bray, M. Glerup, and T.C. Oden, eds.; D.R. Maxwell, trans. (Downers Grove, IL: IVP Academic, 2022), 6.
[97] Ibid., 77.
[98] Genesis 1:28.
[99] Cyril of Alexandria, *Commentaries on Romans, 1-2 Corinthians, and Hebrews*, J.C. Elowsky, G.L. Bray, M. Glerup, and T.C. Oden, eds.; D.R. Maxwell, trans. (Downers Grove, IL: IVP Academic, 2022), 115.
[100] Hebrews 2:8.

> **the one through whom we have been enriched.** You see, he immediately adds, "We see Jesus, who for a little while was made lower than the angels, now crowned with glory and honor because of the suffering of death." The Word of God, who is God by nature as we have often said, lowered himself to the point of emptying and shared our name, as a "man" who "for a little while was lower than the angels," **so that he might become obedient to the Father "even to the point of death,"**[101] and he might crown human nature with glory and honor, since he is crowned as one of us even though he is the "Lord of glory."[102,103]

St. Athanasius, in his commentary on Psalm 68, states, saying, "'Turn not Your face from Your child,'[104] **for God the Father put away humankind because of Adam's transgression.** For the sake of this, he is asking Him to turn His face to us once again."[105]

The Fathers based their interpretations, in this respect, on Holy Scriptures, naturally. For in Paul the Apostle's Epistle to the Romans, chapter five specifically, the Apostle writes of this truth: "Therefore, just as through one man sin entered the world, and death through sin, and thus death spread to all men, because all sinned."[106]

---

[101] Philippians 2:8.
[102] 1 Corinthians 2:8.
[103] Cyril of Alexandria, *Commentaries on Romans, 1-2 Corinthians, and Hebrews*, J.C. Elowsky, G.L. Bray, M. Glerup, and T.C. Oden, eds.; D.R. Maxwell, trans. (Downers Grove, IL: IVP Academic, 2022), 118.
[104] Psalm 68:18 LXX from The Orthodox Study Bible.
[105] Saint Athanasius the Apostolic, *Tafseer Sifr Al-Mazameer Al-Joz' Al-Thalith* [Exegesis on the Book of Psalms Vol. 3], G.M. Andrawis, trans. (Egypt: St. Anthony Press–The Orthodox Center for Patristic Studies in Cairo, 2021), 160. [Translated from Arabic text].
[106] Romans 5:12.

> But the free gift is not like the offense. For if by the one man's offense many died, much more the grace of God and the gift by the grace of the one Man, Jesus Christ, abounded to many. And the gift is not like that which came through the one who sinned. For the judgment which came from one offense resulted in condemnation, but the free gift which came from many offenses resulted in justification. For if by the one man's offense death reigned through the one, much more those who receive abundance of grace and of the gift of righteousness will reign in life through the One, Jesus Christ. Therefore, as through one man's offense judgement came to all men, resulting in condemnation, even so through one Man's righteous act the free gift came to all men, resulting in justification of life. For as by one man's disobedience many were made sinners, so also by one Man's obedience many will be made righteous.[107]

This quote from Holy Scriptures gives a very clear comparison between what humankind[108] contracted in Adam, and what humankind receives in Christ Jesus our Lord: sin as oppose to righteousness, that is, Adam's sin which reached all, as opposed to Christ's righteousness which everyone who believes in Him receives; and death as opposed to life, "for since by man came death, by Man also came the resurrection of the dead. For as in Adam all die, even so in Christ all shall be made alive."[109] And corruption which human nature contracted in Adam, as opposed to the promise of incorruption which we will

[107] Romans 5:15–19.
[108] Literally: all of humankind.
[109] 1 Corinthians 15:21–22.

receive in Christ. "So also is the resurrection of the dead. The body is sown in corruption, it is raised in incorruption."[110]

This Biblical and faith-based concept (the oneness of the human race) is clearly [yet] partially manifest in the story of David and Goliath: "Then he [that is, Goliath] stood and cried out to the armies of Israel, and said to them, 'Why have you come out to line up for battle? Am I not a Philistine, and you the servants of Saul? Choose a man for yourselves, and let him come down to me. If he is able to fight with me and kill me, then we will be your servants. But if I prevail against him and kill him, then you shall be our servants and serve us.'"[111]

The defeat of Goliath was the defeat of all his people, and so Adam's sin became the sin of all human beings. Likewise, the trespass[112] of Achan the son of Carmi was a cause of trouble[113] for all the people of Israel. "But the children of Israel committed a trespass regarding the accursed things, for Achan the son of Carmi, the son of Zabdi, the son of Zerah, of the tribe of Judah, took of the accursed things; so the anger of the LORD burned against the children of Israel."[114]

> Israel has sinned, and they have also transgressed My covenant which I commanded them. For they have even taken some of the accursed things, and

---

[110] 1 Corinthians 15:42.

[111] 1 Samuel 17:8–9.

[112] Literally: betrayal.

[113] On the subject of Achan the son of Carmi, though with his sin he troubled the children of Israel, not all of the children of Israel were destroyed because of his sin. He and his family were destroyed together, however. Therefore, sacrifices used to be offered for the sins of the congregation; assuredly, there are sins of the congregation: negligence might spread among the believers, for example. And perhaps God, by permitting the children of Israel to be troubled for the sin of Achan, desired to awaken them and to give them opportunity to atone for the congregation, but He did not destroy them all. **I here included this story as a proof for the effect of one person's sin on a large congregation.**

[114] Joshua 7:1.

> have both stolen and deceived; and they have also put it among their own stuff. Therefore the children of Israel could not stand before their enemies, but turned their backs before their enemies, because they have become doomed to destruction. Neither will I be with you anymore, unless you destroy the accursed from among you. Get up, sanctify the people, and say, "Sanctify yourselves for tomorrow, because thus says the LORD God of Israel: 'There is an accursed thing in your midst, O Israel; you cannot stand before your enemies until you take away the accursed thing from among you.'"[115]

David's victory was a victory for all his people, and likewise, Christ's victory is for all who believe in His name. "These things I have spoken to you, that in Me you may have peace. In the world you will have tribulation; but be of good cheer, I have overcome the world"[116]

"But thanks be to God, who gives us the victory through our Lord Jesus Christ."[117] Therefore, the Christian person boasts in the cross by which the Lord Jesus overcame the world. "But God forbid that I boast except in the cross of our Lord Jesus Christ, by whom the world has been crucified to me, and I to the world."[118]

The doctrine of the oneness of the human race makes the priest stand and pray in the liturgies with one tongue on behalf of all humankind, in unity in Christ. And this is what the priest prays in Coptic liturgies as an expression of the oneness of

---

[115] Joshua 7:11–13.
[116] John 16:33.
[117] 1 Corinthians 15:57.
[118] Galatians 6:14.

humankind in one person, who is Adam of old, then in the new Adam, the Lord Jesus Christ:

- "O God, the Great, the Eternal, who formed man in incorruption."[119]
- "Who formed us, and placed us in the Paradise of joy."[120]
- "You, as Lover of Mankind, have created me, as man.... Because of the multitude of Your tender mercies, You have brought me into existence when I was not. You have raised heaven as a roof for me, and established the earth for me to walk upon.... And [You have] opened for me Paradise to enjoy, and have given me the learning of Your knowledge. You have manifested to me the tree of life, and made known to me the sting of death. Of one plant have You forbidden me to eat, that of which You have said to me, 'Of it only do not eat.' But according to my will, I did eat. I put Your law behind me by my own counsel, and became slothful toward Your commandments. I plucked for myself the sentence of death."[121]
- "You, O my Master, have turned for me the punishment into salvation. As a good shepherd, You have sought after that which had gone astray. As a true father, You have travailed with me, I who had fallen.... You are He who ministered salvation to me when I disobeyed Your Law. As a true light, You have shone upon the lost and ignorant."[122]
- O You, THE BEING throughout all time, have come to us on earth. You have come into the womb of the Virgin. You, the Infinite, being God, did not consider equality

[119] The Divine Liturgy According to St. Basil – Prayer of Reconciliation.
[120] The Divine Liturgy According to St. Basil – Agios (Holy).
[121] The Divine Liturgy According to St. Gregory – Agios (Holy).
[122] Ibid.

with God a thing to be grasped, but emptied Yourself and took the form of a servant, and blessed my nature in Yourself, and fulfilled Your Law on my behalf. You have shown me the rising up from my fall. You have given release to those who were bound in Hades. You have lifted the curse of the Law. You have abolished sin in the flesh..."[123]

❖ "You have come to the slaughter as a sheep, even to the cross. You have manifested the greatness of Your care for me. You have slain my sin in Your tomb. You have brought my first fruit up to heaven."[124]

The priest, here, prays with the tongue of all of humankind; for God did not create the world[125] for the sake of Adam alone as a person, nor [only] for the sake of the priest who is praying presently, but for the sake of all human beings in Adam. In all the aforementioned words the priest prays with the tongue of all of humankind as though it[126] were one man.

❖ "O God, who in Your ineffable love toward mankind sent Your only-begotten Son into the world that He might return the lost sheep to You."[127]

This is a wonderful interpretation of the Parable of the Lost Sheep,[128] for the Church understood that the lost sheep is all of humankind, which was lost in Adam, and the ninety-nine that were not lost are the angels and the heavenly hosts.

In the verses that are prayed in reverence, which have the same words as the hymn,[129] "He who offered," the priest says:

---

123 Ibid.
124 Ibid.
125 Literally: the universe.
126 That is, humankind.
127 The Divine Liturgy According to St. Basil – Prayer of the Veil.
128 Luke 15:1–7.
129 Ⲫⲁⲓ ⲉ̀ⲧⲁϥⲉⲛϥ

"He opened the gate of Paradise and restored Adam once more to his dominion. Through His cross and holy Resurrection, He returned man once more to Paradise."[130]

The Lord Jesus, of course, did not restore Adam alone but all of humankind which believes and clings to Christ and unites with Him. All of it is called Adam in this beautiful liturgical text.

> **But when he [that is, the devil] saw our glory, he who was envious of our race** from the beginning, **he could not endure [seeing] the glory which we were in, but wished to draw us to himself, to affliction,[131] and wished to deprive us of the enjoyment of the trees of paradise**, except that he could not enter because of the angels surrounding paradise, so he took this opportunity which no one was able to discern, nor was it possible for anyone to know.[132]

This wonderful doctrinal concept is based on our faith in the oneness of God with multiplicity of Hypostases, and on the truth that the human being is created in the image of God. Consequently, human beings, though many, must be one, to realize the image, pattern and likeness of God. This concept explains to us how we were in Adam when he fell, so we contracted his sin and its consequences, that is, death and corruption; and how we come together in Christ to receive in Him and through Him, righteousness, resurrection, eternal life

---

[130] Raising of Incense—Prayer of the Congregation's Confession. The same verses also are chanted in a special tune on Covenant Thursday, Great Friday and the two Feasts of the Cross.

[131] Or: servility.

[132] Bishop Epiphanius, Bishop and Abbot of St. Macarius Monastery, *Kholaji Al-Der Al-Abiad Tarjama An Al-Kobtia Wa Dirasa* [Liturgy Book of the White Monastery Translated from Coptic, with a Study]. (Egypt: School of Alexandria, 2014), 106. [Translated from Arabic text]

and incorruptibility. As we were in Adam when he was created, so we were created in him; likewise, we were in him when he sinned and died and became corrupted, so we sinned in him and died and became corrupted.

The Fall

Considering the great distinctions with which Adam was created to be in the image of God—in intellect, holiness, wisdom, freedom, dominion, and also in oneness with multiplicity—Adam's sin was not a mere mistake and disobedience which require of the person repentance and confession, and that is it. What resulted, however, from this sin was loss and distortion of all that belong to the human being.

St. Athanasius the Apostolic says:

> Nor does repentance recall human beings from what is natural, but merely halts sins. If then there were only offence and not the consequence of corruption, repentance would have been fine. But if, once the transgression had taken off, human beings were now held fast in natural corruption and were deprived of the grace of being in the image.[133]

The human being, in general, and not only Adam,[134] in falling into disobedience, lost the similitude to God's image, and lost all the distinctions which he was granted. So he became a sinner, subject to death, corrupted, ignorant, unwise, bound under Satan's servitude; he also lost sonship to God the Father.

---

[133] Saint Athanasius, *On the Incarnation*, J. Behr, trans. (Yonkers, NY: SVS Press, 2011), 56.

[134] Because of the doctrine of the oneness of the human race, "therefore, just as through one man sin entered the world, and death through sin, and thus death spread to all men, because all sinned" (Romans 5:12).

The human being, thus, inclined to doing evil,[135] erected a wall and enmity between himself and God,[136] and became subject to the judgment and punishment of death.[137]

- ❖ "Being filled with all unrighteousness, sexual immorality, wickedness, covetousness, maliciousness; full of envy, murder, strife, deceit, evil-mindedness; they are whisperers, backbiters, haters of God, violent, proud, boasters, inventers of evil things, disobedient to parents, undiscerning, untrustworthy, unloving, unforgiving, unmerciful; who, knowing the righteous judgement of God, that those who practice such things are deserving of death, not only do the same but also approve of those who practice them."[138]
- ❖ David the Prophet groans with all human beings, saying, "Behold, I was brought forth in iniquity, and in sin my mother conceived me."[139]
- ❖ "Therefore, just as through one man sin entered the world, and death through sin, and thus death spread to all men, because all sinned."[140]

---

[135] "That God made man upright, but they have sought out many schemes" (Ecclesiastes 7:29).
"Then the LORD saw that the wickedness of man was great in the earth, and that every intent of the thoughts of his heart was only evil continually" (Genesis 6:5).
"'For the land is full of adulterers; for because of a curse the land mourns. The pleasant places of the wilderness are dried up. Their course of life is evil, and their might is not right. For both prophet and priest are profane; yes, in My house I have found their wickedness,' says the LORD" (Jeremiah 23:10–11).

[136] "The middle wall You have broken down and the old enmity You have abolished. You have reconciled the earthly with the heavenly" (The Divine Liturgy According to St. Gregory – Prayer of Reconciliation).

[137] "For the wages of sin is death" (Romans 6:23).
"'But of the tree of the knowledge of good and evil you shall not eat, for in the day that you eat of it you shall surely die'" (Genesis 2:17).

[138] Romans 1:29–32.

[139] Psalm 51:5.

[140] Romans 5:12.

- "For as by one man's disobedience many were made sinners."[141]
- "They have all turned aside; they have together become unprofitable; there is none who does good, no, not one."[142]
- "For all have sinned and fall short of the glory of God."[143]

The work of salvation, therefore, requires the restoration of what the human being has lost, and the reformation of what sin has corrupted, and not merely the forgiveness of sin, nor merely the revelation of God's love, nor only paying off the debt, nor the setting free from the bonds; but all these together.

Thus, we view sin, and the breaking of the law, in a holistic view, for sin is not only a sickness,[144] and a weakness,[145] and death,[146] and corruption,[147] but it is also enmity,[148] and a crime,[149] and a debtm[150] and a deviation, and an

---

[141] Romans 5:19.

[142] Romans 3:12.

[143] Romans 3:23.

[144] "Jesus answered and said to them, 'Those who are well have no need of a physician, but those who are sick. I have not come to call the righteous, but sinners, to repentance'" (Luke 5:31–32).

[145] "For when we were still without strength, in due time Christ died for the ungodly" (Romans 5:6).

[146] "For if by the one man's offense many died" (Romans 5:15).
"For if by the one man's offense death reigned through the one" (Romans 5:17).

[147] "[O God,] who formed man in incorruption; and death, which entered into the world through the envy of the devil" (The Divine Liturgy According to St. Basil – Prayer of Reconciliation).

[148] "For if when we were enemies we were reconciled to God through the death of His Son, much more, having been reconciled, we shall be saved by His life" (Romans 5:10).

[149] "Then Jacob was angry and rebuked Laban: 'What is my trespass? What is my sin, that you have so hotly pursued me?'" (Genesis 31:36). [The word "trespass" in the verse in Arabic is a derivative of the word "crime"].

[150] "And when he had begun to settle accounts, one was brought to him who owed him ten thousand talents. But as he was not able to pay, his master commanded that he be sold, with his wife and children and all that he had, and that payment be made. The servant therefore fell down before him, saying, 'Master, have patience with me, and I will pay you all.' Then the master of that servant was moved with compassion, released him, and forgave him the debt" (Matthew 18:24–27).

estrangement,[151] and a transgression,[152] and foolishness,[153] and a rebellion, and disobedience, and a betrayal...etc.

All these meanings were portrayed in the Fall of the first Adam: he disobeyed, deviated, became estranged, transgressed, betrayed, etc. This is expressed in the Holy Scriptures where many terms were used to describe sin, whether in the Hebrew language in the Old testament or in Greek in the New Testament.

The usage of more than one linguistic term about sin does not mean [they are] synonyms, nor is it [for] linguistic eloquence only, but, rather, they describe the multiple aspects of sin.

Therefore, **the Greek terms** used in the Holy Scriptures to express "sin" are many with numerous meanings:

ἁμαρτία (*hamartia*): Missing the mark.

ἀνομία (*anomia*): Breaking the law.

Παραπτώμα (*paraptóma*): A purposeful falling into iniquity.

Παράβασις (*parabasis*): Transgression.

ὀφειλήμα (*opheiléma*): Debt.

---

[151] "And not many days after, the younger son gathered all together, journeyed to a far country, and there wasted his possessions with prodigal living" (Luke 15:13).

[152] "Yes, all Israel has transgressed Your law, and has departed so as not to obey Your voice; therefore the curse and the oath written in the Law of Moses the servant of God have been poured out on us, because we have sinned against Him" (Daniel 9:11).

"Nevertheless death reigned from Adam to Moses, even over those who have not sinned according to the likeness of the transgression of Adam" (Romans 5:14).

"Whoever commits sin also commits lawlessness, and sin is lawlessness" (1 John 3:4).

[153] "For the leaders of My people do not know Me. They are foolish and unwise sons. They are wise to do evil, but do not know how to do good" (Jeremiah 4:22 LXX from Orthodox Study Bible).

ἀδικία (*adikia*): Unrighteousness or injustice.

Likewise, **the Hebrew words:**

חַטָּאָה (*chatta'ah*): Sin.

אָשָׁם (*asham*): Iniquity, offense/betrayal.

מַעַל (*maal*): Trespass.

עָוֹן (*avon*): Iniquity, guilt.

As a reflection to these many aspects of sin, we may understand why the sacrifices in the Old Testament were of many kinds: sin sacrifice, trespass sacrifice, burnt sacrifice, peace sacrifice, grain offering,[154] scapegoat sacrifice,[155] Passover sacrifice.[156]

It is known that all these sacrifices pointed to the one great sacrifice of our Lord Jesus Christ, which is multifaceted.[157] This truth we sing in the Psalmody, that the sacrifice of Christ is the true sacrifice, to which all the Old Testament sacrifices pointed.

> They likened the archpriest to our Savior, the true sacrifice for the forgiveness of sins. He who offered Himself as an acceptable sacrifice upon the Cross for the salvation of our race. His good Father smelled Him in the evening on Golgotha. He opened the gate of Paradise and restored Adam to his authority. Through Mary, the

[154] See Leviticus Chapters 1–7.

[155] "Then Aaron shall cast lots for the two goats: one lot for the LORD and the other for the scapegoat. And Aaron shall bring the goat on which the LORD's lot fell, and offer it as a sin offering. But the goat on which the lot fell to be the scapegoat shall be presented alive before the LORD, to make atonement upon it, and to let it go as a scapegoat into the wilderness" (Leviticus 16:8–10).

[156] See Exodus 12.

[157] This is in response to those who teach that the Old Testament sacrifices have no relation to the cross of our Lord Jesus Christ, the true Sacrifice for the forgiveness of sins.

> daughter of Joachim, we learned of the true sacrifice for the forgiveness of sins.[158]

The same truth, our teacher Paul the Apostle explains, especially in the Epistle to the Hebrews:

> But Christ came as High Priest of the good things to come, with the greater and more perfect tabernacle not made with hands, that is, not of this creation. Not with the blood of goats and calves, but with His own blood He entered the Most Holy Place once for all, having obtained eternal redemption. For if the blood of bulls and goats and the ashes of a heifer, sprinkling the unclean, sanctifies for the purifying of the flesh, how much more shall the blood of Christ, who through the eternal Spirit offered Himself without spot to God, cleanse your conscience from dead works to serve the living God?[159]

St. Athanasius the Apostolic says in this vein: "Whence, by offering to death **the body he had taken to himself, as an offering holy and free of all spot**, he immediately abolished death from all like him, by the offering of a like."[160]

St. Cyril the Great says:

> The holy sacrifice, then, offered for the sake of sin, is nothing but Emanuel, the true Lamb who takes away the sins of the world, and He was offered as a sacrifice instead of the burnt offering. For Christ was not partially holy like us, for "He committed

---

[158] Midnight Praises – Sunday Theotokia, Part 15.

[159] Hebrews 9:11–14.

[160] Saint Athanasius, *On the Incarnation*, J. Behr, trans. (Yonkers, NY: SVS Press, 2011), 58.

no sin"[161] but was wholly a sweet-smelling aroma, and holy and the bestower of holiness to all.[162]

For its sake (the Church) He offered Himself as a sacrifice and built in it His altar. And He, being the One offering the sacrifice, offered Himself as a sacrifice after the form and pattern of the ox threshing the crops, and He became a sacrifice and a burnt offering and a peace offering.[163]

The mystery of the passion may be seen also in another instance. For according to the Mosaic law two goats were offered, differing in nothing from one another, but alike in size and appearance. Of these, one was called "the lord:" and the other, the "sent-away." And when the lot had been cast for that which was called "lord," it was sacrificed: while the other was sent away from the sacrifice: and therefore had the name of the "sent-away." And Who was signified by this? The Word, though He was God, was in our likeness, and took the form of us sinners, as far as the nature of the flesh was concerned. The goat, then, male or female, was sacrificed for sins. But the death was our desert, inasmuch as **by sin we had fallen under the divine curse. But when the Savior of all Himself, so to speak, undertook the charge, He transferred to Himself what was our due,**

---

161 1 Peter 2:22.
162 Cyril the Great, *Al-Sojoud Wa Al-Ibada Bi-Al Rouh Wa Al-Hak* [Worshipping and Serving in Spirit and in Truth], G.A. Ibrahim, trans. (Egypt: The Orthodox Center for Patristic Studies, 2017), 508. [Translated from Arabic text].
163 Ibid., 138.

and laid down His life, that we might be sent away from death and destruction.[164]

From all the aforementioned, it is utterly clear to us that the Law gave the holy and elect nation all kinds of sacrifices and offerings, and also the offerings that are offered for every trespass and for all sins, that is, the trespass offerings and the sin offerings. And because the name of the sacrifices offered for the sake of sins is "sin offering,"[165] **therefore Paul, who is wise concerning the Law, also used the same term about Christ, saying**, "Now then, we are ambassadors for Christ, as though God were pleading through us: we implore you on Christ's behalf, be reconciled to God. For He made Him who knew no sin to be sin for us, that we might become the righteousness of God in Him,"[166] **because the Son, according to Scripture,**[167] **was slain for the sake of our sins as a lamb without blemish. And since the sacrifices were slain for the sake of our sins, the Law therefore gave them the name "sin."**[168]

Summary

- ❖ The human being was created in the image of God.
- ❖ Sin made the human being lose his distinction as an image of God.

---

[164] Cyril of Alexandria, *A Commentary upon the Gospel According to S. Luke* 1, R.P. Smith, trans. (Oxford, ENG: At the University Press, 1859), 239–240.
[165] Or: sin sacrifice.
[166] 2 Corinthians 5:20–21.
[167] Isaiah 53:5.
[168] Cyril the Great, *Al-Sojoud Wa Al-Ibada Bi-Al Rouh Wa Al-Hak* [Worshipping and Serving in Spirit and in Truth], G.A. Ibrahim, trans. (Egypt: The Orthodox Center for Patristic Studies, 2017), 514. [Translated from Arabic text].

- ❖ Salvation is accomplished by restoring man to this image in all its details.
- ❖ This truth is made clear by the Holy Scriptures using many words that denote sin and the diversity of its effects on the fallen human nature in Adam.
- ❖ The same truth is made clear also when God commanded Moses to offer many kinds of sacrifices of blood in the Old Testament.
- ❖ All these sacrifices were an indication for the one sacrifice of Christ which is multifaceted.

The meaning of sin cannot be limited to a single indication, nor can the various consequences of this sin on the human race; consequently, the economy of salvation proceeded, of necessity, in many, various directions.

CHAPTER TWO

Reviewing Previous Research

I will review some of what has been published recently in the Coptic Orthodox Church in the field of the economy of salvation, some of which explains the essence and understanding of the economy of salvation, others explaining the doctrine of the inheritance of Adam's sin.

Studies from the Coptic Orthodox Church

1. Encyclopedia of Comparative Theology, Volume 5

This book deals with theological issues, Pelagianism and the inheritance of sin, by the teacher of generations Pope Shenouda III. The first printing was in November 2019, by St. Mary Church Zeiton Press.

The book is [a collection of] lectures by H.H. Pope Shenouda III, which were published in books posthumously. In the first chapter, the book provides a lecture on Pelagianism and the struggle against it, headed by Augustine in North Africa and Jerome in Palestine. The second chapter is about Original Sin, and includes a response to those who deny this doctrine. His Holiness quoted the teachings of the Fathers before Augustine on the inheritance of sin. Also he answered the question, "What is our fault?" He also discussed the issue of whether marriage should be prohibited if it were a means of transmitting sin.

His Holiness explained the relationship between Baptism and Original Sin, and interpreted Romans 5. He also addressed other issues that are outside the domain of this research.

The book did not discuss the remaining details of the economy of salvation. It focused on our relationship with Adam's sin. However, H.H. Pope Shenouda had written two [other] books on the economy of salvation: "The Heresy of Salvation in a Moment" and "Salvation in the Orthodox Understanding." In these His Holiness was confronting the Protestant deviation in explaining salvation, and he in them confirmed the importance of the Church and the Sacraments, with good works, to obtain salvation. He did not, however, address in these the Neopatristic thought (the subject of this study).

In another domain, His Holiness wrote a book titled "Recent Heresies and Responding to Them," in which His Holiness focused on responding to some of the ideological deviations regarding the economy of salvation which were adopted by the followers of neo-theology and neo-patristic [movement].

2. Original Sin and Actually-Committed Sins Book

This book is written by Dr. Maurice Tawadros, a New Testament professor in the Theological College in Cairo. The first edition was [published] in 1994 by St. John the Beloved Press.

Dr. Maurice Tawadros considers the subject of Original Sin the nucleus of the foundational Christian doctrines, which is related to the human being's state before the Fall, and in his Fall, and to the consequences that resulted from the Fall; therefore, Original Sin is linked essentially to the doctrine of incarnation and redemption.[169]

In Part One, Dr. Maurice reviewed human nature and its components of soul and body, that both are in consistency, in harmony, and tightly bound. The Christian thought is in opposition to the [following] philosophical ideologies: Spiritualism, and Materialism and Darwinism.[170]

Dr. Maurice referred also to the theories of the origin of the human soul, which are: the theory of the prior existence of the soul; and emanationism; and the theory of creation, namely, that God creates the soul or spirit for every person at the time of conception; and the theory which the Church believes, namely reproduction, that is, we receive both the spirit and the body through our parents by reproduction. And this [latter] theory explains our inheritance of Original Sin, because of the oneness of the human race, and also explains the reason for the incarnation of the Son of God for the salvation of the human being in his entirety, body, spirit, and a rational soul.[171]

Of Original Sin, Dr. Maurice says, "The head of the human race did not remain steadfast in the state of the original righteousness in which he was created, but, as he disobeyed God's commandment, he fell (deviated, came down, descended) from this state, and with him fell all the human race which came through reproduction from him. Thus, every individual of the

---

[169] See M. Tawadros, *Al-Khatiah Al-Asliah Wa Al-Khata'iah Al-Fih'liah* [Original Sin and Actually-Committed Sins]. (Egypt: St. John the Beloved Press, 1994), 7 [Translated from Arabic text].
[170] Ibid., 12.
[171] Ibid., 27.

human race carries in himself, by nature, Adam's sin (the head of the human race). So when the human being is born, he is found guilty and under the punishment of God."[172]

Then Dr. Maurice reviewed the beginning and truth of Original Sin, in relation to its essence and the punishment and consequences. Dr. Maurice cited many quotes from Holy Scriptures indicating our relationship with our father Adam's sin, especially Romans 5.

Dr. Maurice also quoted many sayings of the Fathers in this concern, with the Church's teaching about the necessity of Baptism of infants, and the Church's position on the heresy of Pelagius, and the Orthodox Church's position on the teaching of the [Roman] Catholic Church regarding the immaculate birth of the Virgin Mary.[173]

Dr. Maurice reviewed all the interpretations that were opposed to the doctrine of the inheritance of Adam's sin, and ended with the following conclusion:

> Nothing is left after all these discussions but that we accept the matter of Original Sin, in that we inherited sin and guilt, as a matter of the faith. And we are found facing a mystery higher than can be encompassed or comprehended by the human mind, in spite that the human experience and history, in addition to the Holy Scriptures and Tradition, all confirm the truth of the teaching that Original Sin is inherited and was transmitted from Adam to all of the human beings who came from him; therefore, it is

[172] M. Tawadros, *Al-Khatiah Al-Asliah Wa Al-Khata'iah Al-Fih'liah* [The Original Sin and Actually-Committed Sins]. (Egypt: St. John the Beloved Press, 1994), 27. [Translated from Arabic text].
[173] Ibid., 36.

> sufficient that we understand Original Sin correctly.[174]

In Part Two [of the book], Dr. Maurice reviewed the Church's testimony on the commonality of Original Sin and its negative effects on the human race. Then he gave examples of the teachings of some Fathers regarding this: Justin, Theophilus of Antioch, Irenaeus, Hippolytus, Clement of Alexandria, Origen, Athanasius the Apostolic, Basil the Great, Gregory of Nyssa, John Chrysostom, Macarius the Great, Cyril the Great, Didymus the Blind, St. Ephraim the Syrian.[175]

In Part Three [of the book] was reviewed the understanding of Original Sin between the various churches and the Coptic Orthodox Church.[176]

Although Dr. Maurice Tawadros explained, in wonderful details, all that is related to the theological conflict surrounding the matter of the inheritance of Original Sin, he did not address in depth the recent heresies surrounding this topic, which were adopted by the neopatristic movement. Also, his invaluable book did not address the topic of the economy of salvation from this Original Sin.

3. The Economy of the Fullness of Time Book

[This book] deals with the understanding of salvation in the Eastern patristic heritage, by Dr. Imad Maurice Eskander, reviewed by Dr. Joseph Maurice Faltas. The publisher is Panarion Center for Patristic Heritage. The first edition was in June 2019.

This book explains the economy of salvation, beginning, in the first chapter, with the creation of the human being out of

---

[174] Ibid., 63.
[175] Ibid., 76.
[176] Ibid., 93.

nothing according to the image, that he may live in communion with God. It also explains, "Why the commandment?" and explains the ultimate purpose for the creation of man, namely, the adoption by the Father, the true knowledge of God, and deification.

The second chapter speaks about the fall and its consequences, the distortion of the divine image in the human being, the estrangement of the human being from the true knowledge of God, and the obstruction of the human being from reaching deification. The author then addressed the issue of evil and death, and that repentance was not sufficient to treat the problem of the human being's fall.

The third chapter explains the healing of humankind by its union with God, and explains that the incarnation of God the Word was to destroy corruption and overcome death and make it of no effect. This victory is transferred to us through our union with Him in the Sacraments. The author spoke about the re-creation of human beings, to be in the image of God.

In the fourth chapter, the author reviewed the sacrifice of Christ on the cross, focusing on St. Athanasius's explanation of this sacrifice. But the author explained that the death of Christ on our behalf and for our sake does not mean that He died instead of us, but it means that he was the only one able, when dying, to lift away death.[177]

The author explained the Eastern patristic understanding of some terms like the ransom, redemption, propitiation, the price, the debt.

---

[177] See I.M. Eskander, *Tadbeer Mil' Al-Azminah* [The Economy of the Fullness of Times]. (Egypt: Panarion Press, 2019), 129.

Then he spoke about the meaning of the shedding of blood, and reconciliation and forgiveness, and the notions of righteousness and justice, and divine wrath.

In the fifth chapter, the author spoke about the hypostatic union, and our existence and our being in Christ. He also spoke about the salvific substitution, and the mediation of Christ and His priesthood for our sake, and the Church the body of Christ.

In the sixth chapter, he linked together the economy of salvation and the Sacraments, focusing on the Eucharist and our union with Christ.

In the seventh chapter, he spoke about orthodox spirituality.

In the eighth, [he spoke] about gathering everything in Christ.

The book did not provide enough patristic texts speaking about other aspects of the economy of salvation, and did not address the issue of the inheritance of Adam's sin.

4. I have reviewed some of what has been recently published in the Byzantine Orthodox Church in the past decades since AD 1950.

This is pertaining to the topic of Original Sin, with a review of the most important responses from within the Byzantine Church: specifically what Fr. John Romanides (1927-2001) wrote and taught since the late fifties of the past century of new teachings about Original Sin, and how in AD 2012 Vladimir Moss (1949-) responded to them, affirming that they are new heresies. Both of these are of the Byzantine Church.

Studies from the Byzantine Church

In the beginning of his response to Fr. John Romanides, Vladimir Moss wrote:

> We may distinguish between three types of heretical ideas. The first is heresy in the classical sense, an attack on a specific teaching of the faith, such as the Divinity of Christ, the Procession of the Holy Spirit, ... A second type is constituted by the modern heresy of ecumenism, which does not so much attack any specific teaching of the faith, but rather adopts a new attitude to heresy in general, arguing that there is no such thing as One True Faith preserved by the One True Church, that the difference between truth and heresy is unimportant or even non-existent, that all denominations or religions are equally true (or untrue), ... A third type consists in taking a true formula, declaring it to be the central truth of the faith, and then "restructuring" all the other dogmas around it – without specifically denying them, but nevertheless distorting them through the creation of this new dogmatic center of gravity. This is the path adopted by the most influential thinker in modern Greek Orthodoxy, Fr. John Romanides, and the large number of his disciples, including Metropolitan Hierotheos (Vlachos), Protopresbyter George Metallinos, Christos Yannaras and others.[178]

---

[178] Vladimir Moss, *Against Romanides: A Critical Examination of the Theology of Fr. John Romanides*. (E-book: Vladimir Moss, 2018), 3. (Retrieved in June 2022 from https://www.orthodoxchristianbooks.com/downloads/718_AGAINST_ROMANIDES.pdf), (henceforth cited as Moss, Against Romanides).

Vladimir Moss continues:

> Fr. John Romanides (1927-2001) was a member of the new calendarist State Church of Greece, an admirer of the Ecumenical Patriarch Athenagoras, a member of the Central Committee of the World Council of Churches, a participant in many ecumenical conferences ... However, while being actively engaged in the ecumenical movement in this way, ... Romanides constructed a theological system that virulently rejected not only Catholicism and Protestantism, but also certain traditional Orthodox teachings on the grounds that they were "Augustinian" and "scholastic" – that is, heretical. Romanides taught that the theology that was taught in Greece in his day "is of western and Russian origin. No relationship with Byzantium." And so he saw his own work as a revolutionary return to the true Orthodox teaching from the heresy of contemporary Greek and Russian theology.[179]

> The main source for the new soteriologists' theory of original sin is the thesis of John Romanides entitled The Ancestral Sin, which he defended at the University of Athens in 1957. This thesis, not surprisingly, elicited intense debate, being rejected by two of the examiners, Trembelas and Bratsiotis, and was not accepted quickly or unanimously. However, it has now

179 Ibid.

> become a "classic" statement of the new theory of original sin.[180]
>
> Romanides objects to "the peculiar teachings of the Franco-Latin tradition concerning original sin as guilt inherited from Adam, or the need of satisfying divine Justice through the sacrifice of Christ on the Cross". He has a particular contempt for Blessed Augustine of Hippo, whom he accuses of being the "original sinner" in respect of the Franco-Latin doctrine of original sin. His works mention the name of Augustine on almost every page. And yet he very rarely quotes Augustine, and his readers are not given the information necessary in order to judge whether the accusations against him are valid.[181]

According to Moss, the human being in general hates the idea of talking about sin. Therefore, great theories appeared like Marxism, Darwinism and Freudianism "in order to explain how we are supposedly not sinful at all: the real causes of 'sin' are our biological inheritance, our childhood training, our nationality or our position in the class system."[182] But if we do not return to the definition of sin in the traditional Christian sense, it will follow that the traditional divine ways of propitiation will be invalid and founded on a misunderstanding. And since the matter is so, it is no wonder that attempts are creeping in to re-interpret that idea of sin and redemption by some of the theologians in some churches. Perhaps the most dangerous of them is what Fr. John Romanides came out with in the middle

---

180 Vladimir Moss, "The Greek Neo-Soteriology," *Orthodox Christian Books*, 2011, https://www.orthodoxchristianbooks.com/articles/804/-new-soteriology/ The Greek
Neo-Soteriologists.

181 Ibid.

182 Moss, Against Romanides, 25.

of the past century, putting a new definition for sin. Fr. John Romanides, Vladimir Moss says, "has attacked the traditional concepts of sin and expiation from sin at three points: the doctrine of original sin, the doctrine of the Sacrifice for sin on the Cross, and the doctrine of Holy Baptism."[183]

Examination of Fr. John Romanides' Teachings on Original Sin

Moss asks the question, "Can we inherit sin?" And he answers it, saying:

> Nobody pretends that the doctrine of original sin is easy to understand: it is mysterious and to a certain degree counter-intuitive. But then so are several of the deepest and most central teachings of the Orthodox Faith. The temptation for the rationalist mind is to try and strip away the mystery and replace it with something that is clearer, more commonsensical. In the case of original sin, it is difficult for us to understand how sin can be passed down from Adam and Eve to all their descendants; it offends our sense of justice. [184]
>
> However, it is not *personal* responsibility for Adam's *personal* sin that is inherited. For how can we be personally responsible for something that happened before we were even born? What *is* inherited by all those who have the same nature as Adam is a certain sinful pollution of human *nature*. As St. Symeon the New Theologian

[183] Ibid.
[184] Ibid.

writes: "Human nature is sinful from its very conception. God did not create man sinful, but pure and holy. But since the first-created Adam lost this garment of sanctity, not from any other sin than pride alone, and became corruptible and mortal, all people also who came from the seed of Adam are participants of the ancestral sin from their very conception and birth. He who has been born in this way, even though he has not yet performed any sin, is already sinful through this ancestral sin."[185]

This is the teaching of the Orthodox Church. And that is why babies are baptized "for the remission of sins", not because they have committed any *personal* sins – they are too young for that – but because they have inherited *original* sin. So a certain mystery remains: the mystery of *inherited, collective guilt* that is manifest in the fact that every human being comes into this world *already polluted by sin.*[186]

Moss says:

The sin of a single man can be felt to taint his whole family or even his whole nation. But the idea that the sin of the father of mankind could have tainted the whole of the human race is rejected by Romanides and the Romanideans. Of course, this rejection is not new. The British monk Pelagius (ca. 354-420) was perhaps the first openly to question original sin. And although the ideas of Pelagius are not identical to those of

[185] St. Symeon, *Homily 37*, 3 (retrieved from Moss, Against Romanides, 25).
[186] Moss, Against Romanides, 26.

> Romanides, there is much in the old polemic between Pelagius and his main opponent, St. Augustine of Hippo, that is relevant to an evaluation of this neo-Pelagian teaching.[187]

Therefore, we find that Fr. Romanides in all his writings "has a particular contempt for Blessed Augustine of Hippo, whom he accuses of being the 'original sinner' in respect of the Franco-Latin doctrine of original sin."[188]

St. Augustine defends the idea of collective guilt as follows:

> Why did Ham sin and vengeance was declared against his son Canaan?[189] Why was the son of Solomon punished for the sin of Solomon by the breaking up of the kingdom?[190] Why was the sin of Ahab, King of Israel, visited upon his posterity?[191] How do we read in the sacred books: "Returning the iniquity of the fathers into the bosom of their children after them"[192] and "Visiting the iniquity of the fathers upon the children unto the third and fourth generation"?[193]

---

[187] Ibid.

[188] Vladimir Moss, "The Greek Neo-Soteriology," *Orthodox Christian Books*, 2011, https://www.orthodoxchristianbooks.com/articles/804/-new-soteriology/ The Greek
Neo-Soteriologists.

[189] Cf. Genesis 9:22–25.

[190] Cf. 1 Kings 12. God sees the future and sees that the son of Solomon will sin. Therefore, it is accepted in this sense. And so it is about Canaan. God knows his future and his seed as He said: Yet Jacob I have loved; but Esau I have hated; for the children not yet being born. (See Malachi 1:2-3; Romans 9:11,13).

[191] Cf. 1 Kings 21.

[192] Jeremiah 32:18.

[193] Exodus 20:5.

> ... Are these statements false? Who would say this but the most open enemy of the divine words?[194]

Moss goes deeper regarding the idea of collective guilt, in that:

> There are other passages of Holy Scripture that appear to deny the idea of collective or inherited guilt. Thus: "Parents shall not die for their children, nor children for their parents."[195] Moreover, in some cases there may be hidden reasons that explain the apparent injustice of children suffering for their parents. Thus St. John Chrysostom, commenting on Canaan's suffering for his father Ham's sin, writes: "Seeing their children bearing punishment proves a more grievous form of chastisement for the fathers than being subject to it themselves. Accordingly, this incident occurred so that Ham should endure greater anguish on account of his natural affection, so that God's blessing should continue without impairment and so that his son in being the subject of the curse should atone for his own sins. You see, even if in the present instance he bears the curse on account of his father's sin, nevertheless it was likely that he was atoning for his own failings..."[196] Again, Bishop Nikolai wrote ...: "I will ask you also – how else would the Lord God scare the people from sinning except by

---

[194] Saint Augustine, *Against Julian*, M.A. Schumacher, trans. (New York, NY: Fathers of the Church Inc., 1957), 394. This passage is quoted by Moss in Against Romanides, 26.

[195] Deuteronomy 24:16.

[196] Saint John Chrysostom, *Homilies on Genesis 18-45*, R.C. Hill, trans. (Washington, D.C.: The Catholic Church of America Press, 1990), 213.

> visiting their children with the punishment for the sin?"[197,198]

According to what Moss wrote of Archbishop Theophan, that there is a distinction between personal sin and Original Sin or Adam's sin.[199] This is the same distinction between personal sin as a human act and Original Sin as a sickness of human nature. There are indications that St. Paul the Apostle "clearly distinguished in his teaching on original sin between two points:

- παραπτωμα or transgression
- αμαρτια or sin"[200]

> By the first he understood the personal transgression by our forefathers against the will of God that they should not eat the fruit of the tree of knowledge of good and evil, and by the second—the law of sinful disorder that entered human nature as the consequence of this transgression. When he is talking about the inheritance of the original sin, he has in mind not παραπτωμα or transgression, for which only they are responsible, but αμαρτια, that is, the law of sinful disorder which afflicted human nature as a consequence of the fall into sin of our forefathers.[201]

---

[197] Velimirovich, *Missionary Letters of Saint Nikolai Velimirovich* 2, Milorad Loncar, ed. (Grayslake, IL: New Gracanica Monastery, 2009), 215 (retrieved from Moss, Against Romanides, 27).
[198] Moss, Against Romanides, 26–27.
[199] See Romans 7:23.
[200] Archbishop Theophan, "The Patristic Teaching on Original Sin," *Russkoe Pravoslavie*, №
3.20 (2000): 22 (retrieved from Moss, Against Romanides, 27–28).
[201] Moss, Against Romanides, 27-28.

In Romans 5:12, the word ημαρτον (sinned) is mentioned.

"Therefore, just as through one man sin entered the world, and death through sin, and thus death spread to all men, because all sinned."[202]

Archbishop Theophan says:

> And ημαρτον – "sinned" in Romans 5:12 must therefore be understood not in the active voice, in the sense: "committed sin," but in the middle-passive voice,[203] in the sense: αμαρτωλοι in 5:19, that is, "became sinners" or "turned out to be sinners," since human nature fell in Adam.[204]

"For as by one man's disobedience many were made sinners, so also by one Man's obedience many will be made righteous."[205]

And Moss comments, saying:

> We have inherited the law of sin, in the most basic way: through sexual reproduction.[206] For "in sins," says David, - that is, in a nature corrupted by original sin, - "did my mother conceive me" (Psalm 51:5). It follows that even newborn babies, even unborn embryos, are sinners in this sense.

---

[202] Romans 5:12.

[203] According to Vladimir Moss' explanation, which is based on Archbishop Theophan's.

[204] Archbishop Theophan, "The Patristic Teaching on Original Sin," *Russkoe Pravoslavie*, №
3.20 (2000): 22 (retrieved from Moss, Against Romanides, 28).

[205] Romans 5:19.

[206] The Coptic Orthodox Church is at variance here with Moss' idea. Sin is not transmitted to us through marriage, but it is transmitted because we are human beings from Adam's loins. Marriage and sexual relations have nothing to do with the affair, because sin has no biological or genetic entity that is transmitted genetically or biologically. But it is a matter of existence on the ontological level. Had it been a biological matter only, sin would have affected the body only, and not the spirit.

> For "even from the womb, sinners are estranged" (Psalm 58:3). And as Job says: "Who shall be pure from uncleanness? Not even one, even if his life should be but one day upon the earth" (Job 14:4–5[207]).[208]

St. Ambrose of Milan writes commenting on the Lord washing Peter's feet:[209] "Peter was clean, but he needed to wash his feet; for he still had sin by derivation from the first man, when the serpent tripped him and led him into trespass. His foot is washed that hereditary sins may be removed."[210]

The sin of Adam and Eve poisoned the life of all generations after them. This is possible because although human beings are multiple and distinct from each other, yet human nature is one. "For, as **St. Basil the Great** writes, what we inherit from Adam 'is not the personal sin of Adam, but the original human being himself,' who 'exists in us by necessity.'"[211]

St. Cyril the Alexandrian explains, [saying], "Not because they sinned along with Adam, for they did not then exist, but because they had the same nature as Adam, which fell under the law of sin."[212]

---

[207] According to LXX.

[208] Moss, Against Romanides, 28.

[209] The following passage is quoted by Moss in Against Romanides, 28.

[210] St. Ambrose, *On the Mysteries and the Treatise on the Sacraments by an Unknown Author*, T. Thompson, trans. (New York, NY: The Macmillan Company, 1919), 58.
St. Ambrose continues, saying, "For our own sins are remitted by baptism" (ibid.). In the Baptism rites which the saint practiced in Milan, feet were washed after the full immersion (ibid., 93, 98); yet the Fathers unanimously agreed that both Original Sin and personal sins are removed in the three-times immersion in Baptism (ibid., 98–99).

[211] St. Basil, quoted in Demetrios Tzami, *I Protologia tou M. Vasileiou, Thessaloniki*, 1970, p. 135 (retrieved from Moss, Against Romanides, 29).

[212] St. Cyril, *Commentary on Romans*, PG 74: 788–789 (retrieved from Moss, Against Romanides, 30).

Romanides' Radicalism in His Erroneous Understanding of Sin

Moss says:

> But Romanides' radicalism goes further than his denial of the inheritance of sin: it extends to his understanding of sin as such. Thus even Adam's sin is not deemed by him to be sin in the usual sense.[213]

Romanides says:

> Many understand the fall now as an ethical fall, whereas when St. Symeon the New Theologian speaks about the fall, he does not have in mind an ethical fall... Symeon the New Theologian is an ascetic. He teaches asceticism and not ethics. He has in mind that men do not have noetic prayer.[214] That is what he means... In the Augustinian tradition sin has appeared under an ethical form, whereas in the Fathers of the Church it has the form of illness and the eradication of sin is presented under the form of therapy. When we have illness, we have therapy. Sin is an illness of man and not simply a disorder of his when he does not obey God like a subordinate. For sin is not an

---

[213] Moss, Against Romanides, 30.

[214] According to the Byzantine belief, when prayer is recited mentally, repeated in a mystical way within you in stillness, using your inner voice, this is called noetic prayer.
D. Wolf, "Unknown Athonite Monk: 'Concerning Noetic Prayer, Prayer of the Heart, and Watchful Prayer,'" *First Thoughts of God*, 16 Jan. 2017, https://firstthoughtsofgod.com/2017/01/16/unknown-athonite-monk-concerning-noetic-prayer-prayer-of-the-heart-and-watchful-prayer/.

> act and transgression of the commandments of God, as happens with a transgression of the laws of the State, etc. There exist laws, a transgressor transgresses the law and must be punished by the law. Augustine understood sin in this way, that is, that God gave commands, man transgressed the command of God and consequently was punished.[215]

In response to this claim, Moss provides a correction to this in four points, according to the Byzantine thought:

> First of all, the contrast Romanides draws between ethics and asceticism is artificial and false. Sin is the primary category of ethics, and asceticism is the science and art of the struggle against sin. So the sin of Adam and Eve was both an ethical and an ascetic fall. Ascetics train themselves to guard themselves against sinful thoughts coming to them from the world, the flesh and the devil. Eve failed to guard herself and therefore sinned. As St. Paul says, "the woman being deceived was in the transgression" (1 Timothy 2:15) – and transgression (παραβασις) is an ethical category.
>
> Secondly, the darkening of the mind and the loss of noetic prayer are the consequences of the original sin, not the sin itself. Romanides defines the fall as "the identification of the energies of the

[215] Romanides, in Metropolitan Hierotheos (Vlachos), *Empeiriki Dogmatiki tis Orthodoxou Katholikis Ekklesias kata tis Proforikes Paradoseis tou p. Ioannou Romanidi* 2 [The Empirical Theology of the Orthodox Catholic Church according to the Oral Traditions of Fr. John Romanides Vol. 2]. (Levadeia: Monastery of the Nativity of the Theotokos, 2011), 186–188 (retrieved from Moss, Against Romanides, 30). (Henceforth cited as Romanides, in Vlachos).

mind [νους] with the energies of the logical faculty [της λογικης]. When the mind was darkened, [it] was identified in energy with the logical faculty and the passions"[216]... But this is the consequence of the fall, not the fall itself. Nor does St. Symeon the New Theologian teach anything different. As we have seen, his teaching on original sin is completely traditional - what Romanides calls "Augustinian"!

Thirdly, while sin can be called illness, and the process of removing sin – therapy, this in no way implies that the illness is not the illness of sin ... While there are obvious analogies with physical illness, sin is more than a physical illness. Whereas an ordinary physical disease is morally neutral, so to speak, the disease of original sin is far from being such: it is a sinful condition, which therefore requires, not simply treatment, but expiation through repentance and sacrifice - which cannot be identified with any changes in the relationship between the mind and the logical faculty.

For, as Alan Jacobs writes, "Many of us would agree that sin, like the more communicable diseases, transfers to other people; few of us have strong immunity to its ravages. But we would also agree that the affliction of disease is not moral in character. Although it is possible to act in such a

---

[216] Romanides, in Vlachos, Vol. 2, 190 (retrieved from Moss, Against Romanides, 31).

way that one becomes more prone to illness, surely there is no sin in being ill."[217]

Fourthly, it is nonsense to say that "sin is not an act and transgression of the commandments of God". Both the Holy Scriptures and the Holy Fathers understand personal sin as precisely a transgression of the commandments of God. "The strength of sin is the law" (1 Corinthians 15:56), and "where no law is, there is no transgression" (Romans 4:15). Therefore sin is precisely a transgression of the law or the commandment of God—in this case, the law that Adam and Eve were not to eat of the fruit of the tree of life. As for the idea that "sin is an illness of man and not simply a disorder of his when he does not obey God like a subordinate", does Romanides not think that man is God's subordinate?! Of course, man in the unfallen state is not merely a subordinate: he is also God's son. But even the sinless son is subordinate to his father, as Adam was to God in Paradise, and as Christ Himself will be to the Father at the Second Coming (1 Corinthians 15:28[218]).[219]

Sin and Death According to Romanides

According to Romanides, what is passed down from Adam to his descendants is not sin, but death. And death is not considered to be a

---

[217] A. Jacobs, *Original Sin: A Cultural History*. (New York, NY: HarperOne, 2008), 13. (retrieved from Moss, Against Romanides, 31).

[218] "Now when all things are made subject to Him, then the Son Himself will also be subject to Him who put all things under Him, that God may be all in all" (1 Corinthians 15:28).

[219] Moss, Against Romanides, 30-31.

punishment for sin, but God's mercy. "God did not impose death on man as a punishment for any inherited guilt. Rather, God allowed death by reason of His goodness and His love, so that in this way sin and evil in man should not become immortal."[220,221]

Moss responds, [saying]:

This is half true. What is true is that God did not create death, and it is not God but the devil who is the cause of the entrance of death into the world... But none of this entails that death is not *also a punishment*.... So what we inherit from Adam and Eve, according to Romanides, is not sin in any shape or form, but only death, including the process of corruption and ageing that leads to death. It follows that for him every human being is born in complete innocence, and only becomes sinful later.[222]

Romanides says:

The Fathers emphasize that every man is born as was Adam and Eve. And every man goes through the same fall. The darkening of the mind happens to everyone. In the embryo, where the mind [nous] of man exists, it is not yet darkened. Every man suffers the fall of Adam and Eve by reason of the environment.[223]

---

220 Romanides, in Vlachos, Vol. 2, 193 (retrieved from Moss, Against Romanides, 32).

221 Moss, Against Romanides, 32.

222 Ibid.

223 Romanides, in Vlachos, Vol. 2, 197 (retrieved from Moss, Against Romanides, 32).

Moss responds, saying:

> However, Romanides here contradicts the teaching of the Fathers, who assert that every man is *not* born as was Adam and Eve. On the contrary, Adam and Eve were born in innocence, but their descendants in sin - "I was conceived in iniquity" (Psalm 51:5). Nor is it true that the embryo is not yet darkened, for "even from the womb, sinners are estranged" (Psalm 58:3) ... As St. Symeon the New Theologian writes: "Human nature is sinful from its very conception". Again, Nicholas Cabasilas writes: "We have not seen even one day pure from sin, nor have we ever breathed apart from wickedness, but, as the psalmist says, 'we have gone astray from the womb, we err from our birth' (Psalm 58:3)."[224] And St. Gregory Palamas,[225] writes:[226] "Before Christ we all shared the same ancestral curse and condemnation poured out on all of us from our single Forefather, as if it had sprung from the root of the human race and was the common lot of our nature. Each person's individual action attracted either reproof or praise from God, but no one could do anything about the shared curse and condemnation, or the evil inheritance that had been passed down to him

[224] N. Cabasilas, *The Life in Christ.* (Crestwood, NY: SVS Press, 1974), 77 (retrieved from Moss, Against Romanides, 33).

[225] The Coptic Orthodox Church does not believe in the opinions of Palamas concerning deification and other matters which do not have place here in this work.

[226] Gregory Palamas, *The Homilies of Saint Gregory Palamas* 1, C. Veniamin, ed. (South Canaan, PA: Saint Tikhon's Seminary Press, 2002), 52 (retrieved from Moss, Against Romanides, 33).

> and through him would pass to his descendants."[227]

Moss states that:

> Since Romanides regards every human being as pure when he first comes into the world, without any specifically sinful inheritance, he is forced to see the consequent fall of every man as coming, not from inside his nature, but from outside, from his environment.[228]

And Romanides says:

> The fall of the child comes from the environment, from parents, from uncles, from friends, etc. If the child is in the midst of a good environment, this child can grow without a problem, with noetic prayer. The child has less of a problem than the adults. He learns quickly. The child is destroyed by the environment.[229]

Moss marvels that:

> Only one thing from *within* human nature contributes to man's fall, according to Romanides: the process of ageing and corruption. For this engenders the *fear* of death, which in turn engenders the multitude of passions.[230]

---

[227] Moss, Against Romanides, 32–33.
[228] Moss, Against Romanides, 33.
[229] Romanides, in Vlachos, Vol. 2, 197 (retrieved from Moss, Against Romanides, 33).
[230] Moss, Against Romanides, 33.

For Romanides says, "Because of the sins that spring forth from the fear of death 'the whole world lieth in wickedness.' Through falsehood and fear, Satan, in various degrees, motivates sin."[231]

Again Romanides writes:

> All human unrest is rooted in inherited psychological and bodily infirmities, that is, in the soul's separation from grace and in the body's corruptibility, from which springs all selfishness. Any perceived threat automatically triggers fear and uneasiness. Fear does not allow a man to be perfected in love... The fountain of man's personal sins is the power of death that is in the hands of the devil and in man's own willing submission to him.[232]

Romanides goes back later to say:

> In the first place, the deprivation of divine grace impairs the mental powers[233] of the newborn infant; thus, the mind of man has a tendency toward evil from the beginning. This tendency grows strong when the ruling force of corruption becomes perceptible in the body. Through the power of death and the devil, sin that reigns in man gives rise to fear and anxiety and to the general instinct of self-preservation or survival.

---

[231] Romanides, *The Ancestral Sin.* (Ridgewood, NJ: Zephyr, 2002), 77 (retrieved from Moss, Against Romanides, 33).

[232] Romanides, *The Ancestral Sin.* (Ridgewood, NJ: Zephyr, 2002), 116–117 (retrieved from Moss, Against Romanides, 33).

[233] Without a doubt, deprivation of divine grace impairs the human power, but this notion does not annul the doctrine of the inheritance of Original Sin.

> Thus, Satan manipulates man's fear and his desire for self-satisfaction, raising up sin in him, in other words, transgression against the divine will regarding unselfish love, and provoking man to stray from his original destiny. Since weakness is caused in the flesh by death, Satan moves man to countless passion and leads him to devious thoughts, actions, and selfish relations with God as well as with his fellow man. Sin reigns both in death, and in the mortal body because 'the sting of death is sin.' Because of death, man must first attend to the necessities of life in order to stay alive. In this struggle, self-interests are unavoidable. Thus, man is unable to live in accordance with his original destiny of unselfish love. This state of subjection under the reign of death is the root of man's weaknesses in which he becomes entangled in sin at the urging of the demons and by his own consent. Resting in the hands of the devil, the power of the fear of death is the root from which self-aggrandizement, egotism, hatred, envy, and other similar passions spring up.[234]

In another work, Romanides writes: "Because [a man] lives constantly under the fear of death, [he] continuously seeks bodily and psychological security, and thus becomes individualistically inclined and utilitarian in attitude. Sin... is rooted in the disease of death."[235]

Moss responds to this, saying:

---

[234] Romanides, *The Ancestral Sin.* (Ridgewood, NJ: Zephyr, 2002), 162–163 (retrieved from Moss, Against Romanides, 34).
[235] Romanides, "The Ecclesiology of St. Ignatius of Antioch." (Atlanta, 1956). (retrieved from Moss, Against Romanides, 34).

But this is an exaggeration: the fear of death is not the root of all evil. Many pagan vices have nothing to do with the fear of death. When the warrior risks his life in order to rape and plunder, is his motivation the fear of death? No ... Personal sin begins only when out of fear of death we turn away from God's commandments.... The holy martyrs also conquered the fear of death ... They did not allow this fear to turn them away from the confession of Christ.

The root of all evil is the desire to live in defiance of God and His law, which is pride. That was the motivation of Eve when she took of the forbidden fruit. She feared neither God nor the death that God prophesied would take place if she disobeyed Him....Thus if all the blame for Eve's sin could be placed on the devil, it would not be her sin, but the devil's. And if the blame could be placed on her nature alone, again it would not be her sin, but simply an inevitable product of her nature, like the behavior of animals.... The fact that, whatever incitements to sin exist in our nature or in our environment, they do not explain the sin, and therefore do not excuse it.[236]

Romanides reverses the true relationship between sin and death. "Instead of the wages of sin being death," ... "it is turned upside down and the wages of death becomes sin."[237]

---

[236] Moss, Against Romanides, 34–35.
[237] Ibid., 37. In the original quote, this quote is borrowed from Patrick Pummill.

Moss, then, explains his condemnation of Romanides' thought according to the following evidence:

> St. Augustine expressed essentially the same thought, against a very similar error of the Pelagians, as follows: "... For where the apostle says, 'By one man sin entered into the world, and death by sin, and so passed upon all men', they wish the meaning to be not that sin passed over, but death... [But] all die in the sin, they do not sin in the death."[238]
>
> The Council of Orange (529) also condemned the Romanidean thesis: "If anyone asserts that Adam's transgression injured him alone and not his descendants, or declares that certainly of the death of the body only, which is the punishment of sin, but not sin also, which is the death of the soul, passed through one man into the whole human race, he will do an injustice to God, contradicting the Apostle who says: 'As through one man sin entered into the world, and through sin death, so also death passed into all men, in whom all have sinned'" (canon 2).
>
> The fact that original sin taints even children is the reason for the practice of infant baptism. And this practice in turn confirms the traditional doctrine of original sin. Thus the Council of Carthage in 252 under St. Cyprian decreed "not to forbid the baptism of an infant who, scarcely born, has sinned in nothing apart from that which proceeds from the flesh of Adam. He has received

---

[238] Augustine, *Against Two Letters of the Pelagians* 4.7 (NPNF[1] 10) (retrieved from Moss, Against Romanides, 37).

> the contagion of the ancient death through his very birth, and he comes, therefore, the more easily to the reception of the remission of sins in that it is not his own but the sins of another that are remitted."
>
> Still more relevant here is Canon 110 of the Council of Carthage in 419: "He who denies the need for young children and those just born from their mother's womb to be baptized, or who says that although they are baptized for the remission of sins they inherit nothing from the forefathers' sin that would necessitate the bath of regeneration ..., let him be anathema.[239]"[240]

And Moss says, "It follows that the teaching of Romanides on original sin falls under the anathema of the Orthodox Church."[241]

What about the translation of Romans 5:12, on which Romanides bases his erroneous teachings, that death alone is transmitted to humanity and that death is the origin of sin?

This contradiction Moss explains as follows:

> Romanides' seemingly most powerful argument rests on his rejection of the translation of Romans 5:12 used by the Councils of Carthage and Orange above. **His translation goes: "As through one man sin came into the world, and**

[239] This Canon was confirmed by the Sixth and Seventh Ecumenical Councils. Cf. Canons 114,
115 and 116 of the same Council. (This footnote is retrieved from Moss, Against Romanides, 38).

[240] Moss, Against Romanides, 37–38.

[241] Ibid., 38.

through sin death, so also death came upon all men, *because of which* [in Greek] all have sinned." This implies that all men sin because of death; so death is the cause of sin.

Another translation favored by many theologians is as follows: "As through one man sin came into the world, and through sin death, so also death came upon all men, *because* all have sinned." This implies that sin is the cause of death, but everyman's sin, not Adam's.

The traditional translation, however, which was adopted not only in the Orthodox West but also in the Slavonic translation of SS. Cyril and Methodius, is as follows: "As through one man sin came into the world, and through sin death, so also death came upon all men, in whom [i.e. in Adam] all have sinned." This implies that all men are sinners because they are "in" Adam by nature.

If we open Joseph Thayer's authoritative Greek-English Lexicon of the New Testament, and look at the various usages of the preposition επι with the dative case, we find that both the second and third translations are possible from a purely grammatical and linguistic point of view, but not Romanides' translation. Thus επι, according to the Lexicon, is sometimes equivalent to επι τουτω, οτι, meaning "on the ground of this, because", and is used in this sense in II Corinthians 5:4 and Philippians 3:12. On the other hand, in other places – for example, Mark 2:4, Mark 13:2, Matthew 9:16, Luke 5:36, Mark 2:21, Matthew 14, 8, 11, Mark 6:25, Mark 6:55,

Mark 6:39, John 11:38, Acts 8:16 and Revelation 19:14 - επι with the dative case is equivalent to the Latin 'in' with the ablative case, indicating the place where or in which something takes place or is situated. This place can also be a person, as in the famous passage: "Thou art Peter, and on this rock (επι ταυτη τη πετρα) I will build My Church" (Matthew 16:18; cf. Ephesians 2:20).[242]

Romanides' translation is excluded, not only because "because of which" corresponds to neither of the two possible translations of επι, but also because the second half of the verse, in his translation, is in direct contradiction to the first. For while the first half says that death came into the world through sin, the second half says that sin came into the world through death! It seems very unlikely that St. Paul would have meant to contradict himself in one and the same sentence![243]

Archbishop Eleutherius of Lithuania writes:

"The two halves into which we can divide the content of this verse [Romans 5:12] through the conjunctions 'as' (ωσπερ) and 'so also' (και ουτως) represent, not a parallelism, and not a comparison, but a correspondence, according to which the first is the base, the common thesis, while the second is the conclusion from it. This logical connection is indicated by the conjunction 'also'... With the universalism characteristic of the

---

[242] J.H. Thayer, *Greek-English Lexicon of the New Testament.* (Edinburgh: T. and T. Clark, 1901), 232–233 (retrieved from Moss, Against Romanides, 39).
[243] Moss, Against Romanides, 38–39.

> Apostle, and the highly generalizing flight of his thought, St. Paul in the first half speaks about the sin of the forefathers as being the cause of death in the world generally, and not in humanity alone. For the whole of creation is subject to corruption and death, not willingly but 'by reason of Him Who hath subjected the same' (Romans 8:12-22), because of the sin of Adam... From this general proposition the holy Apostle draws the conclusion concerning people that for the very same cause, that is, because of the sin of one man, they also die."[244]

Moss summarized the doctrine of Original Sin briefly, saying:

> This is the doctrine of original sin in a nutshell: Adam's sin made all his descendants sinners – not simply mortal, as Romanides would have it, but precisely sinners. And it is not because of death that all men have sinned, as Romanides would have it, but because of Adam – and more specifically, because of his "disobedience", that is, his sin, which, as the Fathers explain, is inherited by us.[245]

Moss also asks: Are there other passages of the works of St. Paul that are consistent with the traditional interpretation of Romans 5:12, in that it means "in him," that is, in Adam?

Moss explains this also and says:

---

[244] Archbishop Eleutherius, *On Redemption*, Paris, 1937 p. 47 (in Russian) (retrieved from Moss, Against Romanides, 39–40).
[245] Moss, Against Romanides, 40.

> And the answer is: yes. For in 1 Corinthians 15:22 we read: "*As in Adam* (εν τω Αδαμ) all die, so in Christ shall all be made alive." If we all die in Adam, then there can be no objection to saying that we all become sinners *in* him, as the traditionalist translation of Romans 5:12 asserts, insofar as "death is the wages of sin" and sin is "the sting of death". But in what sense are we "in" Adam? In a rather literal, physical sense, as we have seen. Adam, "the original human being himself", "exists in us by necessity" (St. Basil the Great). For all men, "from the first to the last, form one body and one life" (Bishop Nikolai). So if Adam is in us, his sinful human nature is in us, too.[246]

Conclusion

From the examination of the previous research done by Fr. John Romanides from the Byzantine Church in AD 1957, and the examination of another research which was put forward by Vladimir Moss who is also from the Byzantine Church in AD 2012, in response to "the new heretical ideas" adopted by Fr. John Romanides, according to Vladimir Moss, the reader may clearly put his finger on the extreme degree of deviation which Fr. John Romanides embraced, away from the true teaching of the orthodox Fathers and of the Scriptures concerning Ancestral Sin. Accordingly, we expect that there may be other deviations in the teachings and writings of Fr. John Romanides concerning the doctrine of redemption on the cross and the doctrine of Baptism, besides his deviation in the doctrine of Original Sin; this, however, is not the concern of the current research. Therefore, I have studied the doctrine of Original Sin

[246] Ibid.

as the Coptic Orthodox Church received it from the Early Fathers and according to the Holy Scriptures, to contrast it with other studies, whether Byzantine or non-Byzantine that explain the doctrine of Original Sin. And it may be necessary that more research be done to study the ideas, writings and teachings of Fr. John Romanides concerning the rest of the doctrines, to prevent these deviations and new heresies from infiltrating the orthodox world.

CHAPTER THREE

The Original Sin

The relationship between the human race and Adam's sin will be reviewed. Was it [i.e. the human race] affected by his sin or by its consequences only, that is, death and corruption? Or was it not affected at all?

There are three groups:

The first group believes that there is no relationship at all between the human race and Adam's sin. This belief is widespread usually with non-Christians. It is also an extension of a heresy from the fourth and fifth centuries by a heretic named Pelagius, whom the Church excommunicated, and his most famous disciples Celestius.

The second group believes that there is no relationship between the human race and Adam's sin, but it inherited from Adam the consequences of sin, those being, death and corruption. Their explanation is that sin is an act, and the human race did not participate in the act because they[247] were not in existence yet. They descended, however, from a mortal and corruptible root, so they inherited death and corruption.

[247] That is, human beings.

This opinion is adopted by the followers of neopatristic theology.

The third group believes that the human race was in Adam—as human nature and not as individuals—when he was created, when he fell, when he died, and when he became corrupt; so they were accounted sinners, mortal, and corruptible, in him. Although they were not in existence as individuals, but human nature, in its entirety, was in him. This understanding, according to the Fathers, is called the oneness of the human race. And this is what the Holy Scriptures, the exegeses of the Fathers and the orthodox liturgical texts, declare; and this is the understanding which the Coptic Orthodox Church believes, according to what was put forth in this brief study.

Were sin considered not merely an act but a separation from God—and this is what the Greek word *ἁμαρτία* expresses, which is translated to "sin," a term indicating that sin is a straying from the straight path in the relationship with God—we would realize that the second and third groups are close in thought, and that the human race was born in this deviant path which is far from God ([in] sin).

But we must adhere to the terms the Church has settled upon, especially in its liturgical prayers, along with an explanation of the meaning contained in these terms, to eliminate any misunderstanding or any ambiguity.

How Did the Early Church Deal with the Issue of the Inheritance of Adam's Sin?

Concerning the inheritance of Adam's sin, Pelagius[248] and his disciple Celestius and their followers were condemned when they denied the inheritance of Adam's sin and proclaimed the heresy that children have no need of Baptism or that Baptism of children is not for the remission of sins.

The following was stated in **the Second Council of Carthage in AD 418 (Canon 110)**:

> **If any man says that new-born children need not be baptized, or that they should indeed be baptized for the remission of sins, but that they have in them no original sin inherited from Adam which must be washed away in the bath of regeneration**, so that in their case the formula of baptism "for the remission of sins" must not be taken literally, but figuratively, **let him be anathema**; because, according to Rom. v. 12,[249] the sin of Adam has passed upon all.[250]

Note: the text of the Epistle to the Romans here is according to the Latin translation, which is in agreement with the Coptic and ancient Greek translations. H.G. Bishop Gregorius, who has a Ph.D. in the Greek language, translates it thus: "And thus

---

[248] Pelagius (354-418) was a very well-learned monk, spoke both Greek and Latin languages fluently, and studied theology. He spent some time in asceticism as a British monk. Nevertheless, he was later accused of heresy because he taught that human beings were not wounded by Adam's sin, and that they were able to completely fulfill the Law without divine help. Pelagius denied the teaching on Original Sin. The Council of Ephesus denounced Pelagius as a heretic in AD 431. His explanation of the doctrine of free will became known as Pelagianism.
[249] Romans 5:12
[250] C.J. Hefele, *A History of the Councils of the Church* 2, H.N. Oxenham, trans. (Edinburgh: T&T Clark, 1896), 458.

death spread to all men **through whom all sinned in him.**" He explains this, saying, "This Holy Scripture affirms the principle of the spread of sin from the first man Adam to all men." He also comments, saying, "It is to be noted that in the [Arabic] Beirut translation [of the Bible][251] this verse is amputated... But the Greek and the Coptic texts, and the Latin translation known as Vulgate translation, all have the text in the way we have confirmed."[252] His Grace, then, included the texts in the three languages:

In Greek:

"δια τουτο ωσπερ δι ενος ανθρωπου η αμαρτια εις τον κοσμον εισηλθεν και δια" της αμαρτιας ο θανατος και ουτως εις παντας ανθρωπους ο θανατος διηλθεν εφ ω "παντες ημαρτον"

In Latin:

In quo omnes peccaverunt

In Coptic:

Ⲉⲑⲃⲉ ⲫⲁⲓ ⲕⲁⲧⲁ ⲫⲣⲏϯ ⲉⲧⲁ ⲫⲛⲟⲃⲓ ̀ⲓ ⲉ̀ϧⲟⲩⲛ ⲉ̀ⲡⲓⲕⲟⲥⲙⲟⲥ ⲉ̀ⲃⲟⲗ ϩⲓⲧⲉⲛ ⲟⲩⲣⲱⲙⲓ ⲛ̀ⲟⲩⲱⲧ Ⲟⲩⲟϩ ⲉ̀ⲃⲟⲗ ϩⲓⲧⲉⲛ ⲫⲛⲟⲃⲓ ⲁ ⲫⲙⲟⲩ ϣⲱⲡⲓ ⲟⲩⲟϩ ⲡⲁⲓⲣⲏϯ ⲁ ⲡⲓⲙⲟⲩ ϣⲉ ⲉ̀ϧⲟⲩⲛ ⲉⲣⲱⲙⲓ ⲛⲓⲃⲉⲛ ⲫⲏⲉⲧⲁⲩⲉⲣⲛⲟⲃⲓ ⲛ̀ϧⲏⲧϥ.

"Therefore, just as sin entered the world through one man, and through sin death, and thus death entered every man, through whom they sinned in him."[253]

---

[251] Also: Van Dyck version.
[252] Bishop Gregorius, *Mawsouat Al-Lahout Al-Akeadi – Sirai Al-Tajasod Wa Al-Fidah Al-Joz' Althani* [Encyclopedia of Doctrinal Theology 7: The Mysteries of Incarnation and Redemption Part 2]. (Egypt: *Maktabat Al-Motana'ih Anba Gregorius* [The Library of the Late Abba Gregorius], 2004), 237. [Translated from Arabic text].
[253] [Translated from Arabic text].

Therefore, there is no way here to claim that the word death was dropped from the Latin text, and that the Council of Carthage and St. Augustine were mistaken and confused.

And generally, in Church councils, the laid-out topics are examined in an exceedingly detailed manner and with theological research presented by esteemed fathers. And no decision of the council is made without meticulous examination; a decision does not depend on a single verse or one person's opinion.

Therefore, when a decision or a canon is passed by an ecumenical or local Church council, the affair is final and cannot be re-examined.

The **Council of Ephesus, held in AD 431**, headed by **Pope Cyril the Pillar of Faith**, agreed to the decisions of the Council of Carthage. In the Council's letter, which was sent by the Council of Ephesus to Celestine the First, Pope of Rome, the following was stated, informing him of what had taken place in the Council of Ephesus:

> Moreover, the minutes of the actions on the **depositions of the unholy Pelagians and Celestians, Celestius, Pelagius**, Julian, Presidius, Florus, Marcellinus, Orentius, and those who hold the same opinions with them, were read in the Holy Synod, and we also have deemed it right that those things which have been decreed against them by your God-reveringness shall remain strong and firm. And we are all voters on the same side with you, **and hold them deposed.**[254]

[254]*The Third World Council* 2, J. Chrystal, trans. (Jersey City, NJ: James Chrystal, 1904), 177–182.

In another translation of the letter of the ecumenical Council of Ephesus to Pope Celestine, the text is as follows:

> **When there had been read in the holy Synod what had been done touching the deposition of the most irreligious Pelagians and Coelestines, of Coelestius, and Pelagius**, and Julian, and Præsidius, and Florus, and Marcellian, and Orontius, and those inclined to like errors, we also deemed it right (ἐδικαιώσαμεν) that the determinations of your holiness concerning them should stand strong and firm. **And we all were of the same mind, holding them deposed.**[255]

And the Council also issued canons (first and fourth) to depose Celestius, the disciple of Pelagius, and all who agree with him and his teachings:

First Canon:

> **If any Metropolitan of a Province, forsaking the holy and Ecumenical Synod, has joined the assembly of the apostates, or shall join the same hereafter; or, if he has adopted, or shall hereafter adopt, the doctrines of Celestius,** he has no power in any way to do anything in opposition to the bishops of the province, since he is already cast forth from all ecclesiastical communion and made incapable of exercising his ministry; **but he shall himself be subject in all things to those very bishops of the province and to the neighboring orthodox metropolitans,**

[255] *The Letter of the Synod to Pope Celestine* (NPNF[2] 14:239).

> **and shall be degraded from his episcopal rank.**[256]

Fourth Canon:

> **If any of the clergy should fall away, and publicly or privately presume to maintain the doctrines of Nestorius or Celestius, it is declared just by the holy Synod that these also should be deposed.**[257]

It happened, in the first session of the Council of Ephesus, that **the letter of St. Celestine Bishop of Rome to Nestorius, was read:**

> Juvenal, Bishop of Jerusalem, said: Let the Letter of the most holy and most dear-to-God Archbishop of the Romans, Celestine, be read, which he has sent concerning the faith. Peter, a Presbyter of Alexandria, and Chief of the Secretaries, read [as follows]:
>
> A Translation of an Epistle of Celestine, Bishop of Rome, to Nestorius.
>
> **Celestine to the beloved brother Nestorius: The Universal Faith had peace for some days of our lifetime, after the unholy and often condemned doctrine of Pelagius and Celestius, for both the East and the West, had smitten them with the followers of their opinions with the dart of a unanimous sentence. Straightway**

[256] *The Canons of the Two Hundred Holy and Blessed Fathers Who Met at Ephesus* 1 (NPNF[2] 14:225).
[257] *The Canons of the Two Hundred Holy and Blessed Fathers Who Met at Ephesus* 4 (NPNF[2] 14:229).

> **Atticus of holy memory, the teacher of the Universal Faith, and verily successor of the Blessed John, in that same course of thinking and acting also, so pursued them on behalf of the Common King, that no permission was granted them to stay there.**[258]

It is clear from this letter that the faith was in common between the East and West, and that both the East and West condemned Pelagianism.

Also, in the eighth passage of this letter, [the following is written]:

> **And furthermore, in relation to those heretics, regarding whom you, as not knowing [yourself] the matters concerning them, have wished to ask us, [we would say that] a righteous condemnation and decision has thrust them out from their own thrones, on the ground of their having spoken unrighteous things, but we do not wonder that they have found rest there; for they found impious preaching, in comparison with which they deemed themselves innocent. At this point, inasmuch as the proper time to speak has demanded it, we cannot be silent in regard to that at which we are amazed. We have read how you believe well in regard to original sin, and how you show that our nature itself is whelmed in debt, and that you rightly impute that debt to him who is descended from the race of the debtor. What are those who have been condemned for**

---

[258] *The Third World Council* 1, J. Chrystal, trans. (Jersey City, NJ: James Chrystal, 1895), 178–180.

> **denying those truths doing with you? Things which contradict each other are never in agreement with each other without suspicion being excited.** Moreover, they would have been expelled if they had been similarly displeasing to you also. Furthermore, why do you now search for the Actions against them, when it is clear that the Minutes [of those Actions] were sent thence to us by the then Bishop, the Catholic Atticus. Why did not Sisinnius[259] of holy memory have to seek for them? Undoubtedly because he approved of the righteous condemnation of those [heretics] by his predecessor.[260]

St. Cyril the Great, also, said in the Council of Ephesus, in the fifth session:

> **For we have never yet held the errors of** Apolinarius, nor those of Arius, nor those of Eunomius, but from the time when we were little we have learned the sacred Scriptures, and have been brought up in the hands of orthodox and holy fathers. And we anathemize Apolinarius, and Arius, and Eunomius, and Macedonius, Sabellius, Photinus, Paul, and the Manicheans, and every **other heresy**, and, besides them, Nestorius the contriver of the new blasphemies, and **those who commune with him and agree with him, and those who hold the errors of Celestius, that is of Pelagius. We have never held the errors of those men.** Nor have we now by a change of mind become willing to hold the right doctrines; **but, as**

[259] Bishop of Constantinople who reposed in AD 427.

[260] *The Third World Council* 1, J. Chrystal, trans. (Jersey City, NJ: James Chrystal, 1895), 193–194.

I have said, we have been brought up in the right and apostolic dogmas of the Church.[261]

This quote makes it clear that St. Cyril the Great knew of the issue of Pelagius and Celestius, and he considered their opinions erroneous. And this answers the claim that the Council of Ephesus did not discuss the heresy of Pelagius, and that the approval of [the Council] of Ephesus to the decisions of the Council of Carthage was without going into theological details.

And needless to say, deposing someone by a council's decision means banning his teaching and not merely his person, because there are no personal enmities with people. So, there is no room here to claim that the Council of Ephesus agreed to depose people only, without agreeing with the decisions of the Council of Carthage concerning the teaching. Also, there is no council's decision or a saying of the Fathers, throughout the history of the Church, that deposes anyone who teaches about the inheritance of Adam's sin, while the opposite is true in the local Council of Carthage, which was approved by the ecumenical Council of Ephesus.

That some of the sayings of the Fathers and the liturgical texts focus on the inheritance of death and corruption "φθορά" more than focusing on the inheritance of Original Sin, does not mean that they do not approve the inheritance of sin. And this is likely to happen with all the teaching of the Church.

For example, in the Creed of Nicea and Constantinople, there is no mention of the Eucharist, nor the Priesthood, nor the prayer for the departed, nor the intercessions of the saints—

[261] *The Third World Council* 2, J. Chrystal, trans. (Jersey City, NJ: James Chrystal, 1904), 155.

does this mean that the Fathers did not approve of these doctrines?

On the contrary, sometimes not mentioning a subject, or not focusing on it, is a proof that there is no second view about it. In [the Council of] Nicea they did not talk about the divinity of the Holy Spirit, and in the Nicene Creed nothing was mentioned about the Holy Spirit, because the matter of His divinity was not a subject of doubt or examination.

If one found sayings of any of the esteemed Church Fathers, which some may think to be opposed to the inheritance of Adam's sin, these writings must be understood [to mean] that we did not partake in the [act of] eating with Adam because we did not exist yet as individuals. This is exactly what our Church believes in, formerly and currently. Or it may be that the holy Father, in his sayings, is responding to the heresy of Mani which prohibited marriage. The Coptic Orthodox Church, however, teaches what the holy Fathers taught from the beginning, that we were in Adam and were tainted by his sin.

The one who teaches that St. Augustine was the first to talk about Original Sin is like the one who teaches that St. Athanasius was the first to proclaim the equality of the Son with the Father in Essence, where he coined the term ὁμοούσιος in the Council of Nicea.

The Church from the beginning believed in the equality of the Son and the Father in Essence, but St. Athanasius the Apostolic was the first to formally pen this term ὁμοούσιος to express this precious truth of the faith.

Likewise, the Church believed in the inheritance of Original Sin, but St. Augustine may have been the first to sculpt and to formally pen the expression and to focus on it.

The same can be said about some of the non-biblical theological terms, which the Fathers engraved in their times, but this did not indicate that this was the onset of the Church's belief in these terms. For the belief exists in the Church from the beginning, but the heretics pushed the Church to coin these theological terms to set the truth of the Divinity within clear boundaries. Examples of such terms are: The Trinity, Hypostasis, Essence, the Nature, Hypostatic Distinction...

St. Athanasius coined the term ὁμοούσιος as a response to Arianism; in like manner St. Augustine used the term "Original Sin" in response to Pelagianism. The Fathers who were his contemporaries did not object to him using the term Original Sin, especially St. Cyril the Great who was a contemporary of St. Augustine.

It is, likewise, inappropriate to accuse St. Cyril the Great of not having read St. Augustine's writings, written in Latin, because mutual letters between them have come down through history.

For **St. Cyril the Great** had sent a letter to the Council of Carthage while in progress, and he blessed those gathered, in his letter, number 85, to Bishop Aurelius, the head of the Council, and Bishop Valentinus, and "all the most holy synod assembled in Carthage,"[262] Augustine of course being one of them. Then **St. Cyril the Great** said to them at the end of the letter: "May our God and Lord protect your holy synod; this we pray, most honored brethren."[263]

St. Augustine also sent a letter to St. Cyril the Great, around the summer of AD 417, talking to him about Pelagius and his danger, and he thanked him for sending him the proceedings of

---

[262] St. Cyril of Alexandria, *Letters 51–110*, J.I. McEnerney, trans. (Washington, D.C.: The Catholic University of America Press, 1987), 117.
[263] Ibid.

the Council of Jerusalem, Lydda/Diospolis, which is a council that was held in AD 415, in which Pelagius deceived the synod and therefore he was exonerated. **St. Augustine** says in his letter to St. Cyril the Great, which he sent to Cyril with the servant Justus, the servant of God from Alexandria:

> Your Sincerity recalls, I think, that you sent us the acts of the council held in the province of Palestine where the supposedly catholic Pelagius[264] was acquitted, when he succeeded in concealing himself within the clever hiding places of his words and deceived our brothers who then presided as judges when no one representing the other side came forward to expose him. When I had read and studied these proceedings as carefully as I could, I wrote a book about them for our venerable brother and fellow bishop, Aurelius, bishop of the church of Carthage, in which, as much as the Lord permitted to be demonstrated, how it was that catholic judges understood Pelagius' answers so that they came to the verdict that he was a catholic. For many who were caught in that error of his were boasting that since he had been acquitted, his heretical teachings had been confirmed as catholic by the judgment of catholic bishops and with these people spreading this story just about everywhere, very many, not knowing what had really happened, believed what they were saying to the great scandal of the churches.

[264] He means that Pelagius' followers spread that his teaching was in agreement with the teaching of the catholic Church (catholic faith).

> In order to get rid of this misconception, I wrote the book mentioned above. Here, to the best of my ability, I showed that, even though Pelagius had been acquitted—not by God, whom no one can deceive, but in a human court which he was able to deceive—still those pestiferous teachings of his were condemned; even he himself anathematized them.
>
> The servant of God, Justus, the bearer of this letter to your Worship, had a copy of this book of mine.[265]

He also says to St. Cyril:

> Therefore, I commend brother Justus to your most pious Holiness so that you not only may defend him from slanderers but also may deign with pastoral concern and fatherly mildness or even, if necessary, with a doctor's harshness, to correct those very people whom he, not without reason, suspects, lest they both lose their souls and introduce the Pelagian poison into them. Or, if you find them sound in faith, remove from his soul any worries based on his own suspicions (of them). For they are all Latin speakers and have come to those places from the western church, in which we also find ourselves. Thus it is especially necessary for us to commend them to your worship lest it appear that they themselves chose these lands in order to hide with impunity among the Greeks. For there, when they discuss these matters, they are less likely to be understood and

---

265 Augustine of Hippo, *Letters 1*–29**, T.P. Halton, ed.; R.B. Eno, trans. (Washington, DC: The Catholic University of America Press, 1989), 41–42.

> thus their error cannot easily be exposed. And so we are doing things this way, not so that we may be grieved by someone's death but that insofar as this is possible, we might rejoice in the salvation of all.[266]

Also concerning the book St. Augustine pointed to in his letter to St. Cyril, which he sent to St. Cyril the Great, there is an opinion [claiming] that this book was the only book St. Augustine had written which has a Greek translation,[267] to prevent the deception of Pelagius (and the proponents of his heresy) from deceiving those who speak Greek but do not know Latin. This book was translated into English, titled, "On the Proceedings of Pelagius."[268]

I have included this letter as evidence [for the existence] of correspondences between St. Cyril the Great and the Fathers of the West, especially St. Augustine.

And it is worthy of remembrance that St. Augustine was officially invited to attend the Council of Ephesus but he passed away before the council was held. And this we find [stated] in the following:

> **The Emperor had despatched a peculiarly respectful letter to Augustine**, on account of his great celebrity, inviting him to come to the Synod at Ephesus, and had expressly entrusted an official of the name of Ebagnius with the delivery of the

---

[266] Ibid., 43.

[267] N. McCallum. "Original Sin and Ephesus: Carthage's Influence on the East." *Orthodox West Blog*, 4 Jan. 2019, https://journal.orthodoxwestblogs.com/2019/01/04/original-sin-and-ephesus-carthages-influence-on-the-east/.

[268] Augustine of Hippo, *Four Anti-Pelagian Writings*, T.P. Halton, ed.; J.A. Mourant and W.J. Collinge, trans. (Washington, DC: The Catholic University of America Press, 1992), 91–177.

> letter. **But Augustine was already (August 22 [28], 430) dead**, and thus the bearer of the letter could only bring back to Constantinople the news of his death.[269]

In the discourse of the first session, too, of the Council of Ephesus, [the following is mentioned]:

> The edict in which he announced this decree was addressed to all those archbishops and prominent bishops who had previously received special invitations to the Synod of Ephesus, **and probably through an error of the chancery there is still found among them the name of Augustine, who had died eleven months before (August 28, 430).**[270]

Also, a letter was sent from the Fathers of Carthage to the Council of Ephesus, which was read, in which the Archbishop of Carthage apologized for not attending the ecumenical Council due to war:

> The last document which was produced at this first session was the letter of Capreolus, Archbishop of Carthage, in which he asks them, on account of the war in Africa (consequent upon the invasion of the Vandals), to excuse his own inability to be present, or to send any of his suffragan bishops. Besides, he said, the Emperor's letter of invitation had not reached him until Easter 431, and thus too late; **and Augustine, whose presence the Emperor specially wished, had died some time before.** He (the archbishop)

---

[269] C.J. Hefele, *A History of the Councils of the Church* 3. (Edinburgh: T&T Clark, 1883), 41.
[270] Ibid., 82–83.

> therefore sent only his deacon Bessula, and prayed the Synod to tolerate no novelties whatever in matters of religion. In this he does not refer expressly to Nestorius, but he unmistakably indicates that he reckons his doctrines among the unauthorized novelties. The Synod gave its approval to this letter of the African bishop.[271]

And in the letter from John of Antioch and the synod of his bishops to St. Cyril, he says:

> You are a man of such prudence that you need no one to instruct you in such matters. While you may be at a distance, you see each one and regard him no less than those who are present.[272]

St. Augustine was not the only one facing Pelagius but the entire Council of Carthage, in addition to St. Jerome in Palestine also, who faced him with the help of Galatian bishops, Heros and Lazarus, where they presented a list of the errors of Pelagius and his writings. These two bishops could not attend due to illness, even though this council session was held through their efforts and their calling for it. Also, the Pope of Rome in his letter to Nestorius, which was read in the Council of Ephesus, confirmed that the bishops of Constantinople, prior to Nestorius, had condemned Pelagius and his disciple Celestius, and had expelled them. The canons of the Council of Ephesus also condemned them, and also what St. Cyril said in the fifth session of the Council of Ephesus condemned Pelagius and Celestius and their teachings and deposed them. And thus the East, and the West represented in the Council of Carthage

---

[271] Ibid., 50.

[272] St. Cyril of Alexandria, *Letters 51–110*, J.I. McEnerney, trans. (Washington, D.C.: The Catholic University of America Press, 1987), 55.

and St. Augustine, both were united in defending the upright faith in the same sole matter.[273]

The Term Original Sin

Although some may claim that St. Augustine was the first to use the term "Original Sin," the term can be found in the writings of the Fathers before St. Augustine, those who were his contemporaries and those who came after him. Here I do not use the appearance of the term "Original Sin" in the Fathers' writings as evidence of their belief in the inheritance of Adam's sin, for this [latter] has many other proofs which will be provided in this research, but only to fend off the accusation that St. Augustine was the first to use this term, and that the term "Original Sin" was absent in the writings of the Eastern Fathers, as stated in Dr. George Habib Bibawy's book, which is contrary to the faith of the holy Church, in which he said: "Likewise also the subject of the Original Sin was absent, not only from the writings of Athanasius, but from all the works of the Eastern Fathers."[274]

This was in addition to Dr. George Habib Bibawy's other numerous mistakes. It is stated, for example, in one of his writings, that "Athanasius did not mention that the Crucifixion was to pay the price of sins, nor to endure the punishment, nor was it for the forgiveness of sins, as is prevalent now."[275]

---

[273] See C.J. Hefele, *A History of the Councils of the Church* 2, H.N. Oxenham, trans. (Edinburgh: T&T Clark, 1896), 450–451.

[274] G.H. Bibawy, *Mawt Al-Maseeh Ala Al-Saleeb* [The Death of Christ on the Cross]. (Egypt: Center of Coptic and Orthodox Studies, 2006), 256. [Translated from Arabic text].

[275] Ibid.

The Term Ancient Sin, or First, or Original, or Ancestral, in the Writings of the Fathers

St. Severus of Antioch says: "As when we preach the favor of the Resurrection, we indicate that **by it we have risen from the Fall of the Ancient Sin.**"[276]

St. Pope Athanasius the Apostolic says, "Christ offered the sacrifice on behalf of all, delivering His own shrine to death instead of all that He might set all free from the liability of the original transgression."[277]

The word ἀρχαίας which St. Athanasius the Apostolic used in his book "On the Incarnation," Chapter 20, means "the original" or "the beginning of the thing," and does not mean "the first" as a rank or number.

"ὑπὲρ πάντων τὴν θυσίαν ἀνέφερεν, ἀντὶ πάντων τὸν ἑαυτοῦ ναὸν εἰς θάνατον παραδιδούς, ἵνα τοὺς μὲν πάντας ἀνυπευθύνους καὶ ἐλευθέρους τῆς **ἀρχαίας παραβάσεως** ποιήσῃ"[278]

St. Athanasius used it several times, for example, in his explanation of the Book of Psalms:

> "Behold, I was brought forth in iniquity, and in sin my mother conceived me." That is, previously God's purpose was that we would not be born

[276] Severus of Antioch, *Serat Wa Makalat Al-Kidees Sawirus Al-Antaki* [The Biography and Treatises of St. Severus of Antioch], Joseph Habib, trans. (Egypt: Baramous Monastery, 2017) 460. [Translated from Arabic text].

[277] C. Dratsellas, *Questions of the Soteriological Teaching of the Greek Fathers: with Special Reference to St. Cyril of Alexandria*. (Athens: Journal θεολογια, 1969), 25.
[Another translation of this quote is as follows: "He now offered the sacrifice on behalf of all, delivering his own temple to death in the stead of all, in order to make all not liable to and free from the ancient transgression." Saint Athanasius, *On the Incarnation*, J. Behr, trans. (Yonkers, NY: SVS Press, 2011), 70].

[278] Athanasius, *On the Incarnation* 20 (PG 25.132a).

through marriage (the fleshly lust in marriage) and corruption, but the disobedience of the commandment introduced marriage (the lust of the flesh in marriage) because of Adam's transgression, that is, because he disobeyed the commandment which was given unto him by God. **Thus, all of Adam's seed was brought forth in iniquity and is in subjection to the condemnation of its Ancestor.** As for "and in sin my mother conceived me," it means that our mother, all of us, Eve was first to bear sin when the desire for pleasure reigned over her; **therefore, we also fall under the condemnation which is the first[279] mother's, saying, "We were conceived in sin."** This confirms that because of Eve's disobedience, immediately from the beginning human nature fell into sin, and giving birth, subsequently, is subjected to the curse.

On the other hand, he speaks about the events that took place since the beginning, because he wants to show the greatness of God's gift. "Behold, You desire truth in the inward parts, and in the hidden part You will make me to know wisdom." The meaning is the following: He says that You, O Lord, are the truth, and You love the truth, and You desire that we live in the truth. **You will purge us completely from the first sin**; You will purge us with hyssop until we become as white as snow. On the other hand, it resembles the

[279] Literally: uppermost.

work of the Holy Spirit, which is fiery and soaks up all our uncleanness with the hyssop.[280]

In the old Greek text, the word "the first sin" is ἀρχαίας ἁμαρτίας, but a more accurate translation is "the Original Sin."

Ἰδοὺ γὰρ ἀλήθειαν ἠγάπησας, τὰ ἄδηλα καὶ τὰ κρύφια τῆς σοφίας σου ἐδήλωσάς μοι. Ὁ νοῦς οὗτος· Σὺ, φησὶ, Κύριε, ὁ ἀλήθεια ὢν, ἀληθείας ἀγαπῶν, βουλόμενος ἡμᾶς ἐν ἀληθείᾳ διάγειν, ἀποκαθαριεῖς ἡμᾶς **τῆς ἀρχαίας ἁμαρτίας·** καὶ οὕτως ἀποκαθαριεῖς ἡμῖν δι' ὑσσώπου ὡς καὶ ὑπὲρ χιόνα λευκανθῆναι.[281]

This is confirmed by [definitions from] from the following dictionaries:

ἀρχαῖος, from the beginning, original[282]

ἀρχαῖος (archaios), ancient; old; original[283]

ἀρχαῖος, original, primitive; ancient[284]

St. Gregory Nazianzus uses the term "the original nakedness."

"For this reason, a lamb is chosen for its innocence and for the clothing of the original nakedness."[285,286]

---

280 Saint Athanasius the Apostolic, *Tafseer Sifr Al-Mazameer Al-Joz' Al-Thalith* [Exegesis on the Book of Psalms Vol. 3], G.M. Andrawis, trans. (Egypt: St. Anthony Press–The Orthodox Center for Patristic Studies in Cairo, 2021), 66–67. [Translated from Arabic text].

281 Athanasius, Expositions on the Psalms (PG 27.241a).

282 *A Patristic Greek Lexicon*, G.W.H. Lampe, ed. (Oxford, ENG: At The Clarendon Press, 1961). 232.

283 R. Brannan, *The Lexham Analytical Lexicon to the Greek New Testament*. (Logos Bible Software, Lexham Press, 2011).

284 *A Pocket Lexicon to the Greek New Testament*, A. Souter. (Oxford, ENG: Clarendon Press, 1917), 38.

285 St. Gregory of Nazianzus, *Festal Orations*, J. Behr, ed., N.V. Harrison, Trans. (Crestwood, NY: SVS Press, 2008), 172.

286 "καὶ τὸ ἔνδυμα τῆς ἀρχαίας γυμνώσεως" Gregory Nazianzus, Oratio XLV. *In sanctum pascha* (PG 36.640c).

St. Basil the Great used another word, πρωτοτυπον, which means "the original":

St. Basil of Caesarea [At a Time of Famine and Drought 8, 7]:

> Little given, much gotten; **by the donation of food the original sin is discharged. Just as Adam transmitted the sin by his wicked eating,** we destroy that treacherous food when we cure the need and hunger of our brother.[287]

Another translation [of this passage]:

> Give but a little, and you will gain much; **undo the primal sin by sharing your food. Just as Adam transmitted sin by eating wrongfully**, so we wipe away the treacherous food when we remedy the need and hunger of our brothers and sisters.[288]

The original ancient Greek text where the term "Original Sin" is used in the previous quote [is as follows]:

Δὸς ὀλίγα, καὶ πολλὰ κτῆσαι· λῦσον τὴν **πρωτότυπον ἁμαρτίαν** τῇ τῆς τροφῆς μεταδόσει.[289]

την πρωτοτυπον αμαρτιαν: the Original Sin

πρωτοτυπον: original, primal.

"πρωτό-τυπος, ον, original, archetypal. τὸ πρωτότυπον, the original."[290]

---

[287] *The Faith of the Early Fathers* 2, W.A. Jurgens, trans. (Collegeville, MN: The Liturgical Press, 1970–1979), 23.

[288] Basil of Caesarea, *On Social Justice*, C.P. Schroeder, trans. (New York: SVS Press, 2009), 86.

[289] Basil, *Homilia dicta tempore famis et siccitatis* (PG 31.324c).

[290] E.A. Sophocles, *Greek Lexicon of the Roman and Byzantine Periods (From B. C. 146 to A. D. 1100)*. (New York, NY: Charles Scribner's Sons, 1900), 959.

St. Cyril the Great used the term ἀρχαίας several times. I will present two translations in English and a third translation in Arabic[291] of the same text.

> It was impossible for us to be restored, **once we had fallen because of the original transgression**, back to our original beauty except by attaining an ineffable communion and union with God.[292]

Another English translation [of this text]:

> It was, perhaps, impossible **for us who had once fallen away through the original transgression** to be restored to our pristine glory, except we obtained an ineffable communion and unity with God.[293]

It is clear here [from] the term "the original transgression" and "we had fallen" by the Original Sin, that St. Cyril not only mentions the term, but also confirms the inheritance of Original Sin.

Also of the early Syrian Fathers is the saint **Mar Jacob of Serug**, from the 5th century. The following quote was translated from Syriac [to Arabic] by the fathers of the Syrian Church.

> That Christ the Redeemer is the Lord of Peace and is the Sacrifice by which sinners are justified, is the Everlasting King whose kingdom has no beginning nor end; and He became a Mediator, reconciling the two contending sides, breaking the gates of Hades. And no longer is the world in

[291] [The Arabic translation is not included in the English translation of this book].
[292] Cyril of Alexandria, *Commentary on John* 2, J.C. Elowsky, T.C. Oden, and G.L. Bray, eds.; D.R. Maxwell, trans. (Downers Grove, IL: IVP Academic, 2015), 302.
[293] Cyril of Alexandria, *Commentary on the Gospel according to S. John* 2. (London, ENG: Walter Smith, 1885), 545.

> need of Aaron, because the Son took his place **and came to liberate the earthly from the bonds of original sin.**[294]

The founder of monasticism, **St. Abba Anthony the Great** says in his first letter:

> Then the Spirit that is his guide begins to open the eyes of his soul, to give to it also repentance, that it may be purified. The mind also starts to discriminate between the body and the soul, as it begins to learn from the Spirit how to purify both by repentance. And, taught by the Spirit, the mind becomes our guide to the labors of body and soul, showing us how to purify them. **And it separates us from all the fruits of the flesh which have been mingled with all the members of the body since the first transgression, and brings back each of the members of the body to its original condition, having nothing in it from the spirit of satan.** And the body is brought under the authority of the mind, being taught by the Spirit, as St. Paul says: "I keep under my body, and bring it into subjection". (1 Cor. 9:17). For the mind purifies it from food and from drink and from sleep, and in a word from all its motions, until through its own purity it frees the body even from the natural emission of seed.[295]

---

[294] Jacob of Serug, *Mokhtarat Min Kasa'id Mar Yakob Oskof Sirouj* [A Selection of the Poems of Mar Jacob Bishop of Serug], Metropolitan Malatios Barnaba, trans. (Aleppo, Syria: Dar El-Raha,1993), 83–84. [Translated from Arabic text].

[295] *The Letters of Saint Antony the Great*, Derwas J. Chitty, trans. (Oxford, UK: SLG Press, 2005), 2.

The Idea of the Inheritance of Original Sin Apart from the Term Itself

The affair is not a mere expression or term (Original Sin), but is a thought[296] that has permeated the faith of the Church since the beginning. The Fathers used clear and explicit terms to express all of humanity's partaking in Original Sin because of its existence in Adam.

St. Didymus the Blind the Alexandrian (AD 313–398) says in his book *Against the Manichaeans*:

> If Christ had received his body from a marital union and not in another way it would be supposed that he too is liable to an accounting for **that sin, which indeed, all who are descended from Adam contract in succession.**[297]

St. Cyril the Great says, "Of old we were vanquished, and fallen in Adam;[298]... by eating we were conquered in Adam."[299]

> **We became partakers of Adam's offense**, and because of his sins we were punished, the curse reaching all, and wrath extending over his seed. Therefore, the Only-begotten descended and placed Himself in submission to God the Father, and became man and dwelled among us. For it says, "[He] became obedient to the point of death,"[300] blotting out the consequences of the

---

[296] Or: understanding.
[297] *The Faith of the Early Fathers* 2, W.A. Jurgens, trans. (Collegeville, MN: The Liturgical Press, 1970–1979), 64.
[298] Cyril of Alexandria, *A Commentary upon the Gospel According to S. Luke* 1, R.P. Smith, trans. (Oxford, ENG: Oxford Press, 1859), 49.
[299] Ibid., 54.
[300] Philippians 2:8.

> **disobedience of all,**[301] and **the disobedience of each one separately,**[302] and by this He saved us. Paul testifies about this, saying, "Therefore, as through one man's offense judgement came to all men, resulting in condemnation, even so through one Man's righteous act the free gift came to all men, resulting in justification of life. For as by one man's disobedience many were made sinners, so also by one Man's obedience many will be made righteous."[303,304]

The idea of the disobedience of all and the disobedience of each one separately, **St. Cyril the Great** reiterates in the following text:

> Since the first man trampled on the divine command and **human nature succumbed to the propensity to sin**, the Word of God, who is unchangeable by nature and holy and righteous and hating injustice became like us and was anointed a slave. He was enrolled under God the Father because of his human nature, even though he is God, and he is said to have been anointed by him through the Holy Spirit, though he did not receive this for himself. After all, as God he is holy by nature. No, he was leading us by grace through himself, as it were, and making us worthy of the

---

[301] By "the disobedience of all" here is meant Adam's sin, for which all became accountable.

[302] By "the disobedience of each one separately" is meant personal sins. So the Master in the economy of His forgiveness has covered both kinds of sins: Original Sin (the disobedience of all) and the actually-committed sins (the disobedience of each one separately).

[303] Romans 5:18–19.

[304] Cyril the Great, *Al-Sojoud Wa Al-Ibada Bi-Al Rouh Wa Al-Hak* [Worshipping and Serving in Spirit and in Truth], G.A. Ibrahim, trans. (Egypt: The Orthodox Center for Patristic Studies, 2017), 461. [Translated from Arabic text].

> Father's blessing, **even though we offended him long ago both because of the transgression in Adam, and after that because of our own sin that tyrannizes us.**[305]

And this indicates that St. Cyril the Great was convinced that we were defeated and fallen in Adam's sin and [that this was] not a mere expression that was stated by chance in his writings.

He also says:

> **Since on account of the transgression in Adam, sin has reigned against all, and then the Holy Ghost fled away from the human nature and it came therefore to be in all ill**, and it needed that by the Mercy of God, it mounting up to its pristine condition should be accounted worthy of the Spirit:—the Only-Begotten Word of God became Man, and appeared to them on earth with Body of earth, and was made free from sin, that in Him Alone the nature of man crowned with the glories of sinlessness, should be rich in the Holy Ghost, and thus be re-formed unto God through holiness: for thus does the grace pass through to us too, having for its beginning Christ the First-born among us.[306]

---

[305] Cyril of Alexandria, *Commentaries on Romans, 1-2 Corinthians, and Hebrews*, J.C. Elowsky, G.L. Bray, M. Glerup, and T.C. Oden, eds.; D.R. Maxwell, trans. (Downers Grove, IL: IVP Academic, 2022), 113.

[306] Cyril of Alexandria, *Five Tomes Against Nestorius; Scholia on the Incarnation; Christ Is One; Fragments Against Diodore of Tarsus, Theodore of Mopsuestia, the Synousiasts*. (Oxford, ENG: James Parker and Co., 1881), 186.

Also:

> **Therefore, the lot of the necessary endurance of death hung over those on the earth through the transgression in Adam and through sin reigning from him until us.** But the Word of God the Father, being generous in clemency and love of men, became flesh, that is, man, in the form of us who are under sin, and he endured our lot. For as the very excellent Paul writes, "By the grace of God he tasted death for all,"[307] **and he made his life be an exchange for the life of all. One died for all, in order that we all might live to God sanctified and brought to life through his blood**, "justified as a gift by his grace."[308] For as the blessed evangelist John says, "The blood of Jesus Christ cleanses us from all sin."[309,310]

And also:

> "He will smite us and bind us up. After two days, on the third day, he will heal us, and we will arise and live before him and know him. We will pursue knowledge of the Lord, and we will find him ready like the morning."[311] **He struck us because of the transgression in Adam by saying** "Earth you are, and to earth you will return."[312] That which was smitten by decay and death he bound up once again on the third day, that is, not

---

[307] Hebrews 2:9.
[308] Romans 3:24.
[309] 1 John 1:7.
[310] St. Cyril of Alexandria, *Letters 1-50*, J.I. McEnerney, trans. (Washington, D.C.: The Catholic University of America Press, 1987), 174.
[311] Hosea 6:1–3 LXX.
[312] Genesis 2:19 LXX.

> the beginning or the middle but at the end times, when he became human for us.[313]

The same understanding **St. Gregory of Nyssa** offers in the following text:

> The time, then, has come, and bears in its course the remembrance of holy mysteries, purifying man,—mysteries **which purge out from soul and body even that sin which is hard to cleanse away**, and which bring us back to that fairness of our first estate which God, the best of artificers, impressed upon us. Therefore it is that you, the initiated people, are gathered together; and you bring also that people who have not made trial of them, leading, like good fathers, by careful guidance, the uninitiated to the perfect reception of the faith. I for my part rejoice over both;—over you that are initiated, because you are enriched with a great gift: over you that are uninitiated, because you have a fair expectation of hope—remission of what is to be accounted for, release from bondage, close relation to God, free boldness of speech, and in place of servile subjection equality with the angels. For these things, and all that follow from them, the grace of Baptism secures and conveys to us.[314]

Note here that St. Gregory of Nyssa uses the term "sin" and not "sins." This use indicates the sin of the whole world, that is, Adam's sin which became an inheritance borne by all men. This

---

[313] Cyril of Alexandria, *Commentary on John* 1, J.C. Elowsky, T.C. Oden, and G.L. Bray, eds.; D.R. Maxwell, trans. (Downers Grove, IL: IVP Academic, 2015), 91.

[314] Gregory of Nyssa *On the Baptism of Christ* (NPNF^2 5:518).

is in addition to our own sins which we commit every day because of the weakness of our nature.

Apart from the understanding of sin and sins, the Fathers also taught about the entire human nature's partaking of Adam in the sin, without our existence as individuals.

So **St. Gregory Nazianzus** says:

> **We were all without exception created anew, who partake of the same Adam, and were led astray by the serpent and slain by sin**, and are saved by the heavenly Adam and brought back by the tree of shame[315] to the tree of life from whence we had fallen.[316]

Note here how the Fathers are in agreement, in their explanation, on the truth that in Adam, all of humankind is contained when he was created and when he sinned.

St. Cyril the Great confirms, [saying]:

> For that we sinned in Adam first, and trampled underfoot the Divine commandment. For He was dishonored for our sake, in that He took our sins upon Him, as the prophet says,[317] and was afflicted on our account. For as He wrought out our deliverance from death, giving up His own Body to death, so likewise, I think, the blow with which Christ was smitten, in fulfilling the dishonor that **He bore, carried with it our deliverance from the dishonor by which we were burdened through the transgression and**

[315] i.e. the cross.
[316] Gregory Nazianzen *Oration XXXIII. Against The Arians, and Concerning Himself* 9 (NPNF[2] 7:331).
[317] Isaiah 53:4 LXX.

> **original sin of our forefather.** For He, being One, was yet a perfect Ransom for all men, and bore our dishonor.[318]

St. Ambrose says, "**In Adam I fell, in Adam I was cast out of Paradise, in Adam I died**; how shall the Lord call me back, except He find me in Adam; guilty as I was in him, so now justified in Christ."[319]

St. Gregory the Wonderworker says:

> **As sin entered into the world by flesh, and death came to reign by sin over all men**, the sin in the flesh might also be condemned through the selfsame flesh in the likeness thereof;[320] and that that overseer of sin, the tempter, might be overcome, and death be cast down from its sovereignty, and the corruption in the burying of the body be done away, and the first-fruits of the resurrection be shown, and the principle of righteousness begin its course in the world through faith, and the kingdom of heaven be preached to men, and fellowship be established between God and men.[321]

St. Irenaeus says (2nd Century):

> Now He would not have come to do away, by means of that same [image], the disobedience which had been incurred towards our Maker if He proclaimed another Father. But inasmuch as it

---

[318] Cyril of Alexandria, *Commentary on the Gospel according to S. John* 2. (London, ENG: Walter Smith, 1885), 585.

[319] Ambrose *On the Belief in the Resurrection* 6 (NPNF² 10:175).

[320] Romans 5:12; 8:3.

[321] *The writings of Gregory Thaumaturgus, Dionysius of Alexandria, and Archelaus*. In *Ante-Nicene Christian Library* 20. A. Roberts and J. Donaldson, eds. (Edinburgh: T. & T. Clark, 1871), 109.

> was by these things that **we disobeyed** God, and did not give credit to His word, so was it also by these same that He brought in obedience and consent as respects His Word; by which things **He clearly shows forth God Himself, whom indeed we had offended in the first Adam, when he did not perform His commandment.** In the second Adam, however, we are reconciled, being made obedient even unto death. **For we were debtors to none other but to Him whose commandment we had transgressed at the beginning.**[322]

St. Cyril the Great says: "For the whole nature of man became guilty in the person of him who was first formed [Adam]; but now it is wholly justified again in Christ"[323]

He also teaches us:

> "I can will what is right," he says, "but I cannot do it." ... As proof that the flesh is guilty of the dreadful birth of sin within, he skillfully concedes the presence of the good in us, though not the ability to bring it to fruition. Indeed, he is forced to turn away against his will into a state of mind he did not want.[324]

St. John Chrysostom explains the following passage from Scripture, "For until the law sin was in the world, but sin is not imputed when there is no law. Nevertheless death reigned from

---

322 Irenaeus *Against Heresies*. In *Ante-Nicene Fathers* 1, P. Schaff, ed. (Peabody, MA: Hendrickson Publishers, 2012), 544.

323 Cyril of Alexandria, *A Commentary upon the Gospel According to S. Luke* 1, R.P. Smith, trans. (Oxford, ENG: Oxford Press, 1859), 171.

324 Cyril of Alexandria, *Commentaries on Romans, 1-2 Corinthians, and Hebrews*, J.C. Elowsky, G.L. Bray, M. Glerup, and T.C. Oden, eds.; D.R. Maxwell, trans. (Downers Grove, IL: IVP Academic, 2022), 17.

Adam to Moses, even over those who had not sinned according to the likeness of the transgression of Adam, who is a type of Him who was to come."[325] And he says, "It is clear, that it was not this sin, the transgression, that is, of the Law, but that **of Adam's disobedience**, which marred all things. Now what is the proof of this? The fact that even before the Law all died."[326]

With the same meaning, **St. Cyril the Great** says:

> I suppose someone may reasonably make the following argument, he says. Adam was the "type of the one who was to come."[327] **Just as we were made sinners in him because of his transgression**, so also we have been justified in Christ through his obedience. Therefore, justification in Christ had to dawn on the inhabitants of the earth even if no one seized it. What need or necessity was there, then, for the laws of Moses? Paul is all but rising up against such an objection when he adds, "But the law came in, that the trespass may multiply." He says it "came in" meaning that it interposed itself between the condemnation in Adam and the justification in Christ.[328]

St. John Chrysostom tightly binds sin and death such that one cannot be mentioned without mentioning the other, when he says, "What then does the word 'sinners'[329] mean here? To

---

[325] Romans 5:13–14

[326] John Chrysostom *Homilies on the Epistle of St. Paul the Apostle to the Romans* 10 (NPNF[1] 11:402).

[327] Romans 5:14.

[328] Cyril of Alexandria, *Commentaries on Romans, 1-2 Corinthians, and Hebrews*, J.C. Elowsky, G.L. Bray, M. Glerup, and T.C. Oden, eds.; D.R. Maxwell, trans. (Downers Grove, IL: IVP Academic, 2022), 7.

[329] St. John Chrysostom explains Romans 5:19.

me it seems to mean liable to punishment and condemned to death."[330]

The same meaning, that is, the link between sin and death, **St. Cyril the Great** also says:

> This is why the Only-begotten Word of God, who knew no sin, became a human being: **so that just as all were condemned in Adam** when human nature experienced death, so also we will be justified in Christ **and put off sin along with the death that springs from it.**[331]
>
> The Only-begotten became human for us and neutralized the power of death. **He also took away the root of death, which is sin.** He cast out the ruler of this world.[332,333]
>
> **Since there was no other way that what was dominated by death and perishability and sin** could be brought back to its original condition except through Christ alone, the blessed David pleased for the mystery of the incarnation to be fulfilled at the appropriate time, saying, "Why, O Lord, do you stand far off?"[334]

St. Cyril affirms here that sin and death are bound together, and one cannot be mentioned apart from the other, in response

---

330 John Chrysostom *Homilies on the Epistle of St. Paul the Apostle to the Romans* 10 (NPNF[1] 11:403).

331 Cyril of Alexandria, *Commentaries on Romans, 1-2 Corinthians, and Hebrews*, J.C. Elowsky, G.L. Bray, M. Glerup, and T.C. Oden, eds.; D.R. Maxwell, trans. (Downers Grove, IL: IVP Academic, 2022), 74.

332 Cf. John 12:31.

333 Cyril of Alexandria, *Commentaries on Romans, 1-2 Corinthians, and Hebrews*, J.C. Elowsky, G.L. Bray, M. Glerup, and T.C. Oden, eds.; D.R. Maxwell, trans. (Downers Grove, IL: IVP Academic, 2022), 76.

334 Ibid., 120. St. Cyril's explanation on Hebrews 2:14.

to those who claim that we inherited death without inheriting sin!

The same meaning is also explained by **St. Athanasius** in his interpretation of Psalm 70: "'And my soul which You have saved' **from sin and corruption** and subjection to the devil, **and from death** itself."[335]

There are further proofs on sin entering the entire human race. For example, our teacher St. Paul the Apostle says:

"For all have sinned and fall short of the glory of God, being justified freely by His grace through the redemption that is in Christ Jesus."[336] All, here, including children.

> What then? Are we better than they? Not at all. For we have previously charged both Jews and Greeks that they are all under sin. As it is written: "There is none righteous, no, not one; there is none who understands; there is none who seeks after God. They have all turned aside; they have together become unprofitable; there is none who does good, no, not one."[337]

Sin cannot be separated from its consequences, such that we talk about the inheritance of death and corruption, [yet] ignoring the original germ.

"For the law of the Spirit of life in Christ Jesus has made me free from the law of sin and death."[338]

---

[335] Saint Athanasius the Apostolic, *Tafseer Sifr Al-Mazameer Al-Joz' Al-Thalith* [Exegesis on the Book of Psalms Vol. 3], G.M. Andrawis, trans. (Egypt: St. Anthony Press–The Orthodox Center for Patristic Studies in Cairo, 2021), 175. [Translated from Arabic text].
[336] Romans 3:23–24.
[337] Romans 3:9–12.
[338] Romans 8:2.

The skilled physician does not treat the symptoms of the disease, but its root, and this is what the true Physician of our souls did with us.

St. Athanasius the Apostolic says, "For He had to suffer in that place, because He desired to renew the first Adam, so that, by bringing to naught Adam's sin, that sin would disappear from the entire human race."[339]

It is marvelous that St. Athanasius affirms that by the salvation which Christ offered us, sin—Adam's sin, the first, the original—disappears from the human race (human nature).

St. Ambrose comments on the Psalm, [saying,] "Behold, I was brought forth in iniquity, and in sin my mother conceived me,"[340] and he says, "We are told about the piety of his mother;[341] what he means here is **the original sin**; confessing that he is brought forth in this world by the seeds of iniquity. There is no conceiving without sin, as there are no parents who have not fallen."[342]

Teaching the same as St. Ambrose, his disciple **St. Augustine** says:

> Therefore, "Behold, the Lamb of God." He is not a scion[343] stemming from Adam; he took only the flesh from Adam, he did not assume his sin. He

[339] Saint Athanasius the Apostolic, *Izzah Hawl Alam Al-Rab Wa Salibaho* [A Homily on the Lord's Suffering and His Cross], S.H. Jacob, trans. (Egypt: The Orthodox Center for Patristic Studies, 2019), 57. [Translated from Arabic text].
[340] Psalm 51:5.
[341] "I have become a stranger to my brothers, and an alien to my mother's children" (Psalm 69:8); "O LORD, truly I am Your servant; I am Your servant, the son of Your maidservant; You have loosed my bonds" (Psalm 116:16).
[342] Fr. Tadros Malaty, *On the Book of Psalms, A Patristic Commentary*. (Alexandria, Egypt: St. George Coptic Orthodox Church Sporting, 1991), 849.
[343] That is, an heir.

> who has not assumed the sin from our clayey mass
> is the one who takes away our sin.[344]

If some consider that Ambrose and Augustine represent Western theology (this, [however], did not exist before the 11th century, for the Church was one catholic[345] [Church]), so what would they say about St. Basil the Great?

On this **St. Basil the Great** says:

> "No one born of woman is without sin, even if his life is one day on earth;"[346] and David groans, saying: "I was brought forth in iniquity, and in sin my mother conceived me;"[347] and as proclaimed by the apostle: "For all have sinned and fall short of the glory of God; being justified freely by His grace through the redemption that is in Christ Jesus, whom God set forth to be a propitiation by His blood."[348] Hence, the forgiveness of sins is given to those who believe; according to the words of the Lord Himself: "This is My blood of the new covenant, which is shed for many for the remission of sins."[349,350]

The scholar Origen says:

> Everyone who enters this world is said to be made with a certain contamination. This is also why Scripture says, "No one is clean from filth even if

---

[344] Augustine of Hippo, *Tractates on the Gospel of John 1–10*, J.W. Rettig, trans. (Washington, DC: The Catholic University of America Press, 1988), 101.
[345] i.e. universal.
[346] Job 14:4.
[347] Psalm 51:5.
[348] Romans 3: 23–25.
[349] Matthew 26:28.
[350] Fr. Tadros Malaty, *On the Book of Psalms, A Patristic Commentary*. (Alexandria, Egypt: St. George Coptic Orthodox Church Sporting, 1991), 849.

> his life were only one day."[351] Therefore, from the fact that he is placed "in the womb of his mother"[352] and that he takes the material of the body from the origin of the paternal seed, he can himself be called "contaminated in his father and mother."[353] Or do you not know that when a male child is forty days old, he is offered at the altar that he may be purified[354] there as if he were polluted in this conception either by the paternal seed or the uterus of the mother? Therefore, every man "was polluted in his father and mother," but only Jesus my Lord came pure into the world in this birth and "was not polluted in his mother." For he entered "an uncontaminated body."[355] For he was the one who spoke long ago through Solomon, "But since I was better, I came into an undefiled body."[356,357]

The same is also taught by **St. Cyril the Great**, in a very clear text, which we may consider one of the most powerful texts expressing our inheritance of Original Sin, in his interpretation of our teacher Paul the Apostle's Epistle to the Romans:

> The divinely inspired Paul adds a kind of conclusion to the foregoing thoughts when he says, "Therefore, just as one man's trespass," and what follows. **We have all been condemned in Adam**, as I said before, and when the curse of

[351] Cf. Job 14:4–5 LXX.
[352] Cf. Job 3:11.
[353] Cf. Leviticus 21:11.
[354] Cf. Leviticus 12:2f.
[355] For the Holy Spirit overshadowed her and sanctified her.
[356] Wisdom 8:20.
[357] Origen, *Homilies of Leviticus 1–16*, G.W. Barkley, trans. (Washington, D.C.: The Catholic University of America Press, 1990), 223–224.

death came about, the result spread to all as from an original root. But we have also been justified and have blossomed again into life when Christ was justified for us. **Our forefather [Adam] neglected the command he had been given. He offended God and suffered the consequences of divine wrath. Indeed, he fell into decay. That is when sin rushed into human nature.** And that is how "the many were made sinners," which refers to everyone on earth. **Now someone might say: Yes, Adam fell. He disregarded the divine command, and he was condemned to decay and death. But how were "the many made sinners" because of him? Why does his fall affect us? Why have we been condemned with him when we were not even born yet? On the contrary, God says, "Fathers will not be put to death for their children," nor children for their fathers, and, "It is the soul who sins that shall die."[358] What defense could we make for our position?[359] It is indeed the soul who sins that shall die. Nevertheless, we have become sinners through Adam's disobedience in the following way.** He was created in incorruption and life. He lived a holy life in luxurious paradise. His mind completely and continually enjoyed the vision of God. His body was calm and untroubled, since all shameful pleasure was at rest. There was no tumult of alien impulses in him. **When he fell under sin, however, and sank into decay, then pleasures and impurities rushed into the nature**

---

[358] Deuteronomy 24:16.

[359] See here that St. Cyril the Great is convinced of this doctrine which he is about to explain and defend.

> **of the flesh, and a savage law sprang up in our members. So our nature contracted sin "through the disobedience of the one man" (that is, Adam). That is how "the many were made sinners"[360]—not because they transgressed along with Adam (since they did not yet exist), but because they were of his nature, which had fallen under the law of sin.** Just as human nature was enfeebled with decay in Adam through his disobedience (and that is how the passions entered into it), so also it has been freed once again in Christ. He was obedient to God the Father and "committed no sin."[361,362]

St. Severus of Antioch teaches concerning the inheritance of Original Sin:

> The only God the Word who is before the ages, power and wisdom of the Father, in whose image he created rational man, became flesh, I mean man according to the words of John, not that he was changed into flesh (far be it!), but, while he remained invariable as **God, he himself assumed the whole of me by a true and hypostatic union, but still without the sin which had come in upon us.**[363]
>
> Let us see how Peter and John and the rest of the Apostles made the Church according to the

[360] Romans 5:19.
[361] 1 Peter 2:22.
[362] Cyril of Alexandria, *Commentaries on Romans, 1-2 Corinthians, and Hebrews*, J.C. Elowsky, G.L. Bray, M. Glerup, and T.C. Oden, eds.; D.R. Maxwell, trans. (Downers Grove, IL: IVP Academic, 2022), 6–7.
[363] *A Collection of Letters of Severus of Antioch, From Numerous Syriac Manuscripts*, E.W. Brooks, trans. (Paris: Firmin-Didot, 1920), 16–17.

likeness of this lame man,[364] for she used to limp of old, like him, in the knowledge of God. And from her mother's womb she became paralyzed by sin because of the transgression of Adam and Eve, and she used to say, Behold I was formed in iniquity, and in sin my mother conceived me.[365,366]

Now the bush is a thorny plant, and **it illustrates that He was partaker (except for sin) of the nature which is thorny and under sin because of Adam's breaking of the commandment**, so that He may send us power against sin, because He was called the second Adam and became the Beginning of the new creation, as [He] was (the beginning) to the first creation.[367]

St. Gregory of Nyssa says:

Somehow evil is mixed up with our nature through those who first succumbed to passion, and by their transgression made a permanent place for the disease. **Now the nature of living beings is transmitted in each species by its descendants so that, according to the law of**

---

[364] See Acts 3.

[365] Cf. Psalm 51:5.

[366] M. Briere, *Les Homiliae Cathedrales de Severe d'Antioche: Homelies LXX a LXXVI.* (Paris: Firmin-Didot, 1915), 103. [Translated from Arabic text]. Original text in French: "Voyons comment Pierre, Jean et les autres apôtres ont fait lever l'Eglise sous la forme de ce boiteux; autrefois, elle boitait de la même manière sous le rapport de la connaissance de Dieu, et depuis le sein de sa mère, elle était paralysée par le péché à cause de la transgression d'Adam et d'Eve, et elle disait : Car voici, j'ai été conçue dans l'iniquité, et ma mère m'a conçue dans les péchés."

[367] Saint Severus of Antioch, *Mariam Walidat Al-Illah Izzatan Lil-Kidees Sawaros Al-Antaki* [Two Homilies on Mary the Mother of God by Saint Severus of Antioch], Monk-Priest George of St. Anthony Monastery and the late Joseph Habib, trans. (Egypt: School of Alexandria, 2018), 57. [Translated from Arabic text].

> **nature, that which is born is the same as that from which it is born. So man is born from man, the subject of passion from that which is subject to passion, the sinner from the sinner. Hence sin in some way comes into existence together with those who are born**; it is born and grows with them, and at the end of life it also ceases with them.[368]

St. Gregory the Illuminator (the Armenian) says in the 364th passage in the chapter on the Birth of Christ:

> God sent his own son into the world, who came and was born of a woman and was enveloped in our human flesh, he gave life to all flesh by his own flesh. Through him also the Creator of the world succeeded in renewing the just **and in liberating them from births involved in sin** and in making them like angels, and in calling them sons of God, and in rendering mortals immortal through the immortal spirit, and in giving them the honor by the divine glory.[369]

St. Gregory of Nyssa teaches us in his homily on the Baptism of Christ, saying:

> For You verily, O Lord, are the pure and eternal fount of goodness, Who did justly turn away from us, and in loving kindness did have mercy upon us. You did hate, and were reconciled; You did curse, and did bless; You did banish us from Paradise,

---

368 St. Gregory of Nyssa, *St. Gregory of Nyssa: The Lord's Prayer, The Beatitudes*, J. Quasten and J.C. Plumpe, eds.; H.C. Graef, trans. (Mahwah, NJ: Paulist Press, 1954), 150–151.

369 *The Teaching of Saint Gregory: An Early Armenian Catechism.* R.W. Thomson, trans. (Cambridge, MA: Harvard University Press, 1970), 74.

> and did recall us; **You did strip off the fig-tree leaves, an unseemly covering, and put upon us a costly garment; You did open the prison, and did release the condemned; You did sprinkle us with clean water, and cleanse us from our filthiness. No longer shall Adam be confounded when called by You, nor hide himself, convicted by his conscience, cowering in the thicket of Paradise. Nor shall the flaming sword encircle Paradise around, and make the entrance inaccessible to those that draw near; but all is turned to joy for us that were the heirs of sin**: Paradise, yea, heaven itself may be trodden by man: and the creation, in the world and above the world, that once was at variance with itself, is knit together in friendship: and we men are made to join in the angels' song, offering the worship of their praise to God.[370]

Although the principal subject matter which this research focuses on is the bringing to the spotlight the faith of the Fathers of the catholic Church of the first centuries concerning the issue of the inheritance of Adam's sin, nevertheless, the importance is evident of mentioning that there are fathers from the middle ages who referred in their writings to the entire humankind's breaking of God's commandment in the person of Adam. This indicates that the belief in the inheritance of Adam's sin is genuine and ancient, permeating the depths of the Church through the various ages. Of these fathers—as an example but not exhaustively—is Bishop Bulus Al-Bushi (thirteenth century AD), who says in one of his homilies:

---

[370] Gregory of Nyssa *On the Baptism of Christ* (NPNF^2 5:524).

> Truly, the mystery of Your economy, O God, is above every mind and beyond every understanding. And as You have created the world and brought it out of nothing into existence, You have no need of it, but [this was done] out of Your benevolence towards it. **For when we transgressed the commandment, we fell by the just sentence from grace and eternal life.** No created being was able to restore life unending to us, for it is unbefitting of him, and no one was so [able] except the Lord God through whom everything was created, and without Him nothing was made that was made.[371,372]

We are born with a nature that is fallen, sinful, dead, corrupt, because of Adam's fall, sin and death.

The words of the esteemed Fathers here are very clear and explicit, not liable to ambiguity, which do not [themselves] need explanation apart from what they wrote. They can be understood in light of the concept of the oneness of the human race.

Sin is not only the act of transgression, but is the departure from obedience to God, friendship with Him and walking with Him.

Man used to walk with God. Then he left Him and walked in another way, distant, contrary and unyielding. And we were born in this disobedience. "All we like sheep have gone astray;

---

371 See John 1:3.

372 Bishop Bulus Al-Bushi, Homilies on the Divine Feasts, A Homily on the Life-giving Annunciation. Articles of Abba Bulus Al-Bushi, Bishop of Egypt, of the thirteenth century scholars are introduced with revision and classification by Priest Mankarius Awad-Allah, pp. 9–10. [Translated from Arabic text].

we have turned, each one, to his own way; and the LORD has laid on Him the iniquity of us all."[373]

Sin is **hatred of God without a cause**:

> If I had not come and spoken to them, they would have no sin, but now they have no excuse for their sin. He who hates Me hates My Father also. If I had not done among them the works which no one else did, they would have no sin; but now they have seen and also hated both Me and My Father. But this happened that the word might be fulfilled which is written in their law, "They hated Me without a cause."[374]
>
> Yet they say to God, "Depart from us, for we do not desire the knowledge of Your ways. Who is the Almighty, that we should serve Him? And what profit do we have if we pray to Him?"[375]

Sin is **the departure of the soul, and the distancing of the soul, from God, thereby becoming estranged from Him.** And thus the human being makes himself the center of his life, rather than God being the center.

In Greek, ἡ ἁμαρτία (*hamartia*) is a feminine noun, originally meaning "missing the goal."[376] And the goal of the creation of man, principally, was that there might be a relationship of communion and love with God, his Creator. Man failed to realize this goal when he broke the commandment given him by God, and thereby he became a sinner...

---

[373] Isaiah 53:6.
[374] John 15:22–25.
[375] Job 21:14–15.
[376] Or: missing the mark.

Sin, thus, is not the mere committing of a deed only, but:

Sin is disobedience. And we were born in this disobedience, heirs of that backsliding[377] nature which is distant from God in unbelief. "Beware, brethren, lest there be in any of you an evil heart of unbelief in departing from the living God."[378] "For whatever is not from faith is sin."[379]

Sin is the rejection of the knowledge of God. "And even as they did not like to retain God in their knowledge, God gave them over to a debased mind, to do these things which are not fitting."[380]

Sin is also enmity against God. "Because the carnal mind is enmity against God; for it is not subject to the law of God, nor indeed can be."[381]

Therefore, because Adam's sin reached all of the human race, Holy Scriptures refer to us as being weak,[382] ungodly, sinners, enemies, and not only as dead and corrupt.

"For when we were still without strength, in due time Christ died for the ungodly."[383]

"But God demonstrates His own love toward us, in that while we were still sinners, Christ died for us."[384]

---

[377] i.e. nature that departs and turns away from God. The Arabic word is the same as the word "departing" in the following verse.
[378] Hebrews 3:12.
[379] Romans 14:23.
[380] Romans 1:28.
[381] Romans 8:7.
[382] Or: without strength.
[383] Romans 5:6.
[384] Romans 5:8.

"For if when we were enemies we were reconciled to God through the death of His Son, much more, having been reconciled, we shall be saved by His life."[385]

The salvific work of the Lord Christ can be described as having "put away[386] sin," and not only as putting away death and corruption.

"He then would have had to suffer often since the foundation of the world; but now, once at the end of the ages, He has appeared to put away sin by the sacrifice of Himself."[387]

"So Christ was offered once to bear the sins of many. To those who eagerly wait for Him He will appear a second time, apart from sin, for salvation."[388]

And as in Adam we became sinners before we existed as individuals, but we were in him, according to the expression of the Fathers, we became partakers in Adam's offense without partaking in the [act of] eating, of course. Therefore, likewise also, without any merit on our part, we receive the righteousness of Christ, and His victory over death, and the outpouring of His life into us. When we are united with Christ, the Bridegroom of the soul, by Baptism and the Eucharist, we become in Him righteous through His righteousness, and living through His life, and incorruptible in the coming age through His eternal life which is poured out into us; with the necessity of persistence in our uniting with Him until the end, through our Church life which includes continual repentance, prayer and spiritual struggle in Christ.

---

[385] Romans 5:10.
[386] Or: annulled.
[387] Hebrews 9:26.
[388] Hebrews 9:28.

The Lord Christ has treated what previously afflicted our humanity in Adam.

The early catholic Church did not teach that the human race partook as individuals in the act of Adam's sin, but they became sinners in him, and not with him because they did not exist with him. And of the Fathers who taught that the human race did not partake of Adam's sin, they mean [by this] the same as what the Church now teaches, that the human race did not partake with him in the eating, because they did not exist as individuals, but the entire human nature sinned in him.

As the human race became sinners in Adam with no personal guilt they committed, so they become righteous in Christ, without any merit of theirs except [by] accepting the faith in Christ and uniting with Him in Baptism and the Eucharist.

And this is what St. Paul the Apostle meant by saying, "Who is a type of Him who was to come."[389] So Adam is a type of Christ (who is to come), so what happened to the human race in Adam is restored for all of the human race in Christ. If we do not believe that we have become sinners in Adam without partaking with him in the eating, how do we accept that we are justified through Christ?

Further Proofs of the Belief in the Inheritance of Adam's Sin

1. Baptism

We believe that Baptism has many ramifications: the forgiveness of sins, healing of the corrupt nature, creating anew, obtaining of eternal life, becoming members of the Body of

---

[389] Romans 5:14.

Christ,[390] and receiving adoption by God the Father. Why, then, did the Fathers, gathered in Constantinople to formulate the Creed, focus on stating "We confess one baptism for the remission of sins"? And they did not say, "We believe in one baptism to heal the corrupt nature"? Nor, "in one baptism to receive adoption by God the Father"?—though we actually believe in these highly sublime ramifications. The Creed focusing on the forgiveness of sins confirms the belief of the Fathers that our original problem is Adam's sin, especially that the Church from its first day baptized infants, as it did baptize adults, so if the adults do have their own sins, what are the sins of the new-born infants except Adam's sin which is in them?!

The scholar Origen says, in homily 14 of his commentary on the Gospel of St. Luke:

> **Christian brethren often ask a question.** The passage from Scripture read today encourages me to treat it again. **Little children are baptized "for the remission of sins." Whose sins are they? When did they sin?** Or how can this explanation of the baptismal washing be maintained in the case of small children, except according to the interpretation we spoke of a little earlier? **"No man is clean of stain, not even if his life upon the earth had lasted but a single day."[391] Through the mystery of Baptism, the stains of birth are put aside. For this reason, even small children are baptized.** For, "unless a man be born

[390] Literally: sharing in the membership of the Body of Christ.
[391] Job 14:4–5 LXX.

> again of water and spirit, he will not be able to enter into the kingdom of heaven."[392,393]

The scholar Origen also says in his commentary on Leviticus, in the eighth homily:

> But if it pleases you to hear what other saints also might think about this birthday, hear David speaking, "In iniquity I was conceived and in sins my mother brought me forth," **showing that every soul which is born in flesh is polluted by the filth "of iniquity and sin"**; and for this reason we can say what we already have recalled above, "No one is pure from uncleanness even if his life is only one day long." To these things can be added the reason why it is required, since the baptism of the Church is given for the forgiveness of sins, that, according to the observance of the Church, that baptism also be given to infants; **since, certainly, if there were nothing in infants that ought to pertain to forgiveness and indulgence, then the grace of baptism would appear superfluous.**[394]

The scholar Origen also says in his commentary on the Epistle to the Romans:

> **Therefore our body is the body of sin**, for it is not written that Adam knew his wife Eve and became the father of Cain until after the sin. After all, even in the law it is commanded that sacrifices

---

392 John 3:5.

393 Origen, *Homilies of Luke and Fragments on Luke*, T.P. Halton, ed.; J.T. Lienhard, trans. (Washington, D.C.: The Catholic University of America Press, 2009), 58–59.

394 Origen, *Homilies of Leviticus 1–16*, G.W. Barkley, trans. (Washington, D.C.: The Catholic University of America Press, 1990), 157–158.

> be offered for the child who was born: a pair of turtledoves or two young doves; one of which was offered for sin and the other as a burnt offering.[395] **For which sin is this one dove offered? Was a newly born child able to sin? And yet it has a sin for which sacrifices are commanded to be offered, and from which it is denied that anyone is pure, even if his life should be one day long.**[396] It has to be believed, therefore, that concerning this David also said what we recorded above, "in sins my mother conceived me." For according to the historical narrative no sin of his mother is declared. **It is on this account as well that the Church has received the tradition from the apostles to give baptism even to little children. For they to whom the secrets of the divine mysteries were committed**[397] **were aware that in everyone was sin's innate defilement, which needed to be washed away through water and the Spirit.**[398] **Because of this defilement as well, the body itself is called the body of sin.**[399]

St. Gregory the Illuminator (the Armenian) says in the 412th passage of the chapter on the Baptism of Christ:

> He made verdant the womb of generation of the waters, **purifying by the waters and renewing the old deteriorated earthly matter,**[400] **which**

[395] See Leviticus 12:8.
[396] See Job 14:4–5 LXX.
[397] See 1 Corinthians 4:1.
[398] See John 3:5.
[399] Origen, *Commentary on the Epistle to the Romans, Book 1–5*, T.P. Halton, ed.; T.P. Scheck, trans. (Washington, D.C.: The Catholic University of America Press, 2001), 366–367.
[400] i.e. the human body.

> **sin had weakened and enfeebled and deprived of the grace of the Spirit**, then the invisible Spirit opened again the womb by visible water, preparing the newly born fledglings for the regeneration of the font, to clothe with robes of light all who would be born once more.[401]

The martyr St. Cyprian[402] says in a letter he wrote to Bishop Fidus, to exhort him on the Baptism of infants:

> But, in turn, if, in the case of the greatest sinners and those sinning much against God, when afterward they believe, the remission of their sins is granted and no one is prevented from baptism and grace, **how much more should an infant not be prohibited, who, recently born, has not sinned at all, except that, born carnally according to Adam, he has contracted the contagion of the first death from the first nativity. He approaches more easily from this very fact to receive the remission of sins because those which are remitted are not his own sins, but the sins of another.**[403,404]

To those who consider Cyprian a Western bishop, and [thereby declare that] we should not follow his teachings because they represent the Western theology, as they say, here we find that **St. Gregory of Nazianzus** writes praising Cyprian. This indicates the absence of sensitivity to [the idea of] Western vs. Eastern, in their days. He says:

---

[401] *The Teaching of Saint Gregory: An Early Armenian Catechism.* R.W. Thomson, trans. (Cambridge, MA: Harvard University Press, 1970), 89.

[402] He was the Bishop of Carthage, of the 3rd century Latin Fathers.

[403] That is, Adam.

[404] Cyprian of Carthage, *Letters 1–81*, H. Dressler, ed.; R.B. Donna, trans. (Washington, D.C.: The Catholic University of America Press, 1964), 219.

> And you, my Cyprian, are my most precious treasure, both in name and in fact, more than the other martyrs (there is no jealousy among martyrs). Your virtue overwhelms me, the thought of you elates me, and I am, as it were, in transports of joy.[405]

And he also says:

> Gentlemen, I give you Cyprian, so that for those of you who are already familiar with him, the reminder may prove an added source of pleasure, while those who are not may have the opportunity to learn of the finest chapter in our history, one in which all Christians can take pride; this is he, once the great name of the Carthaginians, now of the whole world, a man celebrated for his wealth, respected for his power, high-born (if the fact that he was a member and president of the senate best indicates his family's lineage), the flower of youthfulness, the monument of nature, a bastion of learning not only in philosophical studies but in the other disciplines and any of their divisions you will, so as to be admired more for the range of his learning than for his mastery of any one branch and more for his preeminence in each than for his encyclopedic knowledge of all; or, to make the distinction more clear, he was superior to some in the range of his learning, to others in his mastery of individual subjects, to still others in both, and to everyone in everything.[406]

---

405 Gregory Nazianzus, *Select Orations*, T.P. Halton, ed.; M. Vinson, trans. (Washington, D.C.: The Catholic University of America Press, 2003), 144.
406 Ibid., 145.

2. The Lord Christ Resembled Us in Everything Except for Sin

Why was it said that the Lord Christ resembled us in everything, except for sin alone?

"For we do not have a High Priest who cannot sympathize with our weaknesses, but was in all points tempted as we are, yet without sin."[407]

"And you know that He was manifested to take away our sins, and in Him there is no sin."[408]

It may be understood from this verse that the Lord Christ did not sin, and this is what sets Him apart from the rest of human beings, and therefore He—glory be to Him—said, "Which of you convicts Me of sin?"[409] Likewise of Him Isaiah the Prophet prophesied, saying, "And they made His grave with the wicked—but with the rich at His death, because He had done no violence, nor was any deceit in His mouth."[410]

The Lord Christ said, "For the ruler of this world is coming, and he has nothing in Me."[411] The Church truly believes that the Lord Christ is distinct from all human beings in that He not only did not sin at all, but also that He alone did not inherit Original Sin, for it was said of Him—glory be to Him—as a further proof, that He came "in the likeness of sinful flesh."

"You too O Mary, thousands of thousands, and myriads of myriads, overshadow you, praising their Creator, who was in

[407] Hebrews 4:15.
[408] 1 John 3:5.
[409] John 8:46.
[410] Isaiah 53:9.
[411] John 14:30.

your womb, **and took our likeness, without sin or alteration.**"[412]

3. The Lord Christ Took the Likeness of Sinful Flesh

Why was it said of Christ that He took the likeness of sinful flesh?

"For what the law could not do in that it was weak through the flesh, God did by sending His own Son in **the likeness of sinful flesh**, on account of sin: He condemned sin in the flesh."[413]

Our flesh is sinful flesh, and not only the flesh of death[414] and corruption, but the Lord Jesus took our flesh without sin; therefore, it is said that it is [in] the likeness of sinful flesh.

Our teacher Paul the Apostle spoke about the truth of the sinful flesh with very strong terms:

> But now, it is no longer I who do it, but **sin that dwells in me.** For I know that in me (that is, in my flesh) nothing good dwells; for to will is present with me, but how to perform what is good I do not find. For the good that I will to do, I do not do; but the evil I will not to do, that I practice. Now if I do what I will not to do, it is no longer I who do it, but **sin that dwells in me.** I find then a law, that evil is present with me, the one who wills to do good. For I delight in the law of God according to the inward man. But I see **another law in my members, warring against the law of**

[412] Sunday Theotokia, part 3.
[413] Romans 8:3.
[414] "O wretched man that I am! Who will deliver me from this body of death?" (Romans 7:24).

> **my mind**, and bringing me into captivity to **the law of sin which is in my members.**[415]

St. John Chrysostom says in his explanation of the expression "the likeness of sinful flesh":

> But if he does say that it was "in the likeness" of flesh that he sent the Son, do not therefore suppose that His flesh was of a different kind. For as he called it "sinful," this was why he put the word "likeness." For sinful flesh it was not that Christ had, but **like to our sinful flesh, yet sinless**, and in nature the same with us.[416]

St. Hilary, Bishop of Poitiers, [called] the Athanasius of the West, says:

> He bore our collective humanity in the form of a servant, but He was free from the sins and imperfections of the human body... For His conception was in the likeness of our nature, not in the possession of our faults... He was of Himself born man through the Virgin, and **found in the likeness of our degenerate body of sin**... He was not *found in the fashion of a man*: but *found in fashion as a man*: **nor was His flesh the flesh of sin, but the likeness of the flesh of sin.** Thus the fashion of flesh implies the truth of His birth, and the likeness of the flesh of sin removes Him from the imperfections of human weakness. So the Man Jesus Christ as man was truly born, as Christ had no sin in His nature.[417]

---

[415] Romans 7:17–23.

[416] John Chrysostom *Homilies on the Epistle of St. Paul the Apostle to the Romans* 13 (NPNF[1] 11:432).

[417] Hilary of Poitiers *Book X* 25 (NPNF[2] 9:188–189).

The **scholar Origen** says in his commentary on the Epistle to the Romans:

> What he has said, "in the likeness of the flesh of sin,"[418] **shows that we indeed have flesh of sin, but the Son of God had "the likeness of flesh of sin,"** not the flesh of sin. For all of us human beings who have been conceived from the seed of a man coming together with a woman, must of necessity employ that utterance which David says, "in iniquity I have been conceived and in sins did my mother conceive me."[419] He, however, who came to an immaculate body with no contact from a man, but only by the Holy Spirit coming upon the virgin and by the power of the Most High overshadowing, did indeed possess the nature of our body, **but he possessed in no respect whatsoever the contamination of sin, which is passed down to those who are conceived by the operation of lust.** For this reason, it is said that the Son of God came "in the likeness of flesh of sin."[420]

And **St. Cyril** says:

> For we may suppose that even in the Savior Jesus Christ Himself the human feelings were aroused by two qualities necessarily present in Him. For it must certainly have been under the influence of these that He showed Himself a Man born of woman, not in deceptive appearance or mere

---

[418] Romans 8:3.

[419] Psalm 51:5 LXX.

[420] Origen, *Commentary on the Epistle to the Romans, Book 6–10*, T.P. Halton, ed.; T. P. Scheck, trans. (Washington, D.C.: The Catholic University of America Press, 2002), 49.

> fancy, but rather by nature and in truth, **possessing every human quality, sin only excepted.** And fear and alarm, although they are affections natural to us, have escaped being ranked among sins.[421]

And he also teaches us:

> **What had succumbed had to—had to!—be healed and destroy death through the very flesh that was under the power of sin. When the flesh offended in Adam on account of his transgression, it fell under the power of death.**[422]

4. The Bronze Serpent

When the Lord Jesus said, "And as Moses lifted up the serpent in the wilderness, even so must the Son of Man be lifted up, that whoever believes in Him should not perish but have eternal life,"[423] He meant that as the bronze serpent is like the deadly serpent in everything except that it does not have the venom of death in it, **so is the flesh of the Master like our flesh in everything except the venom of sin.**

About this **St. Gregory of Nyssa** says:

> The Law prefigures for us what is clear in the wood. This figure is a likeness of a serpent and not a serpent itself, as the great Paul himself says, "in the likeness of sinful flesh." **Sin is the real**

---

[421] Cyril of Alexandria, *Commentary on the Gospel according to S. John* 2. (London, ENG: Walter Smith, 1885), 150.
[422] Cyril of Alexandria, *Commentaries on Romans, 1-2 Corinthians, and Hebrews*, J.C. Elowsky, G.L. Bray, M. Glerup, and T.C. Oden, eds.; D.R. Maxwell, trans. (Downers Grove, IL: IVP Academic, 2022), 120.
[423] John 3:14–15.

> **serpent, and whoever deserts to sin takes on the nature of the serpent. Man, then, is freed from sin through him who assumed the form of sin.**[424]

And **St. Augustine** comments on the Holy Scripture, "Behold! The lamb of God who takes away the sin of the world!"[425] And he says:

> **Therefore, "Behold, the Lamb of God." He is not a scion**[426] **stemming from Adam; he took only the flesh from Adam, he did not assume his sin. He who has not assumed the sin from our clayey mass is the one who takes away our sin.**[427]

5. The Testimony of the Liturgies of the Church

The holy Church expresses its belief that we sinned in Adam through liturgical prayers.

First, Texts from the Divine Liturgy Prayers

- ❖ "When we disobeyed Your commandment by the deceit of the serpent, we fell from eternal life and were exiled from the Paradise of joy."[428]
- ❖ "[You] opened for me Paradise to enjoy ... You have manifested to me the tree of life, and made known to me the sting of death. Of one plant have You forbidden me to eat, that of which You have said to me, 'Of it only do

---

[424] Gregory of Nyssa, *The Life of Moses*, R.J. Payne, ed.; A.J. Malherbe and E. Ferguson, trans. (Mahwah, NJ: Paulist Press, 1978), 124.
[425] John 1:29.
[426] That is, an heir.
[427] Augustine of Hippo, *Tractates on the Gospel of John 1–10*, J. W. Rettig, trans. (Washington, DC: The Catholic University of America Press, 1988), 101.
[428] The Divine Liturgy According to St. Basil – Agios (Holy).

not eat.' But according to my will, I did eat. I put Your law behind me by my own counsel, and became slothful toward Your commandments. I plucked for myself the sentence of death.... You have shown me the rising up from my fall.... You have abolished sin in the flesh."[429]

- "Grant them the forgiveness of their sins, and grant them by Your grace that they may be healed from the destroying sin."[430]
- "For You know, as creator of our being, that no one born of a woman shall be justified before You."[431]
- "For no one is pure and without blemish, even though his life on earth be a single day."[432]

Second, From the Prayer Book of the Hours (Agpeya)

In the first centuries, the catholic Church put in place a system for set, daily, liturgical prayers, which went through sequential development in their number and how to use them for prayer.[433] And in the third century AD, the catholic Church developed the daily system for the liturgical prayer of the hours, which was close to what is known [today] as the "Agpeya" in the Coptic Orthodox Church.[434] The fourth century saw a wide spread of the Christian liturgical life throughout the Christian world, and with it the development of the system of the daily prayers of the hours.[435] St. John Cassian left us a detailed description of this system of the prayers of the hours, which was between AD 380–399, that is before the schism of the Church.[436] Fr. Athanasius

[429] The Divine Liturgy According to St. Gregory – Agios (Holy).
[430] Rite of Holy Baptism for Children – Litany.
[431] Prayer of Reconciliation of St. Severus of Antioch.
[432] Litany of the Departed.
[433] Literally: how to pray with them.
[434] Fr. Athanasius of St. Macarius, *Al-Agpeya Ai Salawat Al-Sawa'i* [The Agpeya, That is, the Prayers of the Hours]. (Shobra, Egypt: Dar Nobar Press, 2006), 91.
[435] Ibid., 96.
[436] Ibid., 106.

of St. Macarius monastery mentions in his book *The Agpeya* the testimony of the renowned liturgical scholar Robert Taft, saying, "The basic structure of the office of Scetis described by Cassian is still clearly visible in the hours of the present Coptic *Horologion*."[437]

The liturgical text of the first and second passages [of the litanies] of the sixth hour prayer from the Prayers of the Hours (Agpeya) mentions Adam's sin which was transmitted to the entire human race, and mentions Christ's justification which was also transmitted to all of the human race. Here are the texts:

> O You, who on the sixth day and **in the sixth hour were nailed to the cross, for the sin which our father Adam dared to commit in Paradise, tear the handwriting of our sins, O Christ our God, and save us.** I cried to God, and the Lord heard me. God hear my prayer, and do not refuse my petition. Be attentive to me and hear me in the evening, in the morning, and at midday. I say my words, and He hears my voice and delivers my soul in peace.
>
> O Jesus Christ, our God, who were nailed to the cross in the sixth hour, and **killed sin by the tree**, and by Your death You made alive the dead man, whom You created with Your own hands, and had died in sin. Put to death our pains by Your healing and life-giving passions, and by the nails with which You were nailed. Rescue our minds from thoughtlessness of the earthly deeds and worldly

437 Robert Taft, *The Liturgy of the Hours in East and West.* (Collegeville, MN: Liturgical Press, 1985), 251.

lusts, to the remembrance of Your heavenly commandments, according to Your compassion.

In these prayers we find a very clear entreaty between the person praying and the Lord Christ the Savior who died on the cross.

The first passage: "O You, who on the sixth day and in the sixth hour were nailed to the cross, for the sin which **Adam** dared to commit in Paradise, tear the handwriting of our sins, O Christ our God, and save us." This is the counterpart in the Greek Church,[438] [according to the Byzantine rite]. As to the second passage [from the litanies], it is only mentioned in the Coptic text, and not the Greek.

It is evident from the first passage that the first catholic Church, for the purpose of prayer and teaching the doctrine to its children, would call on Christ, as the One who died for the sake of Adam's sin; then it asks Him to tear "the handwriting of our sins," and to save us (in plural form); that is, to tear "the judgement of condemnation" which fell on all of the human race because of Adam's sin, and to grant us instead, justification. And this is what Paul the Apostle formulated at first in [the Epistle to the] Romans: "Therefore, as through one man's offense judgement came to all men, resulting in condemnation, even so through one Man's righteous act the free gift came to all men, resulting in justification of life."[439]

And it is well-known that we pray with what we believe in. And there are no expressions in Coptic liturgies that may be described as being only for linguistic [purposes] and bearing no concepts of the faith. We have sinned in Adam on the level of

---

[438] Ibid., 314.
[439] Romans 5:18.

human nature which he bore, and not on the level of individuals because we were not in existence as individuals.

Third, Texts from the Baptism Prayers for Newborn Infants

> O Master, Lord Jesus Christ ... **Heal these children ... Grant them the forgiveness of their sins**, and grant them by Your grace that they may be **healed** from the **destroying sin.**
>
> ***
>
> And that they may be purified from the **sin** that is in the world.
>
> ***
>
> O You, THE BEING, Master, God, who formed man in His image and His likeness; who has given us the privilege of everlasting life. **And then, when he fell through sin**, You have not abandoned him, but have prepared the salvation of the world through the Incarnation of Your only-begotten Son, our Lord, Jesus Christ. [440]

Here the Church is asking for the **forgiveness of the sin** of the new-born infant, that he may be healed from **sin that destroys, "Adam's sin."** Then through the tongue of the priest and in place of the infant stepping forward for Baptism for the forgiveness of his sin, the Church entreats the Lord God with this profound prayer in which the priest puts forth **the grounds for asking for forgiveness through Baptism**; and these are: in remembrance of the grace of being formed in His image and His likeness, and then when he fell into sin, the Lord God did not

[440] Rites of Holy Baptism.

abandon him, but He prepared his salvation from sin, and his justification, through the incarnation of the only-begotten Lord Jesus Christ. It becomes clear from the Baptism prayers for a newborn infant that the purpose of baptizing him is the forgiveness of his sin which was brought onto him by the Fall of the first man, Adam.

The Problem of the Translation of Romans Five

> 12 Therefore, just as **through one man sin entered** the world, and death through sin, and thus death spread to all men, **because all sinned**— 13 (For until the law sin was in the world, but sin is not imputed when there is no law. 14 **Nevertheless death reigned from Adam to Moses, even over those who had not sinned according to the likeness of the transgression of Adam**, who is a type of Him who was to come. 15 But the free gift is not like the offense. For if **by the one man's offense many died**, much more the grace of God and the gift by the grace of the one Man, Jesus Christ, abounded to many. 16 And the gift is not like that which came through the one who sinned. For **the judgment which came from one offense resulted in condemnation**, but the free gift which came from many offenses resulted in justification. 17 For if **by the one man's offense death reigned** through the one, much more those who receive abundance of grace and of the gift of righteousness will reign in life through the One, Jesus Christ.)
>
> 18 Therefore, as **through one man's offense judgment came to all men, resulting in**

> **condemnation**, even so through one Man's righteous act the free gift came to all men, resulting in justification of life. 19 For as by **one man's disobedience many were made sinners**, so also by one Man's obedience many will be made righteous.[441]

By going back to some of the ancient translations of the Holy Scriptures, we find the following:

Romans 5:12 in the **Coptic translation** is translated as follows: "Therefore, just as through one man sin entered the world, and death through sin, and thus death spread to all men **through whom all sinned in him.**"[442] This indicates that all people are sinners because they were *in* Adam by nature.

Ⲉⲑⲃⲉ ⲫⲁⲓ ⲕⲁⲧⲁ ⲫⲣⲏϯ ⲉⲧⲁ ⲫⲛⲟⲃⲓ `ⲓ ⲉ̀ϧⲟⲩⲛ ⲉ̀ⲡⲓⲕⲟⲥⲙⲟⲥ ⲉ̀ⲃⲟⲗ ϩⲓⲧⲉⲛ ⲟⲩⲣⲱⲙⲓ ⲛ̀ⲟⲩⲱⲧ Ⲟⲩⲟϩ ⲉ̀ⲃⲟⲗ ϩⲓⲧⲉⲛ ⲫⲛⲟⲃⲓ ⲁ ⲫⲙⲟⲩ ϣⲱⲡⲓ ⲟⲩⲟϩ ⲡⲁⲓⲣⲏϯ ⲁ ⲡⲓⲙⲟⲩ ϣⲉ ⲉ̀ϧⲟⲩⲛ ⲉⲣⲱⲙⲓ ⲛⲓⲃⲉⲛ ⲫⲏⲉⲧⲁⲩⲉⲣⲛⲟⲃⲓ ⲛ̀ϧⲏⲧϥ.

And in the **old Slavonic translation** of[443] Cyril and Methodius in AD 860, we find the text written in the following manner: "As through one man sin came into the world, and through sin death, so also death came upon all men, **when in him**[444] [i.e. in Adam] **all have sinned.**"[445] This is very similar to the Coptic translation.

And the **official Bulgarian Orthodox Bible**, the version authorized by the Bulgarian Orthodox Church, which is known

---

[441] Romans 5:12–19.

[442] Bishop Gregorius, *Mawsouat Al-Lahout Al-Akeadi – Sirai Al-Tajasod Wa Al-Fidah Al-Joz' Althani* [Encyclopedia of Doctrinal Theology 7: The Mysteries of Incarnation and Redemption Part 2]. (Egypt: *Maktabat Al-Motana'ih Anba Gregorius* [The Library of the Late Abba Gregorius], 2004), 237. [Translated from Arabic text].

[443] Text adds "each of."

[444] Or: in whom.

[445] Moss, Against Romanides, 39.

as Библия, синодално издание (BOB), and is described by the Bulgarian Orthodox Church synod as: Bulgarian Orthodox Bible (BOB); the "official liturgical translation." This translation was taken directly from the ancient Greek origins of the Holy Bible and was supported by Ancient Slavonic origins (Church Slavonic[446]) according to the translation of the Greek Saints Cyril and Methodius.

In this translation, Romans 5:12 appears as follows:

Затова, както чрез един човек грехът влезе в света, а чрез греха – смъртта, и по такъв начин смъртта премина във всички люде чрез един човек, в когото всички съгрешиха.[447]

The translation of this text is the following: "Therefore, as through one man sin entered the world, and death through sin, and thus death was transmitted to all men **through one man in whom all sinned.**"[448]

This carries the same meaning as the Coptic translation, "through one man in whom all sinned," and carries the same meaning and understanding as the ancient translation of Cyril and Methodius.

There is a special significance to the translation of Cyril and Methodius in this research on the inheritance of Adam's sin according to our orthodox doctrine. Cyril (826–869) and Methodius (815–885) were brothers, monks from Greece, who were sent to preach in the Slav region (Eastern Europe). They are [considered] saints in the Church of Greece, known as "the

---

[446] "Bible translations into Bulgarian," *Wikipedia*, 20 June 2022, https://en.wikipedia.org/wiki/Bible_translations_into_Bulgarian.
[447] "Bulgarian Orthodox Bible (BOB)," *Bible Gateway*, 2016, https://www.biblegateway.com/passage/?search=romans+5%3A12&version=BOB.
[448] [Translated from Arabic text].

Slav Apostles."[449] The brothers were born in Thessaloniki, Greece, and around AD 860, the Byzantine Emperor Michael III and Patriarch of Constantinople Photios sent them to ancient Eastern Europe to preach. The mission of Cyril and Methodius was very successful among the Slavs because they used the native language of the people instead of Latin or Greek. In AD 863 began the translation of the Holy Bible and the necessary liturgical books into the language that is known now as the Ancient Church Slavonic. From this came out also the Bulgarian translation and the orthodox translations in Eastern Europe. Therefore, you find that some of the ancient translations of the Holy Bible in the orthodox churches are identical to the ancient Coptic translation.

By comparing the translation of Romans 5:12 from the Coptic text, Slavonic text and Bulgarian text, with their counterpart from the uncomplicated[450] Syriac, it becomes clear that it falls back on Adam and not [on] sin.

[رسا و] 12 ܐܝܟܢܐ ܕܒܝܕ ܚܕ ܒܪܢܫܐ ܥܠܬ ܚܛܝܬܐ ܠܥܠܡܐ. ܘܒܝܕ ܚܛܝܬܐ ܡܘܬܐ. ܘܗܟܢܐ ܒܟܠܗܘܢ ܒܢ̈ܝ

كيف لأن أن بيد واحد إنسان دخلت الخطيئة إلى العالم وبيد الخطيئة الموت وهكذا بكلهم -

How For That by hand One Man Entered Sin To the world And by hand Sin Death And so In all of them

ܐܢܫܐ ܥܒܪ ܡܘܬܐ. ܒܗܝ ܕܟܠܗܘܢ ܚܛܘ.

الناس عبر الموت بهذا أنَّ كلُّهم خطئوا

Sinned That all of them In this Death Passed People

"In this (through Adam) that all of them sinned."[451]

---

[449] "Cyril and Methodius," *Wikipedia*, 29 March 2023, https://en.wikipedia.org/wiki/Cyril_and_Methodius.

[450] Or: simple.

[451] [Translated from Arabic text]. The Syriac-Arabic interlinear verse above is taken from original text, to which English translation is inserted under the Arabic words by translator. The original reference is the following: Syriac New Testament, Syriac-Arabic Interlinear Translation, Center for Oriental Studies and Researches, University of Münster, Germany, Antonian University, 2010.

On the other hand, the linguistic analysis concerning the text of Romans 5:12 in the Syriac Peshitta (included below[452]) [reveals the following]:

ܐܝܟܢܐ ܓܝܪ ܕܒܝܕ ܚܕ ܒܪܢܫܐ ܥܠܬ ܚܛܝܬܐ ܠܥܠܡܐ ܘܒܝܕ
ܚܛܝܬܐ ܡܘܬܐ ܘܗܟܢܐ ܒܟܠܗܘܢ ܒܢܝ ܐܢܫܐ ܥܒܪ ܡܘܬܐ
ܒܗܝ ܕܟܠܗܘܢ ܚܛܘ

Some say that the pronoun ܒܗܝ is feminine, and that the word "one man" ܚܕ ܒܪܢܫܐ is masculine, but the word "death" ܡܘܬܐ came in the feminine form; therefore, the pronoun ܒܗܝ refers to the word "death," that is to say, that all men did not sin in Adam, but sinned in death, because of death, and not because of Adam.

In response to this, I would like to clarify the following:

The word "death" in Syriac is *not* feminine, but is masculine, and the word "one man" is [also] masculine; but the word "sin" ܚܛܝܬܐ, Adam's sin, is feminine, and so is the pronoun ܒܗܝ feminine [too]. Thus, the correct translation is: All men became sinners, or sinned, because of Adam's sin.

Perhaps the greatest proof for the correct meaning [of Romans 5:12] is the ancient translations which were done in the era of the ancient text, especially if the translator in the past had a perfect mastery of the two languages. And this is [exactly] what happened in the case of the Coptic translation from ancient Greek, which was done by the Theological School of Alexandria under the leadership of St. Pantaenus.[453] The

---

[452] "Analysis of Peshitta," *Dukhrana*, http://dukhrana.com/peshitta/analyze_verse.php?verse=romans%205%3A12&-font=Estrangelo%20Edessa&fbclid=IwAR1blkm_A3gslQUC7qTOEPg-T_uUym3_3UZagoAJsAf5f_JIhDBmM2n_QII. Last accessed on 7 April 2023.

[453] Pantaenus introduced the Coptic alphabet using Greek letters, adding to them seven letter from the ancient Demotic dialect. Thereby it was possible to translate

translators had mastery of both the Greek and Coptic languages. This gives support to the accuracy of the Coptic translation which very clearly [states] that all sinned in Adam.

Likewise, in the **official translation of the Synod of the Russian Church**, which is taken from the original Greek "*Textus receptus,*" it is translated: "Just as through one man sin entered the world, and death through sin, and thus death spread to all men in whom [of a rational person, that is in Adam] all sinned."[454]

Посему, как одним человеком грех вошел в мир, и грехом смерть, так и смерть перешла во всех человеков, [потому что] в нем все согрешили.[455]

And in the **Jesuit [Arabic] translation**:

"Therefore, just as through one man sin entered the world, and death through sin, and thus death spread to all men through whom all sinned in him."[456]

Note that in the Jesuit translation issued in 1992, it is written "through whom all sinned in him," while the one issued

---

the Holy Bible to Coptic under his supervision. Helping him in this great work were his disciples Clement and Origen. Researchers give this translation great importance for being as old as the original Greek itself. St. Pantaenus also translated a lot of Christian literary works into this language, for it was the latest form of the development of the ancient Egyptian language, and writers began using it.

[454] [Translated from Arabic text].

[455] "Russian Synodal Version," *Bible Gateway*, https://www.biblegateway.com/versions/Russian-Synodal-Version-RUSV/. Last accessed on July 2022.

[456] *Al-Kitab Al-Mukadas, Al-Tarjamah Al-Yaso'iah, Tarjamah Al-Rahbaniah Al-Yaso'iah* [Holy Bible: Jesuit Translation. Translation of the Jesuit Monasticism]. (Beirut, Lebanon: House of the Holy Bible in the Middle East, 1992), 269. [Translated from Arabic text].

in 1994, for the same translation, it is written "because all sinned."[457]

And in the **translation of the Roman Orthodox Diocese of Baghdad, Kuwait and its affiliates**, which is based on the Greek from the original copy of Constantinople:

"Therefore, just as sin entered the world through one man, and through sin death entered, and thus death spread to all men because all sinned in him."[458]

This means that the orthodox doctrine in the ancient orthodox churches was in agreement on the understanding of the inheritance of Adam's sin, and on the need of all men throughout the ages for justification in Christ the Redeemer, for all people throughout the ages are sinners and guilty because they were "in" Adam by nature.

And in truth, the doctrine of the inheritance of Adam's sin is not a linguistic terminological problem connected to a single verse, disagreed upon, in the epistle of our teacher Paul to the Romans (Chapter 5 and verse 12); rather, it is an existing doctrine in the Holy Scriptures, liturgies, and the teachings of the Fathers, as was shown in this research; and tying this doctrine to a single verse which is disagreed upon is like tying the divinity of the Master Christ to the condition of showing an explicit verse wherein the Master Christ says, "I am God, so worship Me." Nevertheless, we have to treat this Holy Scripture with the importance fitting of it.

---

[457] *Al-Kitab Al-Mukadas, Al-Tarjamah Al-Yaso'iah, Tarjamah Al-Rahbaniah Al-Yaso'iah* [Holy Bible: Jesuit Translation. Translation of the Jesuit Monasticism]. (Beirut, Lebanon: Dar El-Mashrik, 1994), 477. [Translated from Arabic text].

[458] *Al-Kitab Al-Mukadas, Al-Ahd Al-Jadeed, Tarjamah Mutraniat Baghdad Wa Al-Kuwait Wa Tawabi'aha Lil-Roum Al-Orthodox* [The Holy Bible: New Testament, Translation of the Roman Orthodox Diocese of Baghdad, Kuwait and its Affiliates]. (Baghdad: Roman Orthodox Diocese of Baghdad, Kuwait and its Affiliates, 2006), 664–665. [Translated from Arabic text].

By Studying the Interconnectedness Between the Verses in Romans Five, We Find the Following:

In Romans 5:12, there is a problem, for (ōeph 'h ‘ἐφ’ ᾧ) could be understood in three ways: “For,” “for all have sinned” (for a rational person); “in him,” “in him (in Adam) all have sinned” (for a rational person); “because of,” “because of it (because of death) all have sinned” (for inanimate). From the context, however, of the remaining verses and their connectedness, it is understood to mean “in him,” that is, in Adam all have sinned, which is as follows:

1. Romanides translated verse 12 as follows: “As through one man sin came into the world, and through sin death, so also death came upon all men, because of which all have sinned.” He also taught that humanity did not inherit Adam’s sin but only inherited death, and from death came sin to all human beings. This means that Paul the Apostle contradicts himself in the same verse, because the second half of the verse is opposite to the first. For it is unreasonable for Paul the Apostle to say in the first half of the verse, “As through one man sin came into the world, and through sin death,” then to go back and say in the second half of the verse, “so also death came upon all men, because of which all have sinned.” God forbid that divine revelation commit this error.
2. In this chapter specifically, St. Paul the Apostle presents a meticulous comparison between Adam and Christ: Adam, in whom and because of whom all of his seed are sinners by fleshly birth, and Christ, in whom all the children of God become righteous by spiritual birth. “Therefore, as through **one man’s offense judgement** came to all men, resulting in **condemnation**, even so through **one Man’s righteous act** the free gift came to all men, resulting in **justification** of life. For as by one

man's **disobedience** many were made **sinners**, so also by one Man's **obedience** many will be made **righteous**."[459] That is to say, we, because of Adam's sin, were sentenced to condemnation though we did not partake in the act of Adam's sin, but we only were in him. If we considered that the phrase "in it/him"[460] means "in death," and not "in Adam," the comparison then is between Christ and death, and not between Christ and Adam.

3. St. Paul continues saying, "Moreover, the law entered that the offense might abound,"[461] meaning that the existence of the law is what makes sin imputed as sin.
4. Then he clarifies that before the law of Moses it was not imputed to the people who did not disobey God like Adam, that is personal sins, for the law did not exist yet. And yet they all died, for he says, "**Nevertheless death reigned from Adam to Moses, even over those who had not sinned according to the likeness of the transgression of Adam**, who is a type of Him who was to come."[462] That is, Adam who is a type of Christ. But death is "the wages of sin."[463] What is, then, the sin that caused them death? There is one answer, that is, Adam's sin. For they were without law, therefore their own trespasses were not imputed to them, but because of Adam's sin they died, and thus death spread to all men because all sinned in Adam.[464]
5. Verse eighteen plainly says that a lawful judgement of condemnation was issued to all men through the trespass of one [man] (that is, Adam's trespass), and not through

[459] Romans 5:18–19.
[460] [In Arabic, the same word is used for animate (him) and inanimate (it), which we translated to "in it/him"].
[461] Romans 5:20.
[462] Romans 5:14.
[463] Romans 6:23.
[464] See Romans 5:12.

the sin of all. "**Through one man's offense judgment came to all men, resulting in condemnation.**"[465]

6. Note that in the text of verse twelve it says, "because all sinned," in the past tense, and not "because all sin," in the present tense. This points to our partaking in Adam's sin in the past.
7. The verb used in 5:12—"all **sinned**"—is in the past tense, as we said, and in Romans 5:19—"For as by one man's disobedience many **were made** sinners"[466]—[the verb] is in the passive tense. That is, through Adam they were made sinners, and not from committing their own sins.
8. The idea that God counts us guilty because of Adam's sin is confirmed to a greater degree in Romans 5:18–19: "Therefore, as **through one man's offense judgement came to all men, resulting in condemnation**, even so through one Man's righteous act the free gift came to all men, resulting in justification of life. For as **by one man's disobedience** many were made sinners, so also by one Man's obedience many will be made righteous."[467]
9. This also is in agreement with Paul the Apostle's declaration: "While we were still sinners, Christ died for us."[468] And, of course, those born after the death of Christ on the cross did not exist when He died on our behalf on the cross. Nevertheless, God considers us sinners and we have need of salvation.
10. In the Divine Liturgy according to St. Basil, the priest prays and says in "Holy":

> Holy, indeed, O Lord our God, who formed us, created us, and placed us in the

[465] Romans 5:18.
[466] Romans 5:19.
[467] Romans 5:18–19.
[468] Romans 5:8.

> Paradise of joy, when **we disobeyed Your commandment by the deceit of the serpent**, we fell from eternal life and were exiles from the Paradise of joy.[469]

The meaning of this is that all were in the Paradise of joy in Adam; and therefore, when Adam fell, all fell from the Paradise of joy in Adam also.

11. If we believe that it is unfair for Adam to represent us and for his sin to be attributed to us, we likewise must believe that it is unfair for Christ to represent us and for His righteousness to be attributed to us.
12. [There are] other passages of the works of St. Paul that are consistent with the traditional interpretation of Romans 5:12, in that it means "in him," that is, in Adam.... [Perhaps the most important] in 1 Corinthians 15:22 we read: "As in Adam (εν τω Αδαμ) all die, so in Christ shall all be made alive." If we all die in Adam, then there can be no objection to saying that we all become sinners in him, as the traditionalist translation of Romans 5:12 asserts, insofar as "death is the wages of sin" and sin is "the sting of death".[470]
13. It is noteworthy that the comparison between our contraction of Adam's sin and receiving Christ's righteousness is similar to the comparison between death, which we contracted as a consequence of Adam's sin, and eternal life which we receive in Christ Jesus our Lord, as is stated in 1 Corinthians, Chapter 15, "For since by man came death, by Man also came the resurrection of the death. For as in Adam all die, even so in Christ all shall be made alive."[471]

---

[469] The Divine Liturgy According to St. Basil – Agios (Holy).
[470] Moss, Against Romanides, 40. [The whole passage is quoted from reference].
[471] 1 Corinthians 5:21–22.

14. The expression that we were "in Adam's loins" when he sinned, has a meaning that is customary for Paul the Apostle. Paul the Apostle also has written about Levi that he was in Abraham's loins when Abraham offered tithes to Melchizedek. St. Paul the Apostle says:

> And indeed those who are of the sons of Levi, who receive the priesthood, have a commandment to receive tithes from the people according to the law, that is, from their brethren, though they have come from the loins of Abraham; but he whose genealogy is not derived from them received tithes from Abraham and blessed him who had the promises. Now beyond all contradiction the lesser is blessed by the better. Here mortal men receive tithes, but these he receives them, of whom it is witnessed that he lives. Even Levi, who receives tithes, paid tithes through Abraham, so to speak, for he was still in the loins of his father when Melchizedek met him.[472]

And concerning this matter, the **scholar Origen** says:

> But in order that what we are saying might become clearer, let us add the following as well. The same Apostle writes as follows to the Hebrews, "Moreover Levi, who received tithes, paid tithes. For he was still in the loins of his father Abraham when Melchizedek met him as he was returning from the slaughter of the kings." **If then Levi, who is born in the fourth generation after**

[472] Hebrews 7:5–10.

> **Abraham, is declared as having been in the loins of Abraham, how much more were all men, those who are born and have been born in this world, in Adam's loins when he was still in paradise.** And all men who were with him, or rather in him, were expelled from paradise when he was himself driven out from there; and through him the death which had come to him from the transgression consequently passed through to them as well, who were dwelling in his loins; and therefore the Apostle rightly says, "For as in **Adam all die, so also in Christ all will be made alive." So then it is neither from the serpent who had sinned before the woman, nor from the woman who had become a transgressor before the man, but through Adam, from whom all mortals derive their origin, that sin is said to have entered, and through sin, death.**[473]

15. It must be noted that Paul the Apostle clearly indicates that the whole of the human race is under sin;[474] therefore, when he says that "many died,"[475] he does not implicitly mean that some did not die because of Adam's sin. And when Paul the Apostle speaks about the beneficiaries of the grace of the righteousness of the faith in Christ,[476] he says that it "abounded to many."[477] This does not mean that just any human being may receive this grace, but only those who believe in Christ;

---

[473] Origen, *Commentary on the Epistle to the Romans, Book 1–5*, T.P. Halton, ed.; T.P. Scheck, trans. (Washington, D.C.: The Catholic University of America Press, 2001), 310–311.

[474] See Romans 3:9–20.

[475] Romans 5:15.

[476] See Romans 3:22 and 5:17.

[477] Romans 5:15.

therefore, Paul the Apostle uses the term "many" only after using the term "the one," as Paul the Apostle's own way of speaking about the death of all [being] inclusive, and about grace only abounding to the many who are believers.

16. Therefore, Paul the Apostle says in verse 19, "By one man's disobedience many were made sinners."[478] This is the doctrine of Original Sin in a nutshell: Adam's sin made all his descendants sinners—not simply mortal, but precisely sinners. And it is not because of death that all men have sinned, as Romanides would have it, but because of Adam—and more specifically, because of his "disobedience", that is, his sin, which, as the Fathers explain is inherited by us. That is, in him we sinned, and were judged and condemned in him.[479]

17. Therefore, Romans 5 does not deal with "the inheritance of corruption," nor is it an indication of "the inheritance of a mortal nature," nor "current personal sins"—rather, it speaks about "the inheritance of Adam's sin," which led to my judgment, me personally, resulting in condemnation. He wrote it in this manner to keep the comparison between Adam and Christ.

18. **Some ask [saying], "Are we punished for something we did not do?"** Why do we accept that we died and were corrupted in Adam without asking [questions] and objecting, [but] then we ask, "Why were we made sinners in Adam?"

    It is the same principle. Just as we were born in death and corruption, likewise we were born in sin and disobedience. God the Word was incarnate to save us from this bad state (sin, death and corruption).

[478] Romans 5:19.

[479] See Moss, Against Romanides, 40.

19. Does our belief in the inheritance of sin mean that we make sin a substance that is mixed into the genes of human beings?

    The inheritance of sin, death and corruption should not be understood biologically and genetically; likewise, we cannot explain our receiving the inheritance of salvation and eternal life in a biological and genetic aspect, but in a true spiritual meaning. For we were in Adam when he sinned, so his sin cleaved to us and its consequences, according to the expression of **St. Cyril the Great**: "**We might escape from the sin that cleaves to us through the original transgression.**"[480]

    And in another translation of the same text, we find it as follows:

    "We might escape the sin of transgression that clings to us."[481]

    And likewise we are justified by the righteousness of Christ and we live through His life, without any biological genetic interpretation.

    "For as by one man's disobedience many were made sinners, so also by one Man's obedience many will be made righteous."[482]

    St. Cyril the Great says:

    > **For the whole nature of man became guilty in the person of him who was first formed [Adam]**; but now it is wholly justified again in Christ. For He became

[480] Cyril of Alexandria, *Commentary on the Gospel according to S. John* 2. (London, ENG: Walter Smith, 1885), 606.

[481] Cyril of Alexandria, *Commentary on John* 2, J.C. Elowsky, T.C. Oden, and G.L. Bray, eds.; D.R. Maxwell, trans. (Downers Grove, IL: IVP Academic, 2015), 333.

[482] Romans 5:19.

> for us the second commencement of our race after that primary one.[483]

> Sin is not something material, nor is righteousness, nor death, nor life. Inheritance here is not understood in a biological genetic aspect, neither in the case of sin, nor of righteousness.

"And if [we are] children, then heirs—heirs of God and joint heirs with Christ."[484]

So sin is disobedience to God; and we are born in this disobedient state, bent [on evil], deviant from the path of God.

---

[483] Cyril of Alexandria, *A Commentary upon the Gospel According to S. Luke* 1, R.P. Smith, trans. (Oxford, ENG: Oxford Press, 1859), 171.
[484] Romans 8:17.

CHAPTER FOUR
The Economy of Salvation

Summary of Our Doctrine of the Economy of Salvation

Salvific theology in Christian thought is founded upon redemption and propitiation which our Lord Jesus Christ worked out on our behalf and for our sake on the cross. We believe that our Lord Jesus is the only-begotten Son of God, the only Savior, and that salvation is through none other than Him.[485] And this salvation is through His precious Blood shed on our behalf,[486] on the holy wood of the cross.[487]

---

[485] "Nor is there salvation in any other, for there is no other name under heaven given among men by which we must be saved" (Acts 4:12).
"For God so loved the world that He gave His only begotten Son, that whoever believes in Him should not perish but have everlasting life" (John 3:16).
"He who believes in Him is not condemned; but he who does not believe is condemned already, because he has not believed in the name of the only begotten Son of God" (John 3:18).
"He who believes in the Son has everlasting life; and he who does not believe the Son shall not see life, but the wrath of God abides on him" (John 3:36).

[486] "And He took bread, gave thanks and broke it, and gave it to them, saying, 'This is My body which is given for you; do this in remembrance of Me'" (Luke 22:19).
"Likewise He also took the cup after supper, saying, "This cup is the new covenant in My blood, which is shed for you" (Luke 22:20).

[487] "In whom we have redemption through His blood, the forgiveness of sins" (Colossians 1:14).
"You were bought at a price; do not become slaves of men" (1 Corinthians 7:23).
"For you were bought at a price; therefore glorify God in your body and in your spirit, which are God's" (1 Corinthians 6:20).

The Church has accepted this faith from the beginning, in simplicity and joy, and lived it daily in its liturgical services,[488] through the continual true, sacramental,[489] and mystical union with her heavenly Bridegroom, our Lord Jesus Christ, in the holy Sacraments, especially in Baptism and the Eucharist.

This is our firm faith, which is immutable, and we will never relinquish it.

How did God cure the deteriorating state humanity reached because of Adam's sin?

St. Athanasius the Apostolic says:

> **For the Word, realizing that in no other way would the corruption of human beings be undone except, simply, by dying,** yet being immortal and the Son of the Father the Word was not able to die, **for this reason he takes to himself a body capable of death, in order that it, participating in the Word who is above all, might be sufficient for death on behalf of all, and through the indwelling Word would remain incorruptible.**[490]

The cure was that God the Word become incarnate, uniting with human nature, and in His own body the judgment of death is fulfilled which was against Adam and his seed. Then He gives us His life that we may unite with Him, to receive in Him righteousness, life, resurrection, and incorruption.

---

488 Literally: liturgical prayers.

489 That is, through the salvific church Sacraments.

490 Saint Athanasius, *On the Incarnation*, J. Behr, trans. (Yonkers, NY: SVS Press, 2011), 58.

The Salvific Works of Christ

The aspects of what Christ worked out with us and in us:

Our saintly Fathers explain that the economy of salvation of our Good God is multifaceted.

St. Athanasius the Apostolic says:

> And thus, taking from ours that which is like,[491] since all were liable to the corruption of death, **delivering it[492] to death on behalf of all, he offered it to the Father**, doing this in his love for human beings, so that, on the one hand, with all dying in him the law concerning corruption in human beings might be undone (its power being fully expended in the lordly body[493] and no longer having any ground against similar human beings), and, on the other hand, that as human beings had turned towards corruption[494] he might turn them again to incorruptibility and give them life from death, by making the body his own and by the grace of the resurrection banishing death from them as straw from the fire.[495]
>
> **For the Word, realizing that in no other way would the corruption of human beings be undone except, simply, by dying,[496] yet being immortal and the Son of the Father the Word was not able to die, for this reason he takes to**

---

[491] Arabic text here adds "the nature of our bodies."
[492] That is, His Body.
[493] "lordly body" is "the Body of the Lord" in the Arabic text.
[494] Arabic text here adds "by the disobedience."
[495] Saint Athanasius, *On the Incarnation*, J. Behr, trans. (Yonkers, NY: SVS Press, 2011), 57.
[496] Arabic text here adds "on behalf of all".

> **himself a body capable of death, in order that it, participating in the Word who is above all, might be sufficient for death on behalf of all, and through the indwelling Word would remain incorruptible, and so corruption might henceforth cease from all by the grace of the resurrection. Whence, by offering to death the body he had taken to himself, as an offering holy and free of all spot, he immediately abolished death from all like him, by the offering of a like. For being above all, the Word of God consequently, by offering his own temple and his bodily instrument as a substitute for all, fulfilled in death that which was required.**[497]

It is clear from the teaching of St. Athanasius the Apostolic, the teacher of the Church, that he did not deem one explanation sufficient, nor one aspect, to interpret what the Lord Christ did for our sake, but had a holistic and multifaceted view.

The error in theological thought begins when a person focuses on one aspect, while ignoring the other aspects. It is like someone who says that the cross is love only, ignoring the rest of the salvific aspects. Noteworthy is that the word "heretic" in its Greek origin means "selection,"[498] that is, selecting one aspect and focusing on, and magnifying it, thereby becoming a heresy

---

[497] Saint Athanasius, *On the Incarnation*, J. Behr, trans. (Yonkers, NY: SVS Press, 2011), 58.

[498] [The word] "heresies" is the plural for heresy, which is an alien word to Arabic; [it comes] from the Greek word αἵρεσις, its adjective αἱρετκός. The word, in its linguistic origin, means "selecting" or "electing" or "choosing" an opinion and favoring it over other opinions.

even though it may be true in its context, and with the other aspects.

What the Lord Jesus worked out for us and for the sake of our salvation, is exceedingly great, multifaceted, and has many results.

The Ramifications of the Incarnation and Redemption

The Incarnation:

- ❖ The revelation of God's love for human beings.
- ❖ He taught humankind about the Father—Christ the Teacher.

Substitution:

- ❖ Christ became the Mediator...
- ❖ Christ is the Head and the Firstborn... A Substitute and an Intercessor...
- ❖ He bore the divine punishment in place of human beings...

The encounter with death:

- ❖ Dying on behalf of human beings.
- ❖ Defeating death.

Privileges:

- ❖ Paying the debt that was on us.
- ❖ Healing human nature.
- ❖ Restoring the divine image in the human being.
- ❖ Restoring adoption by God the Father.
- ❖ Granting us [the privilege] of being partakers of the divine nature.

1. The Revelation of God's Love for Human Beings

"For God so loved the world that He gave His only begotten Son, that whoever believes in Him should not perish but have everlasting life."[499]

"Greater love has no one than this, than to lay down one's life for his friends."[500]

"But God demonstrates His own love toward us, in that while we were still sinners, Christ died for us."[501]

"In this the love of God was manifested toward us, that God has sent His only begotten Son into the world, that we might live through Him. In this is love, not that we loved God, but that He loved us and sent His Son to be the propitiation for our sins,"[502]

Truly Solomon the Wise prophesied in the Song of Solomon saying, "He brought me to the banqueting house,[503] and his banner over me was love."[504] The house of wine is the New Testament altar, and the banner is the cross which waves over the believers' heads with divine love.

That divine love which the Holy Father revealed by the cross of His only-begotten Son: "He who did not spare His own Son, but delivered Him up for us all, how shall He not with Him also freely give us all things?"[505]

Therefore, we, the believers, cannot but love Him. "Who shall separate us from the love of Christ? Shall tribulation, or distress, or persecution, or famine, or nakedness, or peril, or

---

[499] John 3:16.
[500] John 15:13.
[501] Romans 5:8.
[502] 1 John 4:9–10.
[503] Literally: the house of wine.
[504] Song of Solomon 2:4.
[505] Romans 8:32.

sword? As it is written: 'For Your sake we are killed all day long; we are accounted as sheep for the slaughter.' Yet in all these things we are more than conquerors through Him who loved us. For I am persuaded that neither death nor life, nor angels nor principalities nor powers, nor things present nor things to come, nor height nor depth, nor any other created thing, shall be able to separate us from the love of God which is in Christ Jesus our Lord."[506] "We love Him because He first loved us."[507]

"For the love of Christ compels us, because we judge thus: that if One died for all, then all died; and He died for all, that those who live should live no longer for themselves, but for Him who died for them and rose again."[508]

2. He Taught Humankind About the Father (Christ the Teacher)

The Son of God was incarnate, the invisible, the intangible; so seeing Him in the flesh, we may see the Father in Him and are made to know the Father and the Holy Spirit, after human beings had gone astray from their Creator and worshiped idols because of their attachment to perceptible things.

St. Athanasius the Apostolic says:

> Once the mind of human beings descended to perceptible things, the Word himself submitted to appear[509] through a body, so that as a human he might bring humans to himself and return their sense perception to himself, and then, by their seeing him as a human being, he might persuade

[506] Romans 8:35–39.
[507] 1 John 4:19.
[508] 2 Corinthians 5:14–15.
[509] Arabic text adds, "and hid Himself."

> them through the works he effected that he is not a man only but God and the Word, and Wisdom of the true God.[510]

The knowledge of the Father is a salvific knowledge. The Lord Christ saved us, in that He made the Father known to us, when He showed us the light of the Father and granted us true knowledge of the Holy Spirit. (Christ the Teacher). The principal teaching for the sake of which Christ came is that He might make known to us the Father.

"And this is eternal life, that they may know You, the only true God, and Jesus Christ whom You have sent."[511]

"I have manifested Your name to the men whom You have given Me out of the world. They were Yours, You gave them to Me, and they have kept Your word."[512]

"And I have declared to them Your name, and will declare it, that the love with which You loved Me may be in them, and I in them."[513]

It is salvific knowledge in truth.

"Since you have put off the old man with his deeds, and have put on the new man who is renewed in knowledge according to the image of Him who created him."[514]

---

[510] Saint Athanasius, *On the Incarnation*, J. Behr, trans. (Yonkers, NY: SVS Press, 2011), 66.
[511] John 17:3.
[512] John 17:6.
[513] John 17:26
[514] Colossians 3:9-10.

St. Athanasius the Apostolic says, "And he manifested himself through a body that we might receive an idea of the invisible Father."[515]

Therefore we pray in the [Divine] Liturgy according to St. Gregory thanking the only-begotten Son, "who has manifested to us the Light of the Father, who has granted us the true knowledge of the Holy Spirit."[516]

It is truly salvific knowledge because, "My people are destroyed for lack of knowledge."[517]

St. Athanasius the Apostolic says:

> The whole world is filled with the knowledge of God, and those from the Gentiles are abandoning godlessness, and henceforth taking refuge in the God of Abraham through the Word, our Lord Jesus Christ, it should be clear even to those who are exceedingly obstinate that Christ has come, and that he illumines absolutely all with his light and teaches the true and divine teaching concerning his Father.[518]

He also says:

> Demons and human beings were previously deceitful, ascribing to themselves the honor due to God; but when the Word of God appeared in a body and made known to us his own Father, then indeed the deceit of the demons disappears and ceases, while human beings, looking to the true

[515] Saint Athanasius, *On the Incarnation*, J. Behr, trans. (Yonkers, NY: SVS Press, 2011), 107.
[516] The Divine Liturgy According to St. Gregory – Anaphora.
[517] Hosea 4:6.
[518] Saint Athanasius, *On the Incarnation*, J. Behr, trans. (Yonkers, NY: SVS Press, 2011), 92–93.

> God Word of the Father, abandon idols and henceforth recognize the true God.[519]

"And we know that the Son of God has come and has given us an understanding, that we may know God[520] who is true; and we are in Him who is true, in His Son Jesus Christ. This is the true God and eternal life. Little children, keep yourselves from idols. Amen."[521]

The teaching of the Lord Jesus Christ was not a theological, theoretical teaching, but He was also a teacher who taught humankind by a way of life[522] the way of godliness; therefore, seeing Him before us as a perfect example, we may follow His footsteps.

"You call Me Teacher and Lord, and you say well, for so I am. If I then, your Lord and Teacher, have washed your feet, you also ought to wash one another's feet."[523]

"Take My yoke upon you and learn from Me, for I am gentle and lowly in heart, and you will find rest for your souls."[524]

3. Christ Became the Mediator with the Father and the Intercessor of Humankind

Being the Son of the Father, and at the same time being the Firstborn of human beings, the Lord Christ becomes for us a Mediator with the Father, and the One reconciling us with the Father, and a propitiating Intercessor. And because of the

---

[519] Ibid., 108.
[520] The word "God" is according to the Coptic translation in the Lectionary (Katamerous). According to NKJV, "God" appears as "Him." The rest of the passage is taken from NKJV.
[521] 1 John 5:20–21.
[522] "A way of life," i.e. experientially.
[523] John 13:13–14.
[524] Matthew 11:29.

Father's pleasure and acceptance of human beings in Him, after human beings were under the divine wrath which was declared from heaven against all the ungodliness and unrighteousness[525] of people, this reconciliation with God came about because of the righteousness of Christ, His obedience,[526] His victory, and all that He did in the body—all these were assets for the profit of human beings.

So by the incarnation of the Lord Christ and His substitutional death on behalf of human beings, He became a substitute for humankind before the Father, and its representative, interceding for us with His precious Blood,[527] an unending propitiating intercession. (Christ the propitiating Intercessor).

We pray in the [Divine] Liturgy according to St. Gregory saying, "And [You] became for us a mediator with the Father, and the middle wall You have broken down and the old enmity You have abolished. You have reconciled the earthly with the heavenly and made the two into one."[528] This explains the concept of the propitiating intercession of the Lord Christ and His mediation for us with the Father.

---

[525] "For the wrath of God is revealed from heaven against all ungodliness and unrighteousness of men, who suppress the truth in unrighteousness" (Romans 1:18).
"Much more then, having now been justified by His blood, we shall be saved from wrath through Him" (Romans 5:9).

[526] "For as by one man's disobedience many were made sinners, so also by one Man's obedience many will be made righteous" (Romans 5:19).

[527] "Knowing that you were not redeemed with corruptible things, like silver or gold, from your aimless conduct received by tradition from your fathers, but with the precious blood of Christ, as of a lamb without blemish and without spot" (1 Peter 1:18–19).

[528] The Divine Liturgy According to St. Gregory – Prayer of Reconciliation.

"Therefore He is also able to save to the uttermost those who come to God through Him, since He always lives to make intercession for them."[529]

"To Jesus the Mediator of the new covenant, and to the blood of sprinkling that speaks better things than that of Abel."[530]

"But now He has obtained a more excellent ministry, inasmuch as He is also Mediator of a better covenant, which was established on better promises."[531]

"And for this reason He is the Mediator of the new covenant, by means of death, for the redemption of the transgressions under the first covenant, that those who are called may receive the promise of the eternal inheritance."[532]

"For there is one God and one Mediator between God and men, the Man Christ Jesus."[533]

"For Christ has not entered the holy places made with hands, which are copies of the true, but into heaven itself, now to appear in the presence of God for us; not that He should offer Himself often, as the high priest enters the Most Holy Place every year with blood of another."[534]

St. Athanasius the Apostolic says: "Being the Word of the Father and above all, he alone consequently was both able to recreate the universe **and was worthy to suffer on behalf of all and to intercede for all before the Father.**"[535]

---

[529] Hebrews 7:25.
[530] Hebrews 12:24.
[531] Hebrews 8:6.
[532] Hebrews 9:15.
[533] 1 Timothy 2:5.
[534] Hebrews 9:24–25.
[535] Saint Athanasius, *On the Incarnation*, J. Behr, trans. (Yonkers, NY: SVS Press, 2011), 56.

And Christ, by that, became our reconciler with the Father.

"And by Him to reconcile all things to Himself, by Him, whether things on earth or things in heaven, having made peace through the blood of His cross."[536]

"And you, who once were alienated and enemies in your mind by wicked works, yet now He has reconciled in the body of His flesh through death, to present you holy, and blameless, and above reproach in His sight."[537]

St. John Chrysostom says:

> **For God was angry with man**, and we had turned from God our loving Master, and Christ placing Himself between God and man reconciled both natures.
>
> **But in what manner did He make Himself a mediator? By taking upon Himself the punishment the Father[538] must inflict upon us; submitting Himself both to the chastisements decreed against us, and to the humiliations inflicted by us also.** Do you wish to learn how He endured both of these? "Christ," says the Apostle, "has redeemed us from the curse of the law, being made a curse for us."[539] You have seen in what manner **He took upon Himself the punishment decreed from above.** See also how He has endured the humiliations inflicted by men: "The

536 Colossians 1:20.
537 Colossians 1:21-22.
538 παρὰ τοῦ Πατρὸς
539 Galatians 3:13.

> reproaches of them that reproached you have fallen upon me."[540]
>
> Do you perceive in what manner He put an end to enmity, and how He made him who was an enemy into a friend, and pleasing to God; **but not before He had paid in full all that was owing**, and fulfilled all that was to be done and to be suffered? And the proof of all these good things is the festival[541] of this day.[542]

"Who was incarnate of you without change, and became the Mediator of a new covenant. Through the shedding of His holy Blood, He purified the faithful to be a justified people."[543]

"For He has destroyed the middle wall and killed the enmity with perfection."[544]

"The fruit of your womb came and saved the world, and He abolished all enmity and granted us His peace."[545]

"For through your fruit salvation came to our race and God has reconciled with us once again through His goodness."[546]

4. Christ became the Head, Firstborn, New Root for Human Beings, Substitute, Propitiating Intercessor, and the Forerunner for Our Sake

Being our Firstborn, He entered as a forerunner for us into the Holiest above, blessing thereby our human nature and opening for us the door, that we might enter in Him and with Him into

---

540 Psalm 69:10.

541 Feast of the Ascension.

542 *The Sunday Sermons of the Great Fathers* 2, M.F. Toal, trans. (Chicago: Henry Regnery Company, 1964), 433–434.

543 Midnight Praises – Sunday Theotokia, Part 1.

544 Midnight Praises – Monday Theotokia, Part 8.

545 Midnight Praises – Friday Theotokia, Part 5.

546 Midnight Praises – Saturday Theotokia, Part 2.

the Holiest above, and might sit with Him and in Him in the Heavens, in the Age to Come. For because of our uniting with Him through faith, Baptism and the Eucharist, the Lord Christ becomes the Head of the Church, and we members of this great body.

"For the husband is head of the wife, as also Christ is head of the church; and He is the Savior of the body."[547]

"And He is the head of the body, the church, who is the beginning, the firstborn from the dead, that in all things He may have the preeminence."[548]

"Now you are the body of Christ, and members individually."[549]

Thereby the Lord Jesus Christ is the Firstborn for us human beings instead of Adam our first firstborn, who sinned and died and was corrupted; so our human race contracted in Adam, sin, death and corruption. Then the Logos, the Word of the Father, came, to be for us a head, chief, new beginning, root, firstborn, substitute, and an intercessor; so that we may receive in Him and through Him, righteousness in place of Adam's sin, life in place of Adam's death, and incorruption instead of our corruptible inheritance from Adam. Therefore, it is included in the economy of salvation that the Lord Jesus Christ bears our human nature in His own body and enters with it into the Holiest above, as a forerunner and a firstborn, that He may bless our nature in Himself. (Christ the First-fruits,[550] the Firstborn over all creation[551]).

---

[547] Ephesians 5:23.
[548] Colossians 1:18.
[549] 1 Corinthians 12:27.
[550] "But when He again brings the firstborn into the world, He says: 'Let all the angels of God worship Him'" (Hebrews 1:6).
[551] "He is the image of the invisible God, the firstborn over all creation" (Colossians 1:15).

St. John Chrysostom says in his sermon on the glorious Feast of Ascension:

> For as He took upon Himself the first-fruits of our nature, so likewise did He take them up to the Lord. And as happens when the fields are filled with corn, and a man gathers a few of the stalks and makes them into a little sheaf, and offering it to God by this little quantity the whole field is blessed, so has Christ done, Who by means of His one Body, and this the First-fruits, has brought it about that the whole race is to be blessed.
>
> And why did He not offer up the whole of our nature? For the reason that he who offers up the whole does not offer the first-fruits. But if he offers up a little part, through this part he causes the whole to be blessed. But, someone will say, if first-fruits are offered then the first man born should be offered: for the first-fruits are those that are begotten first, and first spring up. We are not held to have offered first-fruits, when the first-fruits we have offered, Beloved Brethren, are poor and weak, but when we have offered what is perfect and worthy. Therefore since the former [Adam] was subject to sin it was not offered, though it came forth the first; but this latter was free of all sin, and this accordingly was offered: for though it was born after, it was the First-fruits.[552]

---

[552] *The Sunday Sermons of the Great Fathers* 2, M.F. Toal, trans. (Chicago: Henry Regnery Company, 1964), 434.

He promised us eternal life and incorruptibility, and we will be like Him, for we will see Him as He is,[553] and we will put on the heavenly image and be transformed into that same image[554]—O what glory!

Our teacher **St. Athanasius the Apostolic** explains the concept of the Lord Christ being the Firstborn for us human beings in *On the Incarnation*: "[He] granted incorruptibility to all through the promise of the resurrection, raising his own body as first-fruits of this and showing it as a trophy over death and its corruption by the sign of the cross."[555]

The Lord Christ entered as a forerunner for us into the Holiest above for our sake. And He promised us that we will sit with Him on His throne, and this to everyone who overcomes,[556] and that we will inherit in Him and with Him everything.[557] (Christ the Co-enthroned with the Father[558]).

This is exactly what we pray with in the Divine Liturgy:

> O Jesus Christ, to whom belongs the name of salvation, ... the High Priest of the good things to come, who ascended into the heavens and has become higher than the heavens. He went within the veil to the Holy place of the Holies, the place into which anyone of human nature cannot enter.

---

[553] "Beloved, now we are children of God; and it has not yet been revealed what we shall be, but we know that when He is revealed, we shall be like Him, for we shall see Him as He is" (1 John 3:2).

[554] "But we all, with unveiled face, beholding as in a mirror the glory of the Lord, are being transformed into the same image from glory to glory, just as by the Spirit of the Lord" (2 Corinthians 3:18).

[555] Saint Athanasius, *On the Incarnation*, J. Behr, trans. (Yonkers, NY: SVS Press, 2011), 83.

[556] "To him who overcomes I will grant to sit with Me on My throne, as I also overcame and sat down with My Father on His throne" (Revelation 3:21).

[557] "He who overcomes shall inherit all things, and I will be his God and he shall be My son" (Revelation 21:7).

[558] The Divine Liturgy According to St. Gregory – Prayer of Reconciliation.

> He became a forerunner on our behalf, having become a High Priest for ever after the order of Melchizedek.[559]

And here, of course, our sitting with Christ on His throne does not mean His own throne—that is, the Divinity—but special thrones befitting of us human beings in His kingdom.[560] And this is a gift that cannot be expressed, but, in any case, it does not mean our equality with Christ in His glory of the Godhead nor His divine majesty.

On this **St. Cyril the Great** says:

> And tell me, I pray, whose is it to sit with the Father, but His Who by nature is the Son? **For of all that is made nothing whatsoever may boast of sitting on the throne of Deity: for every created being is put under the feet of the divine and supreme nature, Which rules over all, and transcends everything whatsoever which has been brought into being. God the Father alone is set upon the throne high and lifted up, but He shares His seat with the Son**, Who is ever with Him, and sprang by nature from Him.[561]

---

[559] Fraction to the Son for Joyous Saturday.

[560] "So Jesus said to them, "Assuredly I say to you, that in the regeneration, when the Son of Man sits on the throne of His glory, you who have followed Me will also sit on twelve thrones, judging the twelve tribes of Israel" (Matthew 19:28). "But you are those who have continued with Me in My trials. And I bestow upon you a kingdom, just as My Father bestowed one upon Me, that you may eat and drink at My table in My kingdom, and sit on thrones judging the twelve tribes of Israel" (Luke 22:28–30).

[561] Cyril of Alexandria, *A Commentary upon the Gospel According to S. Luke* 2, R.P. Smith, trans. (Oxford, ENG: At the University Press, 1859), 709.

[He also says:]

> **For to Christ, as by nature Son, it belongs as a special prerogative to sit at the Father's side, and the glory of this dignity we can ascribe rightly and truly to Him, and Him alone.** But the fact that Christ Who sits there is in all points like unto us, in that He has appeared as Man, while we believe Him to be God of God, seems to confer on us also the privilege of this dignity. **For even if we shall not sit at the side of the Father Himself—for how could the servant ever ascend to equal honor with the master?—yet nevertheless Christ promised the holy disciples that they should sit on thrones.** For He says: "When the Son of Man shall sit on the throne of His glory, ye also shall sit upon twelve thrones, judging the twelve tribes of Israel."[562,563]

This same divine truth is described and explained in Holy Scriptures:

"This hope we have as an anchor of the soul, both sure and steadfast, and which enters the Presence behind the veil, where the forerunner has entered for us, even Jesus, having become High Priest forever according to the order of Melchizedek."[564]

"Seeing then that we have a great High Priest who has passed through the heavens, Jesus the Son of God, let us hold fast our confession."[565]

---

[562] Matthew 19:28.
[563] Cyril of Alexandria, *Commentary on the Gospel according to S. John* 2. (London, ENG: Walter Smith, 1885), 237–238.
[564] Hebrews 6:19–20.
[565] Hebrews 4:14.

5. Bearing the Divine Punishment in Place of Human Beings

This debt which the Lord Christ paid off on our behalf is the death which God sentenced man to as a punishment for his sin. This punishment our teacher Paul the Apostle expressed in the statement, "the handwriting of requirements that was against us, which was contrary to us."

> And you, being dead in your trespasses and the uncircumcision of your flesh, He has made alive together with Him, having forgiven you all trespasses, having wiped out the handwriting of requirements that was against us, which was contrary to us. And He has taken it out of the way, having nailed it to the cross. Having disarmed principalities and powers, He made a public spectacle of them, triumphing over them in it.[566]

And **St. Athanasius the Apostolic** says:

> **That the Lord suffers these things not for his own sake, but for ours.** And it says again through his own lips in Psalm 87, "Your wrath has pressed heavily upon me," and in Psalm 68, "Then I restored that which I did not take away." **For although he was not himself obliged to give account for any crime, he died—but he suffered on our behalf, and he took on himself the wrath directed against us on account of the**

[566] Colossians 2:13–15.

> **transgression,** as it says in Isaiah, "He took on our weaknesses."[567,568]

[He also says:]

> Therefore death upon the cross for our sakes was fitting and suitable, and its cause appeared to be consistent in every way, and there are solid arguments that the salvation of all had to take place in no other way than the cross.[569]

And the same teaching is explained by our father **St. Cyril the Great:**

> But the Word of God the Father, being generous in clemency and love of men, became flesh, that is, man, in the form of us who are under sin, **and he endured our lot.** For as the very excellent Paul writes, "By the grace of God he tasted death for all,"[570] **and he made his life be an exchange for the life of all.** One died for all, in order that we all might live to God sanctified and brought to life through his blood.[571]

The holy Fathers derived this pure unblemished teaching from the Holy Scriptures and from the Fathers before them. In the Book of Isaiah we find a very clear prophecy about the salvific sufferings of the Master Christ:

---

[567] Athanasius takes Isaiah's words not from the Septuagint, but from Matthew 8:17.
[568] Athanasius of Alexandria, *Athanasius: The Life of Antony and the Letter to Marcellinus*, R.C. Gregg, trans. (Mahwah, NJ: Paulist Press, 1980), 105.
[569] Saint Athanasius, *On the Incarnation*, J. Behr, trans. (Yonkers, NY: SVS Press, 2011), 76.
[570] Hebrews 2:9.
[571] St. Cyril of Alexandria, *Letters 1-50*, J.I. McEnerney, trans. (Washington, D.C.: The Catholic University of America Press, 1987), 174.

> Surely He has borne our griefs and carried our sorrows; yet we esteemed Him stricken, smitten by God, and afflicted. But He was wounded for our transgressions, He was bruised for our iniquities; the chastisement for our peace was upon Him, and by His stripes we are healed. All we like sheep have gone astray; we have turned, every one, to his own way; and the Lord has laid on Him the iniquity of us all. He was oppressed and He was afflicted, yet He opened not His mouth; He was led as a lamb to the slaughter, and as a sheep before its shearers is silent, so He opened not His mouth.[572]

"He shall see the labor of His soul, and be satisfied. By His knowledge My righteous Servant shall justify many, for He shall bear their iniquities."[573]

The Lord Jesus was the holy Sacrifice without blemish, which was offered for the life of human beings, "who does not need daily, as those high priests, to offer up sacrifices, first for His own sins and then for the people's, for this He did once for all when He offered up Himself."[574]

"By that will we have been sanctified through the offering of the body of Jesus Christ once for all."[575]

"For indeed Christ, our Passover, was sacrificed for us."[576]

He is the Sacrifice and He is the Priest offering the sacrifice:

---

[572] Isaiah 53:4–7.
[573] Isaiah 53:11.
[574] Hebrews 7:27.
[575] Hebrews 10:10.
[576] 1 Corinthians 5:7.

"For He testifies: 'You are a priest forever according to the order of Melchizedek.'"[577]

The Lord Christ is the Priest and is the Sacrifice:

> He who offered Himself as an acceptable sacrifice upon the Cross for the salvation of our race. His good father smelled Him in the evening on Golgotha. He opened the gate of Paradise and restored Adam to him authority. Through His Cross and holy Resurrection, He returned man once more to Paradise.[578]
>
> Seeing then that we have a great High Priest who has passed through the heavens, Jesus the Son of God, let us hold fast our confession. For we do not have a High Priest who cannot sympathize with our weaknesses, but was in all points tempted as we are, yet without sin.[579]

Therefore our Lord Jesus Christ was called "the Redeemer."

"'Fear not, you worm Jacob, you men of Israel! I will help you,' says the Lord and your Redeemer, the Holy One of Israel."[580]

"All flesh shall know that I, the Lord, am your Savior, and your Redeemer, the Mighty One of Jacob."[581]

The fathers and prophets had prophesied about this great Redeemer.

---

[577] Hebrews 7:17.
[578] The Hymn of the Cross [said] on the two Feasts of the Cross, Covenant Thursday, Great Friday, Sunday Theotokia, and in the verses that are prayed in reverence in Raising of Incense.
[579] Hebrews 4:14–15.
[580] Isaiah 41:14.
[581] Isaiah 49:26.

Prophesies about the redemption:

"He will redeem his soul from going down to the Pit, and his life shall see the light."[582]

"For the Lord has redeemed Jacob, and ransomed him from the hand of one stronger than he."[583]

"Therefore I will divide Him a portion with the great, and He shall divide the spoil with the strong, because He poured out His soul unto death, and He was numbered with the transgressors, and He bore the sin of many, and made intercession for the transgressors."[584]

"Then He is gracious to him, and says, 'Deliver him from going down to the Pit; I have found a ransom'"[585]

"I will whistle for them and gather them, for I will redeem them; and they shall increase as they once increased."[586]

"None of them can by any means redeem his brother, nor give to God a ransom for him—for the redemption of their souls is costly, and it shall cease forever."[587]

"He has sent redemption to His people; He has commanded His covenant forever: holy and awesome is His name."[588]

"Blessed is the Lord God of Israel, for He has visited and redeemed His people."[589]

---

[582] Job 33:28.
[583] Jeremiah 31:11.
[584] Isaiah 53:12.
[585] Job 33:24.
[586] Zechariah 10:8.
[587] Psalm 49:7–8,
[588] Psalm 111:9.
[589] Luke 1:68.

All these prophesies were fulfilled in the Person of our Lord Jesus Christ the Redeemer, and the Ransom at the same time:

"For even the Son of Man did not come to be served, but to serve, and to give His life a ransom for many."[590]

"For there is one God and one Mediator between God and men, the Man Christ Jesus, who gave Himself a ransom for all."[591]

"Knowing that you were not redeemed with corruptible things, like silver or gold, from your aimless conduct received by tradition from your fathers, but with the precious blood of Christ, as of a lamb without blemish and without spot. He indeed was foreordained before the foundation of the world, but was manifest in these last times for you."[592]

"Who Himself bore our sins in His own body on the tree, that we, having died to sins, might live for righteousness—by whose stripes you were healed."[593]

"For He made Him who knew no sin to be sin for us, that we might become the righteousness of God in Him."[594]

"Not with the blood of goats and calves, but with His own blood He entered the Most Holy Place once for all, having obtained eternal redemption. For if the blood of bulls and goats and the ashes of a heifer, sprinkling the unclean, sanctifies for the purifying of the flesh, how much more shall the blood of Christ, who through the eternal Spirit offered Himself without spot to God, cleanse your conscience from dead works to serve the living God? And for this reason He is the Mediator of the

[590] Mark 10:45.
[591] 1 Timothy 2:5–6.
[592] 1 Peter 1:18–20.
[593] 1 Peter 2:24.
[594] 2 Corinthians 5:21.

new covenant, by means of death, for the redemption of the transgressions under the first covenant, that those who are called may receive the promise of the eternal inheritance."[595]

And about this **St. Cyril the Great** says:

> **For no otherwise was it possible that he that has the power of death should be destroyed, and death itself also, had not Christ given Himself for us, a Ransom, One for all, for He was in behalf of all.**[596]

[He also said:]

> **The One died for all**, and He is the only One very suitable to accomplish this work. **He gave His life in place of our life**, and abolished the evil ways of the devil, and stopped the accusation of sin which had dominion over us, and its prating also about the crimes of all.[597]

[Also:]

> **For one Lamb died for all, saving the whole flock on earth to God the Father, One for all, that He might subject all to God, One for all, that He might gain all**: that at length all should not henceforth live to themselves but to Him Which died for them and rose again. **For since we were in many sins, and therefore due to death and corruption, the Father has given the Son a redemption for us.** One for all, since all are in

---

595 Hebrews 9:12–15.

596 Cyril of Alexandria, *Commentary on the Gospel according to S. John* 1. (Oxford, ENG: J. Parker, 1874), 409.

597 Cyril the Great, *Al-Sojoud Wa Al-Ibada Bi-Al Rouh Wa Al-Hak* [Worshipping and Serving in Spirit and in Truth], G.A. Ibrahim, trans. (Egypt: The Orthodox Center for Patristic Studies, 2017), 140. [Translated from Arabic text].

> Him, and He above all. One died for all, that all should live in Him. For death having swallowed up the Lamb for all, has vomited forth all in Him and with Him. For all we were in Christ, Who on account of us and for us died and rose again. But sin being destroyed, how could it be that death which was of it and because of it should not altogether come to nothing? The root dying, how could the shoot yet survive? Wherefore should we yet die, now that sin has been destroyed?[598]

[Again:]

> **For the sentence of death was a consequence of breaking the divine law and of disobeying the divine will.** The Creator, therefore, was made sorrowful over human nature that was corrupted, and the Only-begotten became man and made His body endure death for our sake, **that [death] which crept into us because of sin, that by His death He might annul sin and stop the devil's accusations against[599] us, for we have paid off in the Person of Christ Himself the recompense of our accusations because of sin.** For according to the words of the prophet, "He bore the sin of many and made intercession for the transgressors."[600] Have we not been healed by His sufferings?[601]

---

[598] Cyril of Alexandria, *Commentary on the Gospel according to S. John* 1. (Oxford, ENG: J. Parker, 1874), 132.
[599] Literally: toward.
[600] Isaiah 53:12.
[601] Cyril the Great, *Al-Sojoud Wa Al-Ibada Bi-Al Rouh Wa Al-Hak* [Worshipping and Serving in Spirit and in Truth], G.A. Ibrahim, trans. (Egypt: The Orthodox Center for Patristic Studies, 2017), 141. [Translated from Arabic text].

[He also said:]

> **And rightly I say that they would not have been able to avoid the death that destroyed the firstborn children of the Egyptians**, nor to evade the powerful clutch of the destroying angel, **had they not killed the lamb which is a type of Christ who takes away the sins of the world.**[602]

St. Gregory Nazianzus adds to this and says:

> Now we are to examine another fact and dogma, neglected by most people, but in my judgment well worth enquiring into. **To Whom was that Blood offered that was shed for us, and why was It shed?** I mean the precious and famous Blood of our God and High Priest and Sacrifice. We were detained in bondage by the Evil One, sold under sin, and receiving pleasure in exchange for wickedness. Now, since a ransom belongs only to him who holds in bondage, **I ask to whom was this offered, and for what cause? If to the Evil One, fie upon the outrage! If the robber receives ransom, not only from God, but a ransom which consists of God Himself, and has such an illustrious payment for his tyranny, a payment for whose sake it would have been right for him to have left us alone altogether.** But if to the Father, I ask first, how? For it was not by Him that we were being oppressed; and next, On what principle did the Blood of His Only begotten Son delight the Father, Who would not receive even Isaac, when he was being offered by his Father, but changed the sacrifice, putting a

---

[602] Ibid., 115.

> ram in the place of the human victim?[603] **Is it not evident that the Father accepts Him, but neither asked for Him nor demanded Him; but on account of the Incarnation, and because Humanity must be sanctified by the Humanity of God, that He might deliver us Himself, and overcome the tyrant, and draw us to Himself by the mediation of His Son, Who also arranged this to the honor of the Father, Whom it is manifest that He obeys in all things?**[604]

And on this **St. Athanasius the Apostolic** also says:

> And thus, taking from ours that which is like,[605] since all were liable to the corruption of death, **delivering it[606] to death on behalf of all, he offered it to the Father**, doing this in his love for human beings, **so that, on the one hand, with all dying in him the law concerning corruption in human beings might be undone (its power being fully expended in the lordly body[607]** and no longer having any ground against similar human beings), **and, on the other hand, that as human beings had turned towards corruption[608] he might turn them again to incorruptibility and give them life from death, by making the body his own and by the grace of**

603 Genesis 22:11–13.
604 Gregory Nazianzen *Oration XLV. The Second Oration on Easter* 22 (NPNF[2] 7:431).
605 Arabic text here adds "the nature of our bodies."
606 That is, His Body.
607 "lordly body" is "the Body of the Lord" in Arabic text.
608 Arabic text here adds "by the disobedience."

> **the resurrection banishing death from them as straw from the fire.**[609]

Christ is also the Ransom which was offered to God the Father for the salvation of human beings.[610]

"For even the Son of Man did not come to be served, but to serve, and to give His life a ransom for many."[611]

"Who gave Himself a ransom for all"[612]

St. Athanasius the Apostolic says: "[He] who like a sheep delivered his own body to death as a substitute for the salvation of all."[613]

"Knowing that you were not redeemed with corruptible things, like silver or gold, from your aimless conduct received by tradition from your fathers, but with the precious blood of Christ, as of a lamb without blemish and without spot."[614]

"For you were bought at a price; therefore glorify God in your body and in your spirit, which are God's."[615]

This price is the great propitiation which Christ offered for our sake.

"My little children, these things I write to you, so that you may not sin. And if anyone sins, we have an Advocate with the Father, Jesus Christ the righteous. And He Himself is the

---

[609] Saint Athanasius, *On the Incarnation*, J. Behr, trans. (Yonkers, NY: SVS Press, 2011), 57.

[610] The word "ransom" in this text, in the ancient Greek, is ἀντίψυχον (antípsychon). And it originates from ἀντίψυχος (antípsychos) which means a "a substitute soul" or "substitute," that is, giving the life of one person instead of the life of another as a ransom.

[611] Mark 10:45.

[612] 1 Timothy 2:6.

[613] Saint Athanasius, *On the Incarnation*, J. Behr, trans. (Yonkers, NY: SVS Press, 2011), 89.

[614] 1 Peter 1:18–19.

[615] 1 Corinthians 6:20.

propitiation for our sins, and not for ours only but also for the whole world."[616]

"Being justified freely by His grace through the redemption that is in Christ Jesus, whom God set forth as a propitiation by His blood, through faith, to demonstrate His righteousness, because in His forbearance God had passed over the sins that were previously committed."[617]

"In this is love, not that we loved God, but that He loved us and sent His Son to be the propitiation for our sins."[618]

By this great propitiation the Lord Christ triumphed over the devil and the world and death on our account.

"Having disarmed principalities and powers, He made a public spectacle of them, triumphing over them in it."[619]

"But be of good cheer, I have overcome the world."[620]

"I will ransom them from the power of the grave; I will redeem them from death. O Death, I will be your plagues! O Grave, I will be your destruction! Pity is hidden from My eyes."[621]

And **St. Cyril the Great** says:

> **For our sake He paid the penalty for our sins. For though He was One that suffered, yet was He far above any creature, as God, and more precious than the life of all.** Therefore, as the Psalmist says, "the mouth of all lawlessness was

---

[616] 1 John 2:1–2.
[617] Romans 3:24–25.
[618] 1 John 4:10.
[619] Colossians 2:15.
[620] John 16:33.
[621] Hosea 13:14.

> stopped,"[622] and the tongue of sin was silenced, unable any more to speak against sinners. **For we are justified, now that Christ has paid the penalty for us**; "for by His stripes we are healed,"[623] according to the Scripture. And just as by the Cross the sin of our revolt was perfected, so also by the Cross was achieved our return to our original state, and the acceptable recovery of heavenly blessings; Christ, as it were, gathering up into Himself, for us, the very fount and origin of our infirmity.[624]

6. Dying on Behalf of Human Beings

Being immortal, He took a mortal body, that He may taste death in it, the death with which all are sentenced[625] because of Adam's sin and our own sins; so that He may die on our behalf, thereby paying off our debt and safeguarding the truth of the Father concerning all.[626] For the judgment of the Father is that "the wages of sin is death."[627] He, who is true and the Father of truth, had said, "For in the day that you eat of it you shall surely die."[628]

Therefore death was unavoidable because it is the judgment of the Father, and "the Lord is known in the judgments He

[622] See Psalm 107:42.
[623] See Isaiah 53:5.
[624] Cyril of Alexandria, *Commentary on the Gospel according to S. John* 2. (London, ENG: Walter Smith, 1885), 628.
[625] Or: under judgment.
[626] "For his it was once more both to bring the corruptible to incorruptibility and to save the superlative consistency of the Father. Being the Word of the Father and above all, he alone consequently was both able to recreate the universe and was worthy to suffer on behalf of all and to intercede for all before the Father." Saint Athanasius, *On the Incarnation*, J. Behr, trans. (Yonkers, NY: SVS Press, 2011), 56.
[627] Romans 6:23.
[628] Genesis 2:17.

makes; the sinner is caught in the works of his hands."[629] And an escape from this wretched eternal fate was impossible, except through the substitutional death made on behalf of human beings. And this is what Christ accomplished for our sake because He loved us.

We are taken captive by this divine love.

"For the love of Christ compels us, because we judge thus: that if One died for all, then all died; and He died for all, that those who live should live no longer for themselves, but for Him who died for them and rose again."[630]

"For if by the one man's offense many died, much more the grace of God and the gift by the grace of the one Man, Jesus Christ, abounded to many."[631]

"Just as the Son of Man did not come to be served, but to serve, and to give His life a ransom for many."[632]

"Greater love has no one than this, than to lay down one's life for his friends."[633]

And this is the priceless precious faith which we declare in the Creed: "Who for us men and for our salvation came down from heaven ... And He was crucified for us under Pontius Pilate,"[634] and we pray with it in the timeless Hymn of the Cross: "He who offered Himself as an acceptable sacrifice upon the cross for the salvation of our race."[635]

---

[629] Psalm 9:17 LXX from The Orthodox Study Bible.
[630] 2 Corinthians 5:14–15.
[631] Romans 5:15.
[632] Matthew 20:28.
[633] John 15:13.
[634] The Creed of Nicea and Constantinople.
[635] The Hymn of the Cross on the two Feasts of the Cross, Covenant Thursday, Great Friday, Sunday Theotokia, and in the verses that are prayed in reverence in Raising of Incense.

St. Athanasius the Apostolic, the teacher of orthodoxy, says:

> Being the Word of the Father and above all, he alone consequently was both able to recreate the universe and was worthy **to suffer on behalf of all and to intercede for all before the Father.**[636]
>
> And thus, taking from ours that which is like,[637] **since all were liable to the corruption of death, delivering it[638] to death on behalf of all, he offered it to the Father**, doing this in his love for human beings, so that, on the one hand, with all dying in him the law concerning corruption in human beings might be undone (its power being fully expended in the lordly body[639] and no longer having any ground against similar human beings), and, on the other hand, that as human beings had turned towards corruption[640] he might turn them again to incorruptibility and give them life from death, by making the body his own and by the grace of the resurrection banishing death from them as straw from the fire.[641]
>
> **For the Word, realizing that in no other way would the corruption of human beings be undone except, simply, by dying,**[642] yet being immortal and the Son of the Father the Word was

[636] Saint Athanasius, *On the Incarnation*, J. Behr, trans. (Yonkers, NY: SVS Press, 2011), 56.
[637] Arabic text here adds "the nature of our bodies."
[638] That is, His Body.
[639] "lordly body" is "the Body of the Lord" in Arabic text.
[640] Arabic text here adds "by the disobedience."
[641] Saint Athanasius, *On the Incarnation*, J. Behr, trans. (Yonkers, NY: SVS Press, 2011), 57.
[642] Arabic text adds "on behalf of all".

> not able to die, **for this reason he takes to himself a body capable of death, in order that it, participating in the Word who is above all, might be sufficient for death on behalf of all, and through the indwelling Word would remain incorruptible**, and so corruption might henceforth cease from all by the grace of the resurrection.[643]

This is the salvific substitution which our teacher Peter the Apostle explained in his First Epistle: "For Christ also suffered once for sins, the just for the unjust, that He might bring us to God, being put to death in the flesh but made alive by the Spirit."[644]

Likewise, the wise Paul the Apostle stated, saying, "Who was delivered up because of our offenses, and was raised because of our justification."[645]

And this is what Isaiah the great among the prophets prophesied from antiquity, saying:

> Surely He has borne our griefs and carried our sorrows; yet we esteemed Him stricken, smitten by God, and afflicted. But He was wounded for our transgressions, He was bruised for our iniquities; the chastisement for our peace was upon Him, and by His stripes we are healed. All we like sheep have gone astray; we have turned, every one, to his own way; and the Lord has laid on Him the iniquity of us all.[646]

---

[643] Saint Athanasius, *On the Incarnation*, J. Behr, trans. (Yonkers, NY: SVS Press, 2011), 58.
[644] 1 Peter 3:18.
[645] Romans 4:25.
[646] Isaiah 53:4–6.

And this was fulfilled with power on the cross of our Lord Jesus Christ: "Who gave Himself for us, that He might redeem us from every lawless deed and purify for Himself His own special people, zealous for good works."[647]

"For He made Him who knew no sin to be sin for us, that we might become the righteousness of God in Him."[648]

And the magnificent[649] **St. Cyril the Great** comments on this truth:

> **Thus Christ became a victim "for our sins according to the Scriptures."[650] For this reason, we say that he was named sin; wherefore, the all-wise Paul writes, "For our sakes he made him to be sin who knew nothing of sin,"[651] that is to say, God the Father. For we do not say that Christ became a sinner, far from it, but being just, or rather in actuality justice, for he did not know sin, the Father made him a victim for the sins of the world.[652]**

St. Cyril the Great also says:

> The curse applies to us and not to others. Those who are charged with the transgression of the law and who are very prone to stray from its decrees would be the ones who deserve punishment. **So the one who knew no sin was cursed for us in order to rescue us from the ancient curse. God, who is over all, was sufficient to suffer this on**

[647] Titus 2:14.
[648] 2 Corinthians 5:21.
[649] Or: great.
[650] See 1 Corinthians 15:3.
[651] 2 Corinthians 5:21.
[652] St. Cyril of Alexandria, *Letters 1-50*, J.I. McEnerney, trans. (Washington, D.C.: The Catholic University of America Press, 1987), 174.

> **behalf of all and to purchase redemption for all through the death of his own flesh.**[653]

Another translation of the same text [is as follows]:

> The curse, then, belongs unto us, and not to others. For those against whom the transgression of the Law may be charged, and who are very prone to err from its commandments, surely deserve chastisement. **Therefore, He That knew no sin was accursed for our sakes, that He might deliver us from the old curse. For all-sufficient was the God Who is above all, so dying for all; and by the death of His own Body, purchasing the redemption of all mankind.**[654]

And in explaining why the cross specifically, **St. Athanasius the Apostolic** says:

> **For if he came himself to bear the curse which lay upon us, how else could he have "become a curse" if he had not accepted the death occasioned by the curse? And that is the cross, for thus it is written,** "cursed is he who hangs from the tree." [655] **Moreover, if the death of the Lord is a ransom for all and by his death "the wall of partition"[656] is broken down**, and the call

[653] Cyril of Alexandria, *Commentary on John* 2, J.C. Elowsky, T.C. Oden, and G.L. Bray, eds.; D.R. Maxwell, trans. (Downers Grove, IL: IVP Academic, 2015), 343.
[654] Cyril of Alexandria, *Commentary on the Gospel according to S. John* 2. (London, ENG: Walter Smith, 1885), 623–624.
[655] "Christ has redeemed us from the curse of the law, having become a curse for us (for it is written, 'Cursed is everyone who hangs on a tree')" (Galatians 3:13). Also see Deuteronomy 21:23.
[656] "For He Himself is our peace, who has made both one, and has broken down the middle wall of separation, having abolished in His flesh the enmity, that is, the law of commandments contained in ordinances, so as to create in Himself one new man from the two, thus making peace" (Ephesians 2:14–15).

> of the Gentiles effected, how would he have called us if he had not been crucified?[657]

Indeed the Lord Jesus said: "I am the good shepherd. The good shepherd gives His life for the sheep."[658] "And I lay down My life for the sheep."[659] "Therefore My Father loves Me, because I lay down My life that I may take it again. No one takes it from Me, but I lay it down of Myself. I have power to lay it down, and I have power to take it again. This command I have received from My Father."[660]

And we pray in the [Divine] Liturgy proclaiming our faith in this salvific substitution: "As a ransom on our behalf, [He] gave Himself up unto death, which reigned over us, whereby we were bound and sold on account of our sins."[661]

The death of Christ on the cross had to take place, that He might bear on our behalf the punishment of our sins.

"'The Son of Man must be delivered into the hands of sinful men, and be crucified, and the third day rise again,'"[662] because "without shedding of blood there is no remission."[663]

And our teacher **St. Athanasius the Apostolic** explains the truth of the substitutional death in *On the Incarnation*, in more than one place:

> And thus it happened that both things occurred together in a paradoxical manner: the death of all was completed in the lordly body[664] [on the cross],

[657] Saint Athanasius, *On the Incarnation*, J. Behr, trans. (Yonkers, NY: SVS Press, 2011), 75–76.
[658] John 10:11.
[659] John 10:15.
[660] John 10:17–18.
[661] The Divine Liturgy According to St. Basil – Agios (Holy).
[662] Luke 24:7.
[663] Hebrews 9:22.
[664] "in the Body of the Lord" in Arabic text.

> and also death and corruption were destroyed by the Word in it. For there was need of death, and **death on behalf of all had to take place, so that what was required[665] by all might occur.**[666]

These paradoxical things are: first, the death on behalf of all; second, granting all the grace of eternal life. The first was completed on Great Friday, the second on Covenant Thursday and every day for us in the Eucharist. Therefore, it was said about the Lord Christ that He is the Lamb who carries the sin of the world: "Behold! The Lamb of God who takes away the sin of the world!"[667] And at the same time He is "the bread of God ... who comes down from heaven and gives life to the world."[668]

And it came in **the letter to Diognetus from the second century AD** on Christ's exchange for us:

> But when our wickedness had reached its height, and it had been clearly shown that its reward, punishment and death, was impending over us; and when the time had come which God had before appointed for manifesting His own kindness and power, how the one love of God, ... **showed great long-suffering, and bore with us, He Himself took on Him the burden of our iniquities, He gave His own Son as a ransom for us, the holy One for transgressors, the blameless One for the wicked, the righteous One for the unrighteous, the incorruptible**

---

665 That is, death. Arabic text reads, "so that the debt required by all might be paid."

666 Saint Athanasius, *On the Incarnation*, J. Behr, trans. (Yonkers, NY: SVS Press, 2011), 71.

667 John 1:29.

668 John 6:33.

One for the corruptible, the immortal One for them that are mortal.... O sweet exchange![669]

And by this substitutional death, the Lord Jesus liberated us from the power of sin and death.

"Jesus answered them, 'Most assuredly, I say to you, whoever commits sin is a slave of sin. And a slave does not abide in the house forever, but a son abides forever. Therefore if the Son makes you free, you shall be free indeed.'"[670]

"Stand fast therefore in the liberty by which Christ has made us free, and do not be entangled again with a yoke of bondage."[671]

7. The Defeat of Death

Christ granted us life by His death, after He seized death in our race [which was] because of Adam's sin. And St. Paul the Apostle explains in more than one place the relationship between our inheritance of death from Adam and our being granted life in Christ Jesus our Lord:

"For since by man came death, by Man also came the resurrection of the dead. For as in Adam all die, even so in Christ all shall be made alive."[672]

"Therefore, just as through one man sin entered the world, and death through sin, and thus death spread to all men, because all sinned."[673]

"Nevertheless death reigned from Adam to Moses, even over those who had not sinned according to the likeness of the

---

[669] Mathetes *The Epistle to Diognetus*. In *Ante-Nicene Fathers* 1, P. Schaff, ed. (Peabody, MA: Hendrickson Publishers, 2012), 28.
[670] John 8:34–36.
[671] Galatians 5:1.
[672] 1 Corinthians 15:21–22.
[673] Romans 5:12.

transgression of Adam, who is a type of Him who was to come."[674]

"For if by the one man's offense death reigned through the one, much more those who receive abundance of grace and of the gift of righteousness will reign in life through the One, Jesus Christ."[675]

"But God, who is rich in mercy, because of His great love with which He loved us, even when we were dead in trespasses, made us alive together with Christ (by grace you have been saved)."[676]

The Divine Liturgy also expresses this truth: "As a ransom on our behalf, [He] gave Himself up unto death, which reigned over us, whereby we were bound and sold on account of our sins."[677]

When the Lord Jesus rose from the dead, He declared that He slew death by His death: "O Death, where is your sting? O Hades, where is your victory?"[678] And He promised us the resurrection from the dead and incorruption in the eternal life: "And this is the promise that He has promised us—eternal life."[679]

Truly we glorify Him saying, "O [You], who through His death have slain death, that which had slain all."[680]

---

[674] Romans 5:14.
[675] Romans 5:17.
[676] Ephesians 2:4–5.
[677] The Divine Liturgy According to St. Basil – Agios (Holy).
[678] 1 Corinthians 15:55.
[679] 1 John 2:25.
[680] Annual Fraction [translated from text; also see Fraction to the Son: O Lamb of God.]

"Trampling down death by death and upon those in the tombs bestowing eternal life."[681]

The gift of eternal life is the most important goal for the sake of which our Lord Jesus Christ became incarnate, and He declared this Himself when He said:

> This is the will of the Father who sent Me, that of all He has given Me I should lose nothing, but should raise it up at the last day. And this is the will of Him who sent Me, that everyone who sees the Son and believes in Him may have everlasting life; and I will raise him up at the last day.[682]

"No one can come to Me unless the Father who sent Me draws him; and I will raise him up at the last day."[683]

"Most assuredly, I say to you, he who believes in Me has everlasting life."[684]

"Whoever eats My flesh and drinks My blood has eternal life, and I will raise him up at the last day."[685]

The grace of incorruptibility is linked with the grace of the resurrection from the dead in the last day: "So also is the resurrection of the dead. The body is sown in corruption, it is raised in incorruption."[686]

8. Paying the Debt Which was Upon Us

St. Athanasius the Apostolic, while explaining the salvific works of the Lord Christ, says, "For there was need of death, and

---

[681] Hymn of the Resurrection.
[682] John 6:39–40.
[683] John 6:44.
[684] John 6:47.
[685] John 6:54.
[686] 1 Corinthians 15:42.

death on behalf of all had to take place, so that what was required[687] by all might occur."[688]

It is clear from the last sentence[689] in the previous quote that substitutional death means paying the debt required by all, similar to what the Lord Christ explained in the parable of the unforgiving servant.

> And when he had begun to settle accounts, one was brought to him who owed him ten thousand talents. But as he was not able to pay, his master commanded that he be sold, with his wife and children and all that he had, and that payment be made. The servant therefore fell down before him, saying, "Master, have patience with me, and I will pay you all." Then the master of that servant was moved with compassion, released him, and forgave him the debt.[690]

St. Proclus [of Constantinople] says:

> **Listen to the reason for his coming and glorify the power of the one who became flesh. The human race was deep in debt and incapable of paying what it owed. By the hand of Adam we all signed a bond to sin. The devil held us all in slavery. He kept producing our bills, using our suffering body as his paper. There he stood, the wicked forger, threatening us with our debts and demanding satisfaction. One of two things**

---

[687] That is, death. Also the last sentence in the Arabic text reads, "so that the debt required by all might be paid."

[688] Saint Athanasius, *On the Incarnation*, J. Behr, trans. (Yonkers, NY: SVS Press, 2011), 71.

[689] The last sentence in the Arabic text reads, "so that the debt required by all might be paid."

[690] Matthew 18:24–27.

> **had to happen: either the penalty of death had to be imposed on all, because "all had sinned," or else a substitute had to be provided who was fully entitled to plead on our behalf. No man could save us; the debt would have been his liability too. No angel could buy us out, for such a ransom was beyond his powers. One who was sinless had to die for those who had sinned; that was the only way left by which to break the bonds of evil.**[691]

St. Cyril the Great says:

> For by His sufferings blessings descend to us. **He in our stead paid our debts**: He bore our sins; and as it is written, "in our stead He was stricken."[692] "He took them up in His own body on the tree:"[693] for it is true that "by His bruises we are healed."[694,695]

And the same truth is explained by our blessed father, the lamp of orthodoxy, **St. Athanasius the Apostolic**:

> **But since what was required from all**[696] **still had to be rendered** (for, as I said earlier, it was absolutely necessary to die and for this, in particular, he sojourned among us), for this reason, after the demonstrations of his divinity

691 *Proclus of Constantinople and the Cult of the Virgin in Late Antiquity: Homilies 1-5, Texts and Translations*, N. Constas, trans. (Boston, MA: Brill Publishers, 2003), 141.

692 Cf. Isaiah 53:6.

693 Cf. 1 Peter 2:24

694 Cf. Isaiah 53:5.

695 Cyril of Alexandria, *Commentary on the Gospel according to S. John* 2. (London, ENG: Walter Smith, 1885), 719.

696 Arabic text reads "debt required from all," in place of "what was required from all" in this English translation.

> from his works, he now offered the sacrifice on behalf of all, **delivering his own temple to death in the stead of all, in order to make all not liable to and free from the ancient transgression**, and to show himself superior to death, displaying his own body as incorruptible, the first-fruits of the universal resurrection.[697]

It should be noted that here in the course of the explanation St. Athanasius confirmed the truth of the substitutional death on behalf of all, and that the debt which was upon us is death, and that the Lord wanted to set us free from the first disobedience, that is, the original or ancestral sin.

For the Lord Christ, by His death on the cross on behalf of the human race, paid the punishment that was upon man.

He bore on our behalf the shame and the curse which the human race contracted due to sin; likewise, He also bore on our behalf the punishment for our sins, and turned it into salvation, and this, by His accepting death crucified upon the wood of shame and of the curse, that He may turn it into the greatest sign of honor and blessing.

"Christ has redeemed us from the curse of the law, having become a curse for us (for it is written, 'Cursed is everyone who hangs on a tree')."[698]

"Looking unto Jesus, the author and finisher of our faith, who for the joy that was set before Him endured the cross, despising the shame, and has sat down at the right hand of the throne of God."[699]

---

697 Saint Athanasius, *On the Incarnation*, J. Behr, trans. (Yonkers, NY: SVS Press, 2011), 70.
698 Galatians 3:13.
699 Hebrews 12:2.

St. Cyril the Great says:

> The eighth day on which **Christ came again to life, nailing to His cross the handwriting that was upon us**, "having wiped out the handwriting of requirements that was against us, which was contrary to us. And He has taken it out of the way, having nailed it to the cross."[700] **And He died for the sake of all to take us away from death and sins, and save us from the punishment and sufferings.**[701]

And in his response to those who deny the truth of the incarnation of the Word of God, **St. Cyril the Great** said:

> When they say that the Word of God did not become flesh, or rather did not undergo birth from a woman according to the flesh, they bankrupt the economy of salvation, for if he who was rich did not impoverish himself, abasing himself to our condition out of tender love, then we have not gained his riches but are still in our poverty, still enslaved by sin and death, **because the Word becoming flesh is the undoing and the abolition of all that fell upon human nature as our curse and punishment**. If they so pull up the root of our salvation, and dislodge the cornerstone of our hope, how will anything else be left standing? As I have said, **if the Word has not become flesh then neither has the dominion of death been overthrown, and in no way has sin been abolished, and we are still held captive in**

---

[700] Colossians 2:14.

[701] Cyril the Great, *Al-Sojoud Wa Al-Ibada Bi-Al Rouh Wa Al-Hak* [Worshipping and Serving in Spirit and in Truth], G.A. Ibrahim, trans. (Egypt: The Orthodox Center for Patristic Studies, 2017), 691. [Translated from Arabic text].

> **the transgressions of the first man, Adam, deprived of any return to a better condition**; a return which I would say has been gained by Christ the Savior of us all.[702]

St. Cyril the Great hereby explained, in this, that the curse and death which befell the human race are a punishment, and not a mere consequence only.

Therefore, our Lord Jesus Christ is the true and only Savior of the human race, of whom it was said: "Nor is there salvation in any other, for there is no other name under heaven given among men by which we must be saved."[703] The Lord Jesus saved us, in that He died on our behalf and for our sake, and He wiped out the handwriting of our sins, and He lifted from us the judgment of death which befell our race because of Adam's sin and because of our own actual sins.

> And you, being dead in your trespasses and the uncircumcision of your flesh, He has made alive together with Him, having forgiven you all trespasses, having wiped out the handwriting of requirements that was against us, which was contrary to us. And He has taken it out of the way, having nailed it to the cross. Having disarmed principalities and powers, He made a public spectacle of them, triumphing over them in it.[704]

The Church, therefore, sings praises to our good Savior for the sake of His marvelous precious salvation which He offered humanity on the cross. "This is a faithful saying and worthy of

---

[702] St Cyril of Alexandria, *On the Unity of Christ*, J.A. McGuckin, trans. (Crestwood, NY: SVS Press, 1995), 59–60.
[703] Acts 4:12.
[704] Colossians 2:13–15.

all acceptance, that Christ Jesus came into the world to save sinners, of whom I am chief."[705]

Therefore, the angel preached to the shepherds, saying, "For there is born to you this day in the city of David a Savior, who is Christ the Lord."[706] And the Samaritans confessed that He is the Savior of the world: "Then they said to the woman, 'Now we believe, not because of what you said, for we ourselves have heard Him and we know that this is indeed the Christ, the Savior of the world.'"[707]

Likewise, we, the believers, also confess that He is the Savior of all men: "Because we trust in the living God, who is the Savior of all men, especially of those who believe."[708] The Lord Christ is our good Savior, because He paid by His death the debt human beings owed.

Great is the holy Fathers' explanation of the truth of the Lord Christ's bearing of the punishment instead of us and on our behalf.

St. Cyril the Great says:

> They lead away, then, to death the Author of Life; and for our sakes was this done, for by the power and incomprehensible Providence of God, Christ's death resulted in an unexpected reversal of things. For His suffering was prepared as a snare for the power of death, and the death of the Lord was the source of the renewal of mankind in incorruption and newness of life. Bearing the Cross upon His shoulders, on which He was about to be crucified, He went forth; His doom

[705] 1 Timothy 1:15.
[706] Luke 2:11.
[707] John 4:42.
[708] 1 Timothy 4:10.

was already fixed, **and He had undergone, for our sakes, though innocent, the sentence of death. For, in His own Person, He bore the sentence righteously pronounced against sinners by the Law. For He became a curse for us,[709] according to the Scripture: "For cursed is everyone, it is said, that hangs on a tree."[710] And accursed are we all, for we are not able to fulfil the Law of God**: For in many things we all stumble;[711] and very prone to sin is the nature of man. And since, too, the Law of God says: "Cursed is he who continues not in all things that are written in the book of this Law, to do them,"[712] ... **The Cross, then, that Christ bore, was not for His own deserts, but was the cross that awaited us, and was our due, through our condemnation by the Law. For as He was numbered among the dead, not for Himself, but for our sakes, that we might find in Him, the Author of everlasting life, subduing of Himself the power of death; so also He took upon Himself the Cross that was our due, passing on Himself the condemnation of the Law, that the mouth of all lawlessness might henceforth be stopped, according to the saying of the Psalmist;[713] the Sinless having suffered condemnation for the sin of all.**[714]

---

[709] See Galatians 3:13.
[710] See Deuteronomy 21:23.
[711] See James 3:2.
[712] See Galatians 3:10 and Deuteronomy 27:26.
[713] See Psalm 107:42.
[714] Cyril of Alexandria, *Commentary on the Gospel according to S. John* 2. (London, ENG: Walter Smith, 1885), 623-624.

9. The Healing of Human Nature

The Lord Jesus came as a healing Physician, and saved us, in that He healed us of corruption. (Christ the true Physician).

He is the Physician whom Jeremiah looked for in his prophecy: "Is there no balm in Gilead, is there no physician there? Why then is there no recovery for the health of the daughter of my people?"[715]

Therefore, we glorify the Virgin St. Mary in the daily Psalmody, saying, "Hail to you Mary, the healing of Jeremiah,"[716] that is, from whom our healing came, "Christ," the healing that Jeremiah the prophet looked and searched for.

It is the realization of the prophecy that said: "But to you who fear My name the Sun of Righteousness shall arise with healing in His wings."[717]

The Lord Jesus looked at the sinner as a sick person needing treatment, more so than as a criminal deserving of punishment.

"Those who are well have no need of a physician, but those who are sick. But go and learn what this means: 'I desire mercy and not sacrifice.' For I did not come to call the righteous, but sinners, to repentance."[718]

Christ is the healing Physician as we pray in the Liturgy:

"As for us, too, O Lord, the sicknesses of our souls, heal; and also those of our bodies, cure. O You, the true physician of our souls and bodies."[719]

---

[715] Jeremiah 8:22.
[716] Midnight Praises – Sunday Theotokia, Part 8.
[717] Malachi 4:2.
[718] Matthew 9:12–13.
[719] Morning Offering of Incense – Litany of the Sick.

"O Christ our God ...Those who are sick, heal them. For You are the life of us all, the salvation of us all, the hope of us all, and the resurrection of us all."[720]

"O Lord, visit the sick of Your people, heal them for the sake of Your holy name."[721]

What Christ did with Lazarus the beloved of the Lord, was a model to what He did with all of humankind. For humankind was sick with the sickness of sin: "Lord, behold, he whom You love is sick."[722]

And the appointed result of sin is death: "So when Jesus came, He found that he had already been in the tomb four days."[723]

The four days symbolize the ages prior to the coming of the Lord to our tomb, [that is,] earth. (From Adam to Noah, from Noah to Abraham, from Abraham to Moses, and from Moses to Christ).

He came to heal us from sin and to raise us from our tombs: "Jesus said to her, 'Your brother will rise again.'"[724] "I am the resurrection and the life. He who believes in Me, though he may die, he shall live. And whoever lives and believes in Me shall never die. Do you believe this?"[725]

"Jesus wept."[726] He wept for the fallen, dead and corrupt state of humankind; He wept, knowing He would immediately raise us up from this weakness and from being lost. "Martha, the

---

[720] Morning Offering of Incense – Litany of the Gospel.
[721] The Trisagion [prayed] after "Graciously Accord, O Lord" and "The Gloria" in the Agpeya.
[722] John 11:3.
[723] John 11:17.
[724] John 11:23.
[725] John 11:25–26.
[726] John 11:35.

sister of him who was dead, said to Him, 'Lord, by this time there is a stench, for he has been dead four days.' Jesus said to her, 'Did I not say to you that if you would believe you would see the glory of God?'"[727] "Now when He had said these things, He cried with a loud voice, 'Lazarus, come forth!' And he who had died came out bound hand and foot with graveclothes, and his face was wrapped with a cloth. Jesus said to them, 'Loose him, and let him go.'"[728]

The miracles, which Christ performed for the sick in a visible and perceptible way, were a proof of His plan to heal the soul in an invisible and imperceptible way.

In the story of the healing the paralytic, for example, it was said: "When Jesus saw their faith, He said to the paralytic, 'Son, your sins are forgiven you.'"[729] It was made clear that He cared about healing the soul of sin before healing the body of the manifest sickness, and therefore, some of those standing by objected, saying:

"Why does this Man speak blasphemies like this? Who can forgive sins but God alone?"[730]

Then the Lord Christ explained that He would perform the perceptible visible miracle, in order that all may know that He came to heal the soul from the sickness of sin.

> "Which is easier, to say to the paralytic, 'Your sins are forgiven you,' or to say, 'Arise, take up your bed and walk'? But that you may know that the Son of Man has power on earth to forgive sins"—

---

[727] John 11:39–40.
[728] John 11:43–44.
[729] Mark 2:5.
[730] Mark 2:7.

> He said to the paralytic, "I say to you, arise, take up your bed, and go to your house."[731]

Of the most important signs which the prophets prophesied concerning the coming of the Messiah is that He would heal our sicknesses. And they mean the true sickness, that is, sin and the weaknesses of human nature.

> Jesus answered and said to them, "Go and tell John the things which you hear and see: The blind see and the lame walk; the lepers are cleansed and the deaf hear; the dead are raised up and the poor have the gospel preached to them. And blessed is he who is not offended because of Me."[732]

He pointed out to them that it is He (the Lord Jesus), in the fulfillment of the prophecies of Isaiah about healing:

> Then the eyes of the blind shall be opened, and the ears of the deaf shall be unstopped. Then the lame shall leap like a deer, and the tongue of the dumb sing. For waters shall burst forth in the wilderness, and streams in the desert.[733]

> In that day the deaf shall hear the words of the book, and the eyes of the blind shall see out of obscurity and out of darkness. The humble also shall increase their joy in the Lord, and the poor among men shall rejoice in the Holy One of Israel.[734]

> I, the Lord, have called You in righteousness, and will hold Your hand; I will keep You and give You

---

[731] Mark 2:9–11.
[732] Matthew 11:4–6.
[733] Isaiah 35:5–6.
[734] Isaiah 29:18–19.

> as a covenant to the people, as a light to the Gentiles, to open blind eyes, to bring out prisoners from the prison, those who sit in darkness from the prison house.[735]

The healing of leprosy was the greatest proof of the Lord Christ's power to heal human nature of the corruption it contracted by sin. Leprosy, to a great extent, is like Hansen's disease[736] which causes permanent deformities in the body, which cannot be restored except only by the hand of God the Almighty. The prophecy of the healing of Namaan the Syrian came as a foretelling, that the Christ, the true new Elisha, would heal the leprosy of human nature by dipping it in the water of Baptism.

"So he went down and dipped seven times in the Jordan, according to the saying of the man of God; and his flesh was restored like the flesh of a little child, and he was clean."[737]

Likewise, the healing of the blind represents the healing of human nature which no longer saw the glory of God and His majesty, [but] had inclined to the worshipping of idols as an indication of the lack of sight and insight. The Lord of glory came to enlighten the eyes of our hearts in the sacrament of enlightenment, that is, Holy Baptism.

> That the God of our Lord Jesus Christ, the Father of glory, may give to you the spirit of wisdom and revelation in the knowledge of Him, the eyes of your understanding being enlightened; that you may know what is the hope of His calling, what

---

[735] Isaiah 42:6–7.

[736] Leprosy is a Biblical broad term used in the Old and New Testaments to describe skin diseases which may include what is now known as Hansen's disease. (Translator's note).

[737] 2 Kings 5:14.

> are the riches of the glory of His inheritance in the saints.[738]

"And Jesus said, 'For judgment I have come into this world, that those who do not see may see, and that those who see may be made blind.'"[739]

As for deafness, Christ cured it so as to tell us that He came to open the ears of our hearts, that we may hear His sweet divine voice.

> Then they brought to Him one who was deaf and had an impediment in his speech, and they begged Him to put His hand on him. And He took him aside from the multitude, and put His fingers in his ears, and He spat and touched his tongue. Then, looking up to heaven, He sighed, and said to him, "Ephphatha," that is, "Be opened." Immediately his ears were opened, and the impediment of his tongue was loosed, and he spoke plainly. Then He commanded them that they should tell no one; but the more He commanded them, the more widely they proclaimed it. And they were astonished beyond measure, saying, "He has done all things well. He makes both the deaf to hear and the mute to speak."[740]

As for the miracles of casting out demons, they were [done] so that we may know that He came to release[741] us from the dominion of the devil and the kingdom of darkness into the glorious liberty of the children of God. "Giving thanks to the

---

[738] Ephesians 1:17–18.
[739] John 9:39.
[740] Mark 7:32–37.
[741] Literally: bring us out.

Father who has qualified us to be partakers of the inheritance of the saints in the light. He has delivered us from the power of darkness and conveyed us into the kingdom of the Son of His love, in whom we have redemption through His blood, the forgiveness of sins."[742]

He healed the woman who had a flow of blood, in order that He may stop for us the bleeding of sin which drains us even to death.[743] And He healed the woman who was bent over, in order that He may raise our heads up, that we may not look again to the earth.[744] And He healed the man who had a withered hand, in order that we may stretch out our hands in doing good always.[745]

"For He bruises, but He binds up; He wounds, but His hands make whole."[746]

The cross is the source of healing of the entire human race. As Isaiah the great prophet prophesied:

> Surely He has borne our griefs and carried our sorrows; yet we esteemed Him stricken, smitten by God, and afflicted. But He was wounded for our transgressions, He was bruised for our

742 Colossians 1:12–14.

743 "And suddenly, a woman who had a flow of blood for twelve years came from behind and touched the hem of His garment. For she said to herself, 'If only I may touch His garment, I shall be made well.' But Jesus turned around, and when He saw her He said, 'Be of good cheer, daughter; your faith has made you well.' And the woman was made well from that hour" (Matthew 9:20–22).

744 "And behold, there was a woman who had a spirit of infirmity eighteen years, and was bent over and could in no way raise herself up. But when Jesus saw her, He called her to Him and said to her, 'Woman, you are loosed from your infirmity.' And He laid His hands on her, and immediately she was made straight, and glorified God" (Luke 13:11–13).

745 "And He entered the synagogue again, and a man was there who had a withered hand.... And when He had looked around ... He said to the man, 'Stretch out your hand.' And he stretched it out, and his hand was restored as whole as the other" (Mark 3:1,5).

746 Job 5:18.

> iniquities; the chastisement for our peace was upon Him, and by His stripes we are healed.[747]

Truly our Lord Jesus Christ was the Redeemer, "who Himself bore our sins in His own body on the tree, that we, having died to sins, might live for righteousness—by whose stripes you were healed."[748]

He is the true bronze serpent which brought to us healing from the bite of the old serpent. "Then the Lord said to Moses, 'Make a fiery serpent, and set it on a pole; and it shall be that everyone who is bitten, when he looks at it, shall live.' So Moses made a bronze serpent, and put it on a pole; and so it was, if a serpent had bitten anyone, when he looked at the bronze serpent, he lived."[749]

Truly Isaiah prophesied, whose eyes were opened, before the time about the salvation by the cross, saying, "Look to Me, and be saved, all you ends of the earth! For I am God, and there is no other."[750]

The Lord Christ spoke of this salvific look, of which Isaiah the prophet spoke, saying, "And as Moses lifted up the serpent in the wilderness, even so must the Son of Man be lifted up, that whoever believes in Him should not perish but have eternal life."[751]

Therefore, the Lord Jesus said about His healing, and life-giving cross:

---

[747] Isaiah 53:4–5.
[748] 1 Peter 2:24.
[749] Numbers 21:8–9.
[750] Isaiah 45:22.
[751] John 3:14–15.

"'And I, if I am lifted up from the earth, will draw all peoples to Myself.' This He said, signifying by what death He would die."[752]

It is truly the healing from the defilement of sin which humankind felt, and Isaiah declared this; and his healing was completed by the holy coal from the altar, which represents the holy Body and Blood of the Lord, and the tongs represent the holy spoon.[753]

> So I said: "Woe is me, for I am undone! Because I am a man of unclean lips, and I dwell in the midst of a people of unclean lips; for my eyes have seen the King, the Lord of hosts." Then one of the seraphim flew to me, having in his hand a live coal which he had taken with the tongs from the altar. And he touched my mouth with it, and said: "Behold, this has touched your lips; your iniquity is taken away, and your sin purged."[754]

He is the true Physician of our souls, our bodies and our spirits:

> And Jesus went about all Galilee, teaching in their synagogues, preaching the gospel of the kingdom, and healing all kinds of sickness and all kinds of disease among the people. Then His fame went throughout all Syria; and they brought to Him all sick people who were afflicted with various diseases and torments, and those who were

---

[752] John 12:32–33.

[753] "Now O God the Father, the Pantocrator, extend Your hand on these spoons with which they will dispense the precious blood … Bless them, consecrate them, and grant them the power and glory of the seraphim's tongs held in his right hand" (Prayer for the Consecration of the Spoons).

[754] Isaiah 6:5–7.

> demon-possessed, epileptics, and paralytics; and He healed them.[755]

And He gave the power of healing sicknesses to the Fathers the Apostles and their heirs in the Church, not to perform perceptible miracles only, but rather to deliver the healing message of Christ to every person through Baptism, and repentance, and the Eucharist, the Mysteries of the true healing.

"Then He appointed twelve, that they might be with Him and that He might send them out to preach, and to have power to heal sicknesses and to cast out demons."[756]

"Heal the sick, cleanse the lepers, raise the dead, cast out demons. Freely you have received, freely give."[757]

St. Clement of Alexandria says:

> **Many passions are healed by punishment and by the imposition of severe commands and, more particularly, by the teaching of certain principles.** Reproof is like surgery performed on the passions of the soul; **the passions are like a disease of truth, which need to be removed by the surgeon's knife.**[758]

By this work of healing, corruption, which human nature contracted, was treated.

St. Athanasius the Apostolic says:

> **Being with all through the like [body], the incorruptible Son of God consequently**

[755] Matthew 4:23–24.

[756] Mark 3:14–15.

[757] Matthew 10:8.

[758] Clement of Alexandria, *Christ the Educator*, P.S. Wood, trans. (Washington, DC: The Catholic University of America Press, 1954), 58.

> **clothed all with incorruptibility in the promise concerning the resurrection.** And now the very corruption of death no longer holds ground against human beings because of the indwelling Word, in them through the one body.[759]

St. Cyril the Great says:

> **The Only Begotten and Word of God the Father lending us the Stability of His Own Nature, because the nature of man had been condemned in Adam as powerless for stability and falling (and that most easily) into perversion. As then in the turning of the first the loss of good things passes through unto the whole nature: in the same way I deem in Him too Who knows not turning will the gain of the abidance of the Divine Gifts be preserved to our whole race. And if we seem to any not to think and speak altogether what is proper, let him come forward and tell us why the Savior has been called by the Divine Scriptures the Second Adam. For in that first one, the human race proceeds from not being unto being, and having come forth, decayed, because it had broken the Divine Law: in the Second, Christ, it rises up again unto a second beginning, reformed unto newness of life and unto a return of incorruption, for if ought be "in Christ, a new creature.**[760]"[761]

---

[759] Saint Athanasius, *On the Incarnation*, J. Behr, trans. (Yonkers, NY: SVS Press, 2011), 58.

[760] 2 Corinthians 5:17.

[761] Cyril of Alexandria, *Commentary on the Gospel according to S. John* 1. (Oxford, ENG: J. Parker, 1874), 549.

And he also says:

> **And now the Likeness to God was through the inroad of sin defaced and no longer was the Impress bright, but fainter and darkened because of the transgression.** But when the race of man had reached to an innumerable multitude, and **sin had dominion over them all**, manifoldly despoiling each man's soul, **his nature was stripped of the ancient grace; the Spirit departed altogether, and the reasonable creature fell into extremest folly**, ignorant even of its Creator.... **The first man**, being earthy, and of the earth, and having, placed in his own power, the choice between good and evil, being master of the inclination to each, **was caught of bitter guile, and having inclined to disobedience, falls to the earth, the mother from whence he sprang, and over-mastered now at length by corruption and death, transmits the penalty to his whole race**. The evil growing and multiplying in us, and our understanding ever descending to the worse, **sin reigned, and thus at length the nature of man was shown bared of the Holy Ghost Which indwelt him**. *For the Holy Spirit of wisdom will flee deceit*, as it is written, *nor dwell in the body that is subject unto sin.*[762] Since then the first Adam preserved not the grace given him of God, **God the Father was minded to send us from Heaven the second Adam. For He sends in our likeness His own Son Who is by Nature without variableness or change, and wholly**

[762] Wisdom of Solomon 1:5,4 LXX.

> **unknowing of sin, that *as by the disobedience*[763] of the first, we became subject to Divine wrath, so through the obedience of the Second**, we might both escape the curse, and its evils might come to nought. But when the Word of God became Man, He received the Spirit from the Father as one of us, (not receiving ought for Himself individually, for He was the Giver of the Spirit); **but that He Who knew no sin, might, by receiving It as Man, preserve It to our nature, and might again inroot in us the grace which had left us.** For this reason, I deem, it was that the holy Baptist profitably added, *I saw the Spirit descending from Heaven, and It abode upon Him.* **For It had fled from us by reason of sin, but He Who knew no sin, became as one of us, that the Spirit might be accustomed to abide in us, having no occasion of departure or withdrawal in Him.**
>
> **Therefore through Himself He receives the Spirit for us, and renews to our nature, the ancient good.**[764]

For our Lord Jesus Christ's own body, because of its unity with the immortal Divinity, became stronger than death.[765] And He defeated death and demolished it, and He became a source of life from death and healing from the corruption of our nature, which we contracted because of Adam's sin and our own

763 Romans 5:19.

764 Cyril of Alexandria, *Commentary on the Gospel according to S. John* 1. (Oxford, ENG: J. Parker, 1874), 141–142.

765 "Whom God raised up, having loosed the pains of death, because it was not possible that He should be held by it" (Acts 2:24).

sins, and this [He granted] to all who unite with Him in Baptism and the Eucharist.

"Heal me, O Lord, and I shall be healed; save me, and I shall be saved, for You are my praise."[766]

> Bless the Lord, O my soul, and forget not all His benefits: Who forgives all your iniquities, who heals all your diseases, who redeems your life from destruction, who crowns you with lovingkindness and tender mercies, who satisfies your mouth with good things, so that your youth is renewed like the eagle's.[767]

10. Restoring the Divine Image in the Human Being

The Lord Jesus Christ is the image of God.[768] And the human being is created in the image of God, and this image was distorted because of Adam's sin, so it was befitting of Him alone that He comes to us, in order that He may restore to us the divine image, by uniting us with Him and by the work of the Holy Spirit in our life, until we are like Him in the blissful eternity, because we will see Him as He is in His Second Coming.

Because this divine image was distorted in the human being, as a result of the disobedience and Adam's sin, **St. Athanasius the Apostolic** says: "But then what need was there in the beginning for human beings to come into being in the image of God? He should have come into being simply irrational, or

---

[766] Jeremiah 17:14.

[767] Psalm 103:2–5.

[768] "Who, being in the form of God, did not consider it robbery to be equal with God, but made Himself of no reputation, taking the form of a bondservant, and coming in the likeness of men" (Philippians 2:6–7).

having been rational not live the life of the irrational creatures."[769]

Therefore, the Lord Christ our God restored[770] the divine image within the human being, which was distorted in Adam because of the disobedience, for, **says St. Athanasius the Apostolic**, "it was not for another to turn what was corruptible to incorruptibility except the Savior himself, who in the beginning created the universe from nothing; and that it was not for another to recreate again the 'in the image' for human beings, except the Image of the Father; and that it was not for another to raise up the mortal to be immortal, except our Lord Jesus Christ, who is Life itself."[771]

"So the Word of God came himself, **in order that he being the image of the Father, the human being 'in the image' might be recreated.**"[772]

"Since you have put off the old man with his deeds, and have put on the new man who is renewed in knowledge according to the image of Him who created him."[773] And this is fulfilled in Holy Baptism. And we continue in the transformation to the image of God once again through spiritual struggle.

"That you put off, concerning your former conduct, the old man which grows corrupt according to the deceitful lusts, and be renewed in the spirit of your mind, and that you put on the new man which was created according to God, in true righteousness and holiness."[774]

---

[769] Saint Athanasius, *On the Incarnation*, J. Behr, trans. (Yonkers, NY: SVS Press, 2011), 62.
[770] Text adds "to us."
[771] Saint Athanasius, *On the Incarnation*, J. Behr, trans. (Yonkers, NY: SVS Press, 2011), 70.
[772] Ibid., 63.
[773] Colossians 3:9–10.
[774] Ephesians 4:22–24.

"Therefore, if anyone is in Christ, he is a new creation; old things have passed away; behold, all things have become new."[775]

"For whom He foreknew, He also predestined to be conformed to the image of His Son, that He might be the firstborn among many brethren."[776]

And the Holy Spirit has the greatest role in inscribing the image of Christ in us. "But we all, with unveiled face, beholding as in a mirror the glory of the Lord, are being transformed into the same image from glory to glory, just as by the Spirit of the Lord."[777]

The features are finished in truth in the Resurrection of the dead and the life of the Age to Come.

> Behold what manner of love the Father has bestowed on us, that we should be called children of God!... Beloved, now we are children of God; and it has not yet been revealed what we shall be, but we know that when He is revealed, we shall be like Him, for we shall see Him as He is.[778]

"For you died, and your life is hidden with Christ in God. When Christ who is our life appears, then you also will appear with Him in glory."[779]

"For our citizenship is in heaven, from which we also eagerly wait for the Savior, the Lord Jesus Christ, who will transform our lowly body that it may be conformed to His glorious body."[780]

---

[775] 2 Corinthians 5:17.
[776] Romans 8:29.
[777] 2 Corinthians 3:18.
[778] 1 John 3:1–2.
[779] Colossians 3:3–4.
[780] Philippians 3:20–21.

"And as we have borne the image of the man of dust, we shall also bear the image of the heavenly Man. Now this I say, brethren, that flesh and blood cannot inherit the kingdom of God; nor does corruption inherit incorruption."[781]

"In a moment, in the twinkling of an eye, at the last trumpet. For the trumpet will sound, and the dead will be raised incorruptible, and we shall be changed. For this corruptible must put on incorruption, and this mortal must put on immortality."[782]

Therefore the Lord Christ says: "'And I, if I am lifted up from the earth, will draw all peoples to Myself.' This He said, signifying by what death He would die."[783] He will draw us towards the imitation of Him and being followers of His holy Person.

11. Restoring the Adoption by God the Father

He being the Son of the Father by nature and in truth, and we having lost sonship to the Father because of Adam's sin, He came down and became the Son of Man, so that He may make the sons of men, sons of God by the grace of adoption through uniting with Him.

"For you are all sons of God through faith in Christ Jesus."[784]

> But when the fullness of the time had come, God sent forth His Son, born of a woman, born under the law, to redeem those who were under the law, that we might receive the adoption as sons. And because you are sons, God has sent forth the Spirit of His Son into your hearts, crying out, "Abba,

[781] 1 Corinthians 15:49–50.
[782] 1 Corinthians 15:52–53.
[783] John 12:32–33.
[784] Galatians 3:26.

> Father!" Therefore you are no longer a slave but a son, and if a son, then an heir of God through Christ.[785]
>
> For as many as are led by the Spirit of God, these are sons of God. For you did not receive the spirit of bondage again to fear, but you received the Spirit of adoption by whom we cry out, "Abba, Father." The Spirit Himself bears witness with our spirit that we are children of God, and if children, then heirs—heirs of God and joint heirs with Christ.[786]
>
> But as many as received Him, to them He gave the right to become children of God, to those who believe in His name: who were born, not of blood, nor of the will of the flesh, nor of the will of man, but of God.[787]

St. Cyril the Great says, commenting on this holy Scripture:

> **For since they received the Son through faith, they receive the power to be ranked among the sons of God. For the Son gives what is His alone and specially and of nature to be in their power, setting it forth as common**, making this a sort of image of the love for man that is inherent to Him, and of His love for the world. **For in none other way could we who bore the image of the earthy escape corruption, unless the beauty of the image of the heavenly[788] were impressed upon us, through our being called to sonship. For**

---

[785] Galatians 4:4–7.
[786] Romans 8:14–17.
[787] John 1:12–13.
[788] See 1 Corinthians 15:49.

> **being partakers of Him through the Spirit, we were sealed unto likeness with Him and mount up to the primal character of the Image after which the Divine Scripture says we were made.**[789] For thus hardly recovering the pristine beauty of our nature, and re-formed unto that Divine Nature, shall we be superior to the ills that have befallen us through the transgression. **Therefore we mount up unto dignity above our nature for Christ's sake, and we too shall be sons of God, not like Him in exactitude, but by grace in imitation of Him. For He is Very Son, existing from the Father; we adopted by His Kindness**, through grace receiving "I have said, Ye are gods and all of you are children of the Most High."[790,791]

And **St. Athanasius the Apostolic** likewise says:

> How then has He chosen us, before we came into existence, but that, as he says himself,[792] in Him we were represented beforehand? And **how at all, before men were created, did He predestinate us unto adoption**, but that the Son Himself was "founded before the world," taking on Him that economy which was for our sake? Or how, as the Apostle goes on to say, have we "an inheritance being predestinated," but that the Lord Himself was founded "before the world," inasmuch as He had a purpose, for our sakes, **to take on Him**

789 See Genesis 1:27.
790 Psalm 82:6.
791 Cyril of Alexandria, *Commentary on the Gospel according to S. John* 1. (Oxford, ENG: J. Parker, 1874), 104–105.
792 Ephesians 1:3–5.

> **through the flesh all that inheritance of judgment which lay against us, and we henceforth were made sons in Him**?[793]

"Having predestined us to adoption as sons by Jesus Christ to Himself, according to the good pleasure of His will, to the praise of the glory of His grace, by which He made us accepted in the Beloved."[794]

And **St. Athanasius the Apostolic** expounded the explanation on this theological truth:

> **For adoption there could not be apart from the real Son**, who says, "No one knows the Father, save the Son, and he to whomsoever the Son will reveal Him." **And how can there be deifying apart from the Word** and before Him? Yet, says He to their brethren the Jews, "If He called them gods, unto whom the Word of God came." **And if all that are called sons and gods, whether in earth or in heaven, were adopted and deified through the Word, and the Son Himself is the Word, it is plain that through Him are they all**, and He Himself before all, or rather He Himself only is very Son, **and He alone is very God from the very God, not receiving these prerogatives as a reward for His virtue, nor being another beside them, but being all these by nature and according to essence.** For He is Offspring of the Father's essence, so that one cannot doubt that after the resemblance of the unalterable Father, the Word also is unalterable.[795]

---

[793] Athanasius *Four Discourses Against the Arians* 2.22.76 (NPNF^2 4:389).
[794] Ephesians 1:5–6.
[795] Athanasius *Four Discourses Against the Arians* 1.11.39 (NPNF^2 4:329).

And we pray in the Liturgy According to St. Cyril, in the Prayer of Submission Addressed to the Father after the Fraction:

> O God, who loved us so, and granted us the rank of sonship, so as to be called the sons of God, and as such, we are indeed heirs of You, O God, the Father, and joint heirs of Your Christ. Incline Your ear, O Lord, and hearken to us, we who bow our heads to You. And cleanse our inner man according to the manner in which Your only-begotten Son is holy. He is the One we intend to take hold of.
>
> ***
>
> Having become partakers of the Body, partakers of the form, and partakers in the succession of Your Christ.[796]

O the depth of these glorious prayers!

12. Granting That We May Be Partakers of the Divine Nature

Because of the grace of adoption by God the Father, which we received by uniting with the true only-begotten Son, by faith and Baptism, we, by this, become partakers of the divine nature in Him and we become gods because of His condescension. For He is God by nature, and became man in truth, in order to deify us in Him, that is, we become gods by grace, and partakers of His eternal inheritance, inheriting eternal life and incorruptibility.

> As His divine power has given to us all things that pertain to life and godliness, through the

796 The Divine Liturgy According to St. Cyril – The Prayer of Submission Addressed to the Father.

> knowledge of Him who called us by glory and virtue, by which have been given to us exceedingly great and precious promises, that through these you may be partakers of the divine nature, having escaped the corruption that is in the world through lust.[797]

And **St. Athanasius the Apostolic** says:

> **For he was incarnate that we might be made god**; and he manifested himself through a body that we might receive an idea of the invisible Father; **and he endured the insults of human beings, that we might inherit incorruptibility.** He himself was harmed in no way, being impassible and incorruptible and the very Word and God; but he held and preserved in his own impassibility the suffering human beings, on whose account he endured these things.[798]

The concept of deification which we are granted is, in its simplest explanation, the union with Christ—for He saved us—by uniting with Him through Baptism and the Eucharist, so that we might become His members, and in Him we become children of the Father, the dwelling of the Holy Spirit, and heirs of the Kingdom of Heaven. And Christ became the Head of the body, and we the members of this body; it is an ontological union, leading to our salvation.

"Now you are the body of Christ, and members individually."[799]

> But, speaking the truth in love, may grow up in all things into Him who is the head—Christ—from

---

[797] 2 Peter 1:3–4.

[798] Saint Athanasius, *On the Incarnation*, J. Behr, trans. (Yonkers, NY: SVS Press, 2011), 107.

[799] 1 Corinthians 12:27.

> whom the whole body, joined and knit together by what every joint supplies, according to the effective working by which every part does its share, causes growth of the body for the edifying of itself in love.[800]

The essence of salvation is the union with the Lord Christ. By virtue of the union between the divinity and humanity, perfect hypostatical union, One of the Trinity—with respect to His divinity—became One of us—with respect to His humanity. And because He bears our human nature in Himself, after the union, His death and His victory were accounted in favor of humankind. And He gave us the authority, by faith in Him, so that we may unite with His body and become His members. And as through our kinship with the first Adam, we inherited sin, death and corruption, so through our kinship with the new Adam, and our uniting with Him by faith and Baptism and the Eucharist, we become through Him and in Him victorious over death, and inherit in Him and through Him life.

> For if by the one man's offense death reigned through the one, much more those who receive abundance of grace and of the gift of righteousness will reign in life through the One, Jesus Christ. Therefore, as through one man's offense judgment came to all men, resulting in condemnation, even so through one Man's righteous act the free gift came to all men, resulting in justification of life. For as by one man's disobedience many were made sinners, so also by one Man's obedience many will be made righteous.[801]

[800] Ephesians 4:15–16.
[801] Romans 5:17–19.

"For since by man came death, by Man also came the resurrection of the dead. For as in Adam all die, even so in Christ all shall be made alive."[802]

"And as we have borne the image of the man of dust, we shall also bear the image of the heavenly Man."[803]

St. Athanasius the Apostolic speaks of this partaking of the divine nature using the expression that God clothed us with incorruptibility:

> **Being with all through the like [body],[804] the incorruptible Son of God** consequently clothed all with incorruptibility in the promise concerning the resurrection. And now the very corruption of death no longer holds ground against human beings because of the indwelling Word, in them through the one body.[805]

The Coptic Orthodox liturgy expresses in its prayers this great grace, with all simplicity using the expression "oneness." And this is the true meaning which the Fathers mean by the term "deification" θεοποισες.[806]

"For He who sits upon the cherubim came and was incarnate of you, and He united us with Him, through His goodness."[807]

---

[802] 1 Corinthians 15:21–22.

[803] 1 Corinthians 15:49.

[804] Arabic text adds here: "of all human beings and His uniting with them".

[805] Saint Athanasius, *On the Incarnation*, J. Behr, trans. (Yonkers, NY: SVS Press, 2011), 58.

[806] St. Athanasius the Apostolic used it in his first discourse in *Against the Arians*: "Οὐκ ἄρα ἄνθρωπος ὢν ὕστερον γέγονε Θεός· ἀλλὰ Θεὸς ὤν ὕστερον γέγονεν ἄνθρωπος, ἵνα μᾶλλον ἡμᾶς θεοποιήσῃ" Athanasius, *Against the Arians* 1.39 (PG 26.34c).

[807] Midnight Praises – Friday Theotokia, Part 2.

"He took our body and gave us His Holy Spirit, and made us one with Him, through His goodness."[808]

"He took what is ours and gave us what is His, we praise and glorify Him, and exalt Him."[809]

"For you know the grace of our Lord Jesus Christ, that though He was rich, yet for your sakes He became poor, that you through His poverty might become rich."[810]

[808] Midnight Praises – Friday Theotokia, Part 3.
[809] Midnight Praises – Friday Theotokia, Chorus.
[810] 2 Corinthians 8:9.

CHAPTER FIVE

The Results of This Study

The purpose of this research is to study the following hypotheses, to confirm whether they are completely or partially true:

- That the one catholic Church in the first centuries, in the period from Pentecost on the fiftieth day to the time before the schism of AD 451 in Chalcedon, had one specific doctrine regarding the understanding of the economy of salvation which was accomplished by the Lord Christ.
- That the first catholic Church taught that the human race had inherited Adam's Original Sin without partaking in the act.
- That the economy of salvation cannot be implemented nor understood except in light of understanding the truth of the inheritance of Adam's sin by the entire human race. "Therefore, as through one man's offense judgement came to all men, resulting in condemnation, even so through one Man's righteous act the free gift came to all men, resulting in justification of life."[811]

---

[811] Romans 5:18.

- ❖ That the Coptic Orthodox Church has kept through the ages what it has received from the first catholic Church regarding the doctrine of salvation. There is a direct and clear connection between what the first catholic Church taught and what the Coptic Church currently teaches, which has not changed through the ages.
- ❖ The new notions concerned with the doctrine of salvation which have infiltrated into the Coptic Orthodox Church from some theologians of the Byzantine Church since the middle of the past century, are considered contrary to what the Coptic Orthodox Church has received from the first catholic Church.

Therefore, the aforementioned hypotheses have been studied to arrive at their validity or invalidity, entirely or partially, for the purpose of answering the **research's principal question**, which is:

Has the Coptic Orthodox Church kept until today what it has received from the one catholic Church, from its founding on Pentecost to the time before the schism of AD 451 in Chalcedon?

The **problem we are facing** is that some are sowing doubt in the teaching of the fathers which was handed down to the Church concerning the matter of salvation, and they accuse the Church of wallowing in—of having adopted—Western theology and the theology of the Middle Ages in Europe

Therefore, research has been conducted in several domains regarding what the first catholic Church had left us, which include Biblical texts, sayings of the Fathers, liturgical texts, and canons of the local and ecumenical Councils.

This methodical research has permitted me to go deeper[812] in understanding the mind of the first catholic Church on the economy of salvation.

After going back to the original Biblical texts in the deeply-rooted Orthodox Churches and to the sayings of the Early Fathers of the catholic Church before the schism, and after examining the liturgical texts the first catholic Church left us and the canons it decreed in the local and ecumenical Councils, and with testing the hypotheses of the research and performing deductive analysis on my findings in the aforementioned domains, I have ascertained that the Coptic Orthodox Church is teaching up to the present, concerning the doctrine of salvation, what it received from the first catholic Church, which was founded on Pentecost until its schism in the Council of Chalcedon in AD 451, and that [was] concerning the doctrine of salvation.

The research results which I reached on "the economy of salvation according to the first catholic Church," through these domains, are based on two premises.

The first premise: the doctrine of the inheritance of Adam's sin is a foundational doctrine which must be accepted to understand the economy of the Lord Christ in the salvation of the human race.

The second premise: the work of the Lord Christ in the economy of salvation is multifaceted and has many results.

First, Research Results on the First Premise:

The doctrine of the inheritance of Adam's sin is a foundational doctrine for the understanding of the economy of the Lord Christ in the salvation of the human race. Understanding the

[812] Literally: to widen or broaden.

inheritance of Original Sin or Ancestral Sin is considered an essential element in understanding our justification by the Lord Christ. The doctrine of the oneness of the human race was explained at length, as an important entrance to understand our relationship with Adam, [and] then the gathering of all in Christ as being the new Adam.

Concerning Original Sin, the Fathers focused on the truth that we did not partake with Adam in the [very] act, because we were not in existence, but they employed many expressions, like: Human nature is sinful; we sinned in Adam; we became partakers of Adam's offense, and because of his sins we were punished, the curse reaching all, and wrath extending over his seed.

The Church does not teach that human beings as individuals partook with Adam in his disobedience, because they did not exist [at that time] as individuals, but all of humankind was accounted sinful in the person of Adam who sinned first.

These results [of this research] may be placed in the following categories:

Results concerning Biblical texts:

- Romans 5:12–20 makes it clear that we inherited Adam's sin, and consequently all of the human race was condemned (verse 18). It gives a comparison between our inheritance of Adam's sin as humankind and the gift [we received] by the righteousness of the Lord Christ. And Romans 5:12 cannot be understood in isolation from the remaining verses and apart from the theological thought of Paul the Apostle on why we inherited Adam's sin. The meaning that we were in Adam when he sinned is a well-known understanding of Paul the Apostle, which is made clear in his writing about Levi being in the loins of Abraham when Abraham offered tithes to Melchizedek.[813]

- There are ancient translations of Romans 5, authorized by the ancient orthodox churches, which make it clear that we inherited sin from Adam, like the Coptic translation, the old Slavonic translation, the official Bulgarian Orthodox translation of the Holy Bible, authorized version by the Bulgarian Orthodox Church, and official translation of the Synod of the Russian Church, which is taken from the original Greek "*Textus receptus.*".

Results concerning liturgical texts:

- The inheritance of Adam's sin by all of the human race is made clear in the texts of the liturgical prayers of the Divine Liturgy which were handed down from the first centuries, which believe in the doctrine of the oneness of the human race. These liturgical prayers make the priest stand and pray in the liturgies with one tongue on behalf of all of humankind, in unity in Christ. And what the priest prays in the Coptic Liturgy expresses the oneness of the human race in one person, who is Adam of old, then in the new Adam, the Lord Jesus Christ.
- The doctrine of the inheritance of sin is made clear in the Liturgy of Baptism and the Creed, where we say: "We confess one baptism for the remission of sins." Even if an infant's life is but one minute on earth, he is in need of Baptism for the remission of sins. What sins?

---

[813] See Hebrews 7:5–10.

Results concerning the sayings of the [Church] Fathers:

Many of the holy Early Fathers have mentioned the inheritance of Adam's sin. And some have called it different terms as follows, which are listed according to historical chronology:

- ❖ The scholar Origen (AD 185–254): "that in everyone was sin's innate defilement."[814]
- ❖ The martyr St. Cyprian of Carthage (AD 210–258): "an infant ... because those [sins] which are remitted are not his own sins, but the sins of another."[815]
- ❖ St. Gregory Thaumaturgus (AD 213–270)[816]
- ❖ St. Gregory the Armenian (AD 240–330): "and in liberating them from births involved in sin."[817]
- ❖ St. Pope Athanasius the Apostolic (AD 296–373): "the original sin."[818]
- ❖ St. Anthony the Great (AD 251–356): "the first transgression."[819]
- ❖ St. Basil the Great (AD 330–379): "the original sin."[820]
- ❖ St. Gregory Nazianzus (AD 329–390): "original nakedness."[821] "We ... who partake of the same Adam."[822]

---

[814] Origen, *Commentary on the Epistle to the Romans, Book 1–5*, T.P. Halton, ed.; T.P. Scheck, trans. (Washington, D.C.: The Catholic University of America Press, 2001), 366–367.
[815] Cyprian of Carthage, *Letters 1–81*, H. Dressler, ed., R. B. Donna, trans. (Washington, D.C.: The Catholic University of America Press, 1964), 219.
[816] *The writings of Gregory Thaumaturgus, Dionysius of Alexandria, and Archelaus*. In *Ante-Nicene Christian Library* 20. A. Roberts and J. Donaldson, eds. (Edinburgh: T. & T. Clark, 1871), 109.
[817] *The Teaching of Saint Gregory: An Early Armenian Catechism*. R.W. Thomson, trans. (Cambridge, MA: Harvard University Press, 1970), 74.
[818] Athanasius, Expositions on the Psalms (PG 27.241a).
[819] *The Letters of Saint Antony the Great*, Derwas J. Chitty, trans. (Oxford, UK: SLG Press, 2005), 2.
[820] *The Faith of the Early Fathers* 2, W.A. Jurgens, trans. (Collegeville, MN: The Liturgical Press, 1970–1979), 23.
[821] St Gregory of Nazianzus, *Festal Orations*, J. Behr, Ed., N. V. Harrison, Trans. (Crestwood, NY: SVS Press, 2008), 172.
[822] Gregory Nazianzen *Oration XXXIII. Against The Arians, and Concerning Himself* 9 (NPNF² 7:331).

- St. Gregory of Nyssa (AD 335–395): "all is turned to joy for us that were the heirs of sin."[823]
- St. Ambrose (AD 340–397): "In Adam I fell."[824]
- St. Didymus the Blind the Alexandrian (AD 313–398): "all who are descended from Adam contract [it] in succession."[825]
- St. John Chrysostom (AD 349–407).[826]
- St. Augustine (AD 354–430): "Therefore, 'Behold, the Lamb of God.' He is not a scion[827] stemming from Adam; he took only the flesh from Adam, he did not assume his sin. He who has not assumed the sin from our clayey mass is the one who takes away our sin."[828]
- St. Cyril the Great (AD 376–444): "We offended him long ago both because of the transgression in Adam, and after that because of our own sin that tyrannizes us."[829]
- St. Jacob of Serug (AD 451–521): "the original sin."[830]
- St. Severus of Antioch (AD 465–538): "but [God the Word is] still without the sin which had come in upon us."[831]

---

[823] Gregory of Nyssa *On the Baptism of Christ* (NPNF[2] 5:524).
[824] Ambrose *On the Belief in the Resurrection* 6 (NPNF[2] 10:175).
[825] *The Faith of the Early Fathers* 2, W.A. Jurgens, trans. (Collegeville, MN: The Liturgical Press, 1970–1979), 64.
[826] John Chrysostom *Homilies on the Epistle of St. Paul the Apostle to the Romans* 10 (NPNF[1] 11:403).
[827] That is, an heir.
[828] Augustine of Hippo, *Tractates on the Gospel of John 1–10*, J. W. Rettig, trans. (Washington, DC: The Catholic University of America Press, 1988), 101.
[829] Cyril of Alexandria, *Commentaries on Romans, 1-2 Corinthians, and Hebrews*, J.C. Elowsky, G.L. Bray, M. Glerup, and T.C. Oden, eds.; D.R. Maxwell, trans. (Downers Grove, IL: IVP Academic, 2022), 113.
[830] Jacob of Serug, *Mokhtarat Min Kasa'id Mar Yakob Oskof Sirouj* [A Selection of the Poems of Mar Jacob Bishop of Serug], Metropolitan Malatios Barnaba, trans. (Aleppo, Syria: Dar El-Raha,1993), 83–84. [Translated from Arabic text].
[831] *A Collection of Letters of Severus of Antioch, From Numerous Syriac Manuscripts*, E.W. Brooks, trans. (Paris: Firmin-Didot, 1920), 16–17.

It is clear from studying the sayings of the Early Fathers that St. Augustine was not the first to mention and talk about the inheritance of Adam's sin.

St. Augustine used the term "Original Sin" to respond to Pelagianism, and the Fathers who were his contemporaries did not object on the use of the term Original Sin, especially St. Cyril the Great who was a contemporary of St. Augustine. And there are reciprocal letters between St. Cyril the Great and St. Augustine.[832]

Results concerning the decisions of the local and ecumenical Councils in the first centuries:

Pelagius, his disciple Celestius and their followers were condemned when they denied the inheritance of Adam's sin and proclaimed the heresy that infants have no need of Baptism or that the Baptism of infants is not for the remission of sins.

The following was stated in the Second Council of Carthage in AD 418 (Canon 110):

> If any man says that new-born children need not be baptized, or that they should indeed be baptized for the remission of sins, but that they have in them no original sin inherited from Adam which must be washed away in the bath of regeneration, so that in their case the formula of baptism "for the remission of sins" must not be taken literally, but figuratively, let him be anathema; because, according to Rom. v. 12,[833] the sin of Adam has passed upon all.[834]

---

832 Augustine of Hippo, *Letters 1*–29**, T.P. Halton, ed.; R.B. Eno, trans. (Washington, DC: The Catholic University of America Press, 1989), 41–42.
833 Romans 5:12.
834 C.J. Hefele, *A History of the Councils of the Church* 2, H.N. Oxenham, trans. (Edinburgh: T&T Clark, 1896), 458.

The Council of Ephesus, held in AD 431, headed by Pope Cyril the Pillar of Faith, approved the decisions of the Council of Carthage, which was mentioned the Council's letter which was sent by the Council of Ephesus to Celestine the First, Pope of Rome, and they informed him of what took place in the Council of Ephesus.[835]

Second, Research Results on the Second Premise

The work of the Lord Christ in the economy of salvation is multifaceted and has many results.

1. The Early Fathers did not adopt one way only to explain the economy of salvation, but adopted many ways, and viewed them as being complementary and not contradictory. Here I mean specifically the legal judicial aspect with the ontological healing aspect. For the salvific works of Christ are numerous and glorious, and cannot be exhaustively investigated.

   For **St. Athanasius the Apostolic** said:

   > It was not for another to turn what was corruptible to incorruptibility except the Savior himself, who in the beginning created the universe from nothing; and that it was not for another to recreate again the 'in the image' for human beings, except the Image of the Father; and that it was not for another to raise up the mortal to be immortal, except our Lord Jesus Christ, who is Life itself; and that it was not for another to teach about the Father and destroy the worship of idols, except

[835] *The Third World Council* 2, J. Chrystal, trans. (Jersey City, NJ: James Chrystal, 1904), 177–182.

> the Word who arranges all things and is alone the true only-begotten Son of the Father."[836]

Note that St. Athanasius in his explanation of the mystery of the incarnation and redemption did not consider a single aspect sufficient to comprehend what God did for us and in us, for the sacrifice of Christ has many ramifications and facets. It is in truth "the ways of salvation," as the Coptic Liturgy of St. Basil expresses it. Therefore, the Church does not limit the cross to a single meaning, but is joyful in the multifaceted work of God for our sake, and His overflowing love which is inexpressible.

2. Faith is a mystery whose perfection cannot be comprehended, is a mystery which the human being will never finish understanding.
3. The path to understanding this economy begins at the explanation of the human being's creation out of nothing in the image of God, and this image is the only and sufficient cause for human beings to have the promise of eternal life.
4. When the first human being fell, all of humankind fell in him and sinned, and the divine image was distorted, and the human being lost the cause which gives him eternal life, and thereby began walking in the path of death and eternal perdition.

Perhaps the reader marvels at what the new theologians teach, teachings that are different from what the Church has received from the first centuries through the hands of the holy Fathers. Therefore, and with all faithfulness, I would like to pose a summary of the many inquiries surrounding these branched issues, so that they may be within reach of any seeker. It may have been, perhaps, sufficient that we

[836] Saint Athanasius, *On the Incarnation*, J. Behr, trans. (Yonkers, NY: SVS Press, 2011), 70.

pray the liturgies with understanding, thereby learning everything without going into extremes;[837] the movement of sowing doubt, however, which some have adopted made it necessary to undertake this study, to bring to light the depth of the truths of the faith that is preserved in the conscience of the Coptic Orthodox Church.

A Brief List of the Sub-questions of This Research and Their Answers

Did we inherit Adam's sin, or only its consequences, that is, death and corruption only?

We believe that we have inherited Adam's sin, and death and corruption which resulted from it, because of the oneness of the human race in Adam. We believe that all of human nature was in him when he was created, sinned and was judged with death and corruption. Therefore, the Logos came, taking our human nature, that He may be for us a new Adam, permitting those who accept Him by faith and Baptism to be re-created, and to be granted the righteousness of Christ instead of the sin of Adam, and the life of Christ instead of death that seeped into us from Adam, with the promise of eternal life and incorruptibility in the Age to Come.

What is the difference between the Eastern and Western theology, and when did the disagreement emerge? And how were the East (Constantinople) and the West (Rome) in communion together until the 11th century (AD 1054)?

The theology between the East and West: The Church was one, only, holy, catholic, apostolic until the first schism which took place in Chalcedon; then the Great Schism between

[837] "Without going into extremes" is literally "in a balanced way."

Constantinople and Rome in the eleventh century. Consequently, we cannot talk about one Eastern theology and another Western in the first centuries, except concerning the geographic origin of the [Early Church] Father and the language he wrote in; and if some instructions were found that are associated with the culture, they were viewed in a complementary manner and not contradictory or disagreeing, so no [Church] Father was judged for being Western.

Nevertheless, there is a clear example of Saint Pope Theophilus the Alexandrian, the brother of St. Cyril the Great's mother (his uncle) and his teacher also, in which he testifies to St. Ambrose and his wise stands which benefited the catholic Church. Although [the following] is not related to the subject of the research, St. Theophilus' testimony of St. Ambrose, nevertheless, confirms the existing relationship between the Fathers of the East and West:

> Knowing that our holy Fathers dealt with greater[838] difficulties than that, and became, by the wise opinion, "as without law to those who are without law,"[839] and quieted down (matters) difficult to deal with, and did not destabilize the whole body of the Church, and therefore Ambrose—the mention of whose name is sweet—had accepted those who had received the ordination from Auxentius, who was earlier in Milan.[840]

[838] Literally: more.

[839] Cf. 1 Corinthians 9:21.

[840] The writings of Pope Theophilus the Alexandrian preserved in Syriac. It was translated from Syriac and introduced by Fr. Zakka Faiz Labib, a lecturer in the theological school in Cairo, who has a certificate in Syriac Studies from Mar Ephraim the Syrian Theological College. [Translated from Arabic text].

This letter was sent by Saint Pope Theophilus the Alexandrian, the 23rd Patriarch, who was a disciple of Pope Athanasius the Apostolic, and was raised up near him and learned from him the spiritual manners. And when Pope Timothy the Great passed away, this father was selected in his place. He was a scholar, virtuous, who had committed the Church books to memory, and was well-versed in their interpretations. Pope Cyril the Great, the 24th Patriarch, testified to his orthodoxy, for he was a disciple of his, saying, "Through the grace of our Savior I always was orthodox and I was reared also by an orthodox father."[841]

This example is very powerful, for an Alexandrian pope to testify to St. Ambrose in a letter [sent] to the Patriarch of Antioch. We are before a letter from an Eastern Patriarch to an Eastern Patriarch, and the idea did not exist in the Fathers' mind that this saint is Western [or] Latin, and that his teaching is not sound or not obligatory for us [to heed]; we do not see such divisions, for what is more important than the geographic and linguistic divisions, is the soundness of the faith. The [Church] Father is accepted on the basis of his uprightness of faith and of not being excommunicated by the Church. And [the Church] does not accept any person whose teaching is not upright, whether he be from the West or East or any region or [speaking] any language; but rejecting a person for merely being in a region located in the West geographically, or because the language is Latin or any other language!—this logic is not sound.

St. Irenaeus says, confirming the unity of the faith of the Church from the beginning:

---

[841] St. Cyril of Alexandria, *Letters 1-50*, J.I. McEnerney, trans. (Washington, D.C.: The Catholic University of America Press, 1987), 132.

As I have already observed, **the Church, having received this preaching and this faith, although scattered throughout the whole world, yet, as if occupying but one house, carefully preserves it. She also believes these points [of doctrine] just as if she had but one soul, and one and the same heart, and she proclaims them, and teaches them, and hands them down, with perfect harmony, as if she possessed only one mouth. For, although the languages of the world are dissimilar, yet the import of the tradition is one and the same. For the Churches which have been planted in Germany do not believe or hand down anything different**, nor do those in Spain, nor those in Gaul, nor those in the East, nor those in Egypt, nor those in Libya, nor those which have been established in the central regions of the world. But as the sun, that creature of God, is one and the same throughout the whole world, so also the preaching of the truth shines everywhere, and enlightens all men that are willing to come to a knowledge of the truth. **Nor will any one of the rulers in the Churches, however highly gifted he may be in point of eloquence, teach doctrines different from these (for no one is greater than the Master)**; nor, on the other hand, will he who is deficient in power of expression inflict injury on the tradition. **For the faith being ever one and the same**, neither does one who is able at great length to discourse

> regarding it, make any addition to it, nor does one, who can say but little diminish it.[842]

Was death, which befell Adam and his seed, a consequence or a punishment from God? And does God really punish the wicked? And did He create Hades and Hell? Or is it merely a psychological state as a consequence of the separation from God and His glory?

We believe that death which has befallen the human race was a consequence of Adam's sin and at the same time was a punishment issued to him from the mouth of God, the Just Judge. The Lord Christ turned this punishment into salvation by His death instead of us on the holy cross.

We believe that God, generally, punishes evil people if they persist in their evil and do not repent until death. The eternal punishment will be in Hades, then the lake of fire, according to the Holy Scriptures and the teaching of the Lord Christ and the Fathers' interpretations.

Had Adam not sinned, would the only-begotten Son have been incarnate?

We believe that the incarnation of the Son the Word was for the sake of our salvation, and because of Adam's sin and the entrance of sin and death into human beings.

St. Athanasius the Apostolic says: "He gave them a law, so that if they guarded the grace and remained good, they might have the life of paradise—without sorrow, pain, or care besides having the promise of their incorruptibility in heaven."[843]

---

[842] Irenaeus *Against Heresies*. In *Ante-Nicene Fathers* 1, P. Schaff, ed. (Peabody, MA: Hendrickson Publishers, 2012), 331.

[843] Saint Athanasius, *On the Incarnation*, J. Behr, trans. (Yonkers, NY: SVS Press, 2011), 52.

Is it wrong to say, "Christ died on our behalf," and use instead, "died for our sake"? What is the difference? Is the idea that Christ died on our behalf, instead of us, and in our place, a Western idea, which is not accepted by the Fathers of the East?

The catholic Church used from the beginning the expressions "died on our behalf," "died for our sake," "instead of us", and "in our place." And these expressions have appeared in the liturgies,[844] the Creed, and the Fathers' interpretations.

What is the meaning of "the redeemer"? And "the ransom"? And the price paid off to purchase us? To whom was the price paid off? What is the debt we owed? How did the Lord Christ pay it off by His cross? What is the meaning of, "who through the eternal Spirit offered Himself without spot to God"?[845]

We do not believe that the Father punished the Son by His death on the cross—God forbid! We believe, however, that it is us who deserve the punishment, curse and death, but the only-begotten Son of God accepted of His own will and the pleasure of His Father and the Holy Spirit,[846] to suffer in place of all, and to take our curse upon Himself by the cross, and to die and bear the punishment instead of us.

The understanding of redemption, as it appeared in the Holy Scriptures and the explanation of the Fathers and liturgical texts, is "life shall be for life,"[847] and the Lord Christ is the Redeemer and the Ransom, and He bought us by His

[844] i.e. liturgical texts.
[845] Hebrews 9:14.
[846] See Morning Doxology.
[847] Deuteronomy 19:21.

precious Blood from death which reigned over us and with which our race was bound.[848]

We believe that the Lord Jesus offered Himself to God His Father through the eternal Spirit for redemption on our behalf, and He bought us by His Blood, [offered] to God His Father in that He gave Himself up to death instead of us.[849]

Has the West truly adopted the judicial theory in explaining the economy of salvation? Did the Fathers of the East not accept it? Did the word "justice" not appear at all in the writings of the Eastern Fathers, as they claim? Are the writings of the Western Fathers devoid of the healing aspect of the cross of Christ and His precious salvation?

The judicial theory in explaining the economy of salvation focuses on sin as being a crime, a moral transgression of God's commandment and a disobedience against the Most High, and deserving of a very severe punishment, that is, death. Salvation of the human being is accomplished by the death of the Redeemer instead of human beings, and the punishment is executed in this Redeemer, so that the divine justice may receive its due.

The healing theory, or the ontological, in explaining the economy of salvation focuses on sin as being a separation from God, the Source of life, so the resulting death from it is a mere natural consequence and not a punishment. In their view, sin is not an act or a trespass of God's commandments. Salvation is accomplished by uniting with God, so the human being may be restored to life, the image and eternal glory. This theory sees that the human being is in need of salvation by healing and not by punishment.

---

848 See The Divine Liturgy According to St. Basil – Agios (Holy).
849 See The Divine Liturgy According to St. Basil – The Institution Narrative.

In this study, it was made clear to me that the Fathers of the catholic Church before the schism adopted both theories in explaining the economy of salvation, without contradiction nor conflict in the concepts: for sin is a crime and disease, is a transgression and separation; and following one way or the other only in the explanation is contrived and erroneous. Therefore, salvation from sin is deserving of punishment, and the sinner is in need of healing. And this is what Christ accomplished through the cross and through the healing Sacraments of the Church.

Were all human beings crucified with Christ on Golgotha? What is the meaning of, "the death of all was completed in the lordly body?"[850,851] What is the meaning of, "I have trodden the winepress alone, and from the peoples no one was with Me?"[852]

The Fathers use the expression, "His own body," "His instrument," and "His temple," about the body of Christ which He took from the Virgin St. Mary for the sake of our salvation. This body is without spot or sin or blemish, in which He lived a blameless life, and tasted death in place of all, and defeated death by His resurrection from the dead, as a Firstborn of those who have fallen asleep, and ascended into the heavens in this His own body and sat at the right hand of His Father, as a Forerunner for our sake. And all that the Lord Jesus did in the body was for our sake and on our account, being the Firstborn, the Head, the Chief, the Leader, the Governor, the New Root, and a Substitute for human beings and their Representative before the Father.

---

[850] Arabic text reads: in the body of the Lord.

[851] Saint Athanasius, *On the Incarnation*, J. Behr, trans. (Yonkers, NY: SVS Press, 2011), 71.

[852] Isaiah 63:3.

As for human beings, they are invited to unite with Christ, by faith, Baptism and the Eucharist, so that they may receive by Him and in Him all that He did in His own body for our sake.

Did all human beings rise with Him? Did they ascend with Him, and sit with Him at the right hand of the Father? Including the unbelievers, atheists, and the evil [human beings]? Did we all ascend with Him, or did He bring our first-fruit up to heaven?

We believe that the Logos took our human nature in its entirety—body, human spirit and rational soul—and united with it through a perfect, unique and hypostatic union, without mingling, confusion, alteration, impermanence, disruption, separation, nor impossibility. And He came to have His own body and His instrument and His temple, which He used for our salvation, so in this His own body, He passed through sufferings, the cross, death, burial, resurrection, ascension, and sitting at the right hand of the Father. But being the New Firstborn for human beings and the Head who is not targeted for death, all that He worked in the body was accounted for the good of human beings: so His righteousness became ours, His sufferings became our sufferings, His death became ours, and His burial and His resurrection and His ascension and His sitting at the right hand of His Father—all these became the human beings' because Christ is the Head, Chief, Root, Substitute, Forerunner and Conqueror on our account. And we human beings are called to receive of these His treasures, by faith, Baptism, the Eucharist and abiding in Him to the last breath. So we may live His life here on earth, with the promise of eternal life and incorruptibility in the Age to Come.

In Baptism and the Eucharist we are granted by Christ the first resurrection with which we defeat the second death, and Christ will raise us up in the last day. He arose alone as the Firstborn of those who have fallen asleep, and we arise through Him and in Him in His coming.

As for the expressions, "with Christ I was crucified," "He raised us up with Him," "made us sit with Him in the heavens," and "we were buried with Him," all these expressions mean two things: what was accomplished in the body of Christ was on account of humankind, and that these gifts are granted to us in Baptism, as our teacher Paul the Apostle said:

"[You were] buried with Him in baptism, in which you also were raised with Him through faith in the working of God, who raised Him from the dead."[853]

"Therefore we were buried with Him through baptism into death, that just as Christ was raised from the dead by the glory of the Father, even so we also should walk in newness of life."[854]

"Blessed and holy is he who has part in the first resurrection. Over such the second death has no power, but they shall be priests of God and of Christ, and shall reign with Him a thousand years."[855]

What do the Fathers mean by their emphasis on the expression, "His own body, His own temple, and His instrument"?

The Fathers used the expression "His own body; His temple, and His instrument" to distinguish Christ's body, with which He accomplished redemption for us by His death on our behalf and His tasting suffering and death by means of this body, from the concept that we have all become members of His body by faith and Baptism and the Eucharist, and *not* on the day He was born from the Virgin, nor on the day of His death on the cross,

---

853 Colossians 2:12.

854 Romans 6:4.

855 Revelations 20:6.

nor His resurrection as a Firstborn of those who have fallen asleep, nor His sitting alone on the right hand of His Father.

What does "our unity in Christ" mean? Do we become God? Or gods exactly like Him? Or we become deified? Or what?

The deification of the human being, according to the thought of the Early Fathers, means the restoration of the divine image in the human being, through uniting with Christ and the receiving of eternal life in Him and eternal glory and incorruptibility which He grants us by His grace. Christ remains the only Son of God, and we sons of God by the grace of adoption because of faith and Baptism. And He, alone with the Father and the Holy Spirit, has immortality in Himself; we, however, are created by His grace, and we live forever as a gift from Him. He alone is everlasting, [but] we have a beginning and by His grace we will live forever. And the glory we will be granted in eternity is not the glory of Divinity which created natures cannot endure, but the glory which Christ received from the Father in His humanity through the resurrection from the dead. "And the glory which You gave Me I have given them, that they may be one just as We are one."[856]

What is meant by "gathering all in Christ"?

Gathering all in Christ is the fulfillment of the principle of the oneness of the human race, that principle which was not fulfilled in Adam because of disobedience, death and corruption. Christ fulfilled it for us because of His righteousness, His redemption and His resurrection. And He called human beings to unite with Him by faith, Baptism, the Eucharist and continual repentance, that we may be in Him and with Him and may receive by this the adoption by God the

[856] John 17:22.

Father and the indwelling of the Holy Spirit in us, and eternal life in Christ.

What is the value of the Old Testament sacrifices? Do they have a connection with the sacrifice of the Master Christ on the cross?

The Old Testament sacrifices were commanded by God as symbols and preludes for the perfect sacrifice of the Lord Christ on the cross for the salvation of human beings. Of old, some of them were offered for sins committed in ignorance, and others for premeditated sins; some [were offered] for personal sins, others for the sins of all the holy congregation. All [of these] were a symbol for the sacrifice of Christ on the cross.

What does "and without shedding of blood there is no remission"[857] mean? Why shedding of blood? And why death, to begin with, as a means for forgiveness?

It was said that "and without shedding of blood there is no remission," because the shedding of blood carries the meaning of redemption, because "the wages of sin is death."[858] And had Christ died a natural death without shedding of blood, His death would have been His own and would have had no salvific nor redemptive aspect.

How do we understand the salvific works of Christ?

- ❖ In understanding what Christ did for us, it is important that we know that:
    - Salvation is the work of the entire Trinity, for the Father saves us, by the Son, in the Holy Spirit.
    - The incarnation, cross and resurrection were for us human beings and for our salvation.

---

[857] Hebrews 9:22

[858] Romans 6:23.

- The salvific works of Christ cannot be separated, for the incarnation is connected to the cross, and the resurrection, and the ascension, and the sitting down at the right hand of the Father, and the sending of the Holy Spirit the Comforter, and the Sacraments, which are Baptism, Myron, the Eucharist, and repentance and confession, that convey to us the ramifications of salvation.
- Our great salvation revealed to us—and we tasted in it—the love of the Father and the grace of the only-begotten Son and the communion of the Holy Spirit.

❖ Knowing that the Church now enjoys the forgiveness of sins as the most important blessing of the blessings of the incarnation and redemption; as to receiving life and incorruptibility, they are now a pledge, but they will be in truth in the blissful eternity.

- "For as in Adam all die, even so in Christ all shall be made alive. But each one in his own order: Christ the firstfruits, afterword those who are Christ's at His coming."[859]
- "So also is the resurrection of the dead. The body is sown in corruption, it is raised in incorruption."[860]
- "Now this I say, brethren, that flesh and blood cannot inherit the kingdom of God; nor does corruption inherit incorruption."[861]
- "In a moment, in the twinkling of an eye, at the last trumpet. For the trumpet will sound, and the dead will be raised incorruptible, and we shall be changed. For this corruptible must put on incorruption, and this mortal must put on immortality. So when this

[859] 1 Corinthians 15:22–23.
[860] 1 Corinthians 15:42.
[861] 1 Corinthians 15:50.

corruptible has put on incorruption, and this mortal has put on immortality, then shall be brought to pass the saying that is written: 'Death is swallowed up in victory.'"[862]

- "Blessed and holy is he who has part in the first resurrection. Over such the second death has no power, but they shall be priests of God and of Christ, and shall reign with Him a thousand years."[863]

❖ The first resurrection is Baptism and repentance; as to the second resurrection, it is the promise we were promised in Christ Jesus our Lord, which is the resurrection of the body and incorruptibility.
"And this is the promise that He has promised us—eternal life."[864]

❖ This promise the Lord Jesus declared repeatedly in John Chapter six "I will raise him up at the last day."

- "This is the will of the Father who sent Me, that of all He has given Me I should lose nothing, but should raise it up at the last day. And this is the will of Him who sent Me, that everyone who sees the Son and believes in Him may have eternal life; and I will raise him up at the last day."[865]
- "No one can come to Me unless the Father who sent Me draws him; and I will raise him up at the last day."[866]
- "Whoever eats My flesh and drinks My blood has eternal life, and I will raise him up at the last day."[867]

---

[862] 1 Corinthians 15:52–54.
[863] Revelation 20:6.
[864] 1 John 2:25.
[865] John 6:39–40.
[866] John 6:44.
[867] John 6:54.

- ❖ It is a calling to reconciliation around Christ, in whom God reconciled the world to Himself and put in us the service of reconciliation.

CHAPTER SIX
Recommendations

Rejecting Heresies and Radical Exaggerations

Accepting all opinions that are complementary and true, excluding, of course, what the Church has rejected since the beginning of heretical opinions which are not befitting of the Person and work of our Lord Jesus Christ, or [what the Church has rejected] of exaggerated opinions.

1. An example is that which depicted the Father as an angry cruel God who needs to be pacified, and He stands watching, taking delight in His Son's punishment, and that the Son became incarnate to please Him.

   It is as though the matter of the incarnation and salvation is to resolve a problem in God Himself, yet the Church declares in the Creed: "Who for us men and for our salvation came down from heaven, was incarnate of the Holy Spirit and of the Virgin Mary, and became man..." For this [aforementioned] deviant explanation separates between the Father and the Son, depicting the Father as a cruel wrathful God, and the Son as a gentle and good God. This ruins our understanding of the equality of the Son and the Father in everything, in essence, will and work, and it ignores the Father's love for the human being, and it overlooks the role of the Holy Spirit as a Hypostasis who is of the same one essence with the Father and the Son, ignoring His role in the salvific economy.

For the wrath of God which is revealed from heaven against all ungodliness and unrighteousness of men,[868] according to St. Paul's expression, is the wrath of the Holy Trinity, and not the wrath of the Father only. And God's remission of humankind by the salvific sacrifice of Christ is a work of the Trinity also, and not the work of the Son only. The work of salvation concerns us human beings, and there is no problem with God which Christ came to resolve it.

It is for certain that God forgives us for free, for He does not ask for any recompense. But the only-begotten Son of His own will, and the pleasure of His Father and the Holy Spirit, "as a ransom on our behalf, gave Himself up unto death, which reigned over us, whereby we were bound and sold on account of our sins."[869]

2. The Church also rejects the opinions which imagine a conflict between justice and mercy in the Trinity, as though God has gotten Himself into a predicament, which obliged and forced Him to become incarnate and to die to resolve this conflict. Our fathers have taught that the justice of God is merciful, and the mercy of God is just. (Pope Shenouda III).
3. The Church rejects the idea of paying ransom to the devil, so that he may set us free.[870]

---

[868] "For the wrath of God is revealed from heaven against all ungodliness and unrighteousness of men, who suppress the truth in unrighteousness" (Romans 1:18).

[869] The Divine Liturgy According to St. Basil – Agios (Holy).

[870] The Lord Christ offered Himself as a sacrifice to God His Father on behalf of human beings: "How much more shall the blood of Christ, who through the eternal Spirit **offered Himself without spot to God**, cleanse your conscience from dead works to serve the living God?" (Hebrews 9:14).

St. Gregory Nazianzus says:

> To Whom was that Blood offered that was shed for us, and why was It shed? I mean the precious and famous Blood of our God and High priest and Sacrifice. We were detained in bondage by the Evil One, sold under sin, and receiving pleasure in exchange for wickedness. Now, since a ransom belongs only to him who holds in bondage, I ask to whom was this offered, and for what cause? If to the Evil One, fie upon the outrage! If the robber receives ransom, not only from God, but a ransom which consists of God Himself.[871]

"How does God pay the price to the devil, the indebted? How does the one who is indebted take the debts? So, it is impossible for the indebted devil to take the price. What will the devil benefit from his taking the blood of Christ?" (Pope Shenouda III).

4. Likewise, [the Church rejects] the opinions which limited the accomplishment of salvation to the action of the Son only.
5. And the opinions which limited the work of salvation to the cross only, ignoring the other salvific works of Christ, namely, the incarnation, the teaching, the healing, the resurrection, the ascension, the sending of the Holy Spirit,

---

"And walk in love, as Christ also has loved us and given Himself for us, an offering and a sacrifice to God for a sweet-smelling aroma" (Ephesians 5:2). "For **He offers Himself a sacrifice to His Father**, and surely not for His own sake according to the upright teaching, but for our sake, we who were under the yoke and weight of sin" (Cyril the Great, *Al-Sojoud Wa Al-Ibada Bi-Al Rouh Wa Al-Hak* [Worshipping and Serving in Spirit and in Truth], G.A. Ibrahim, trans. (Egypt: The Orthodox Center for Patristic Studies, 2017), 420. [Translated from Arabic text]).

[871] Gregory Nazianzen *Oration XLV. The Second Oration on Easter* 22 (NPNF[2] 7:431).

the work of the Holy Spirit in the Church, in addition to the glorious cross, of course.

6. The Church rejects the interpretations which annul the understanding of the inheritance of Adam's sin, like the understanding adopted of old by Pelagius and his disciple Celestius in the fifth century AD, which is revived recently by some who are Greek like John Romanides and others. And we consider the Church's accepting the Baptism of newborn infants a very powerful testimony of the Church's belief in the inheritance of Original Sin, in addition to the proofs which I have provided in this study.
7. Owing to there being extreme deviations in Fr. John Romanides' understanding of the inheritance of Ancestral Sin, far removed from the right orthodox Patristic and Biblical teaching, we predict, therefore, that there may be other deviations in the teaching and writings of Fr. John Romanides, especially in other important doctrines like the doctrine of redemption on the cross and the doctrine of Holy Baptism, and others. Therefore, further research should be done to study the thoughts and teachings of Fr. John Romanides on other doctrines, to put an end to the infiltration of these deviations and new heresies into our Coptic Church and the remaining orthodox churches.
8. In all this, the truths of the faith must be viewed as being higher than the academic scientific research whose scope is narrow. The truths of the faith, however, are seen with the broad eye of the spirit, through the understanding of the Fathers. Scientific research begins from doubt in any theory, in the manner of Thomas the Apostle [who said], "Unless I see ... and put my finger ..." The truth of the faith, however, is shining like the sun, needing no evidence nor examination; therefore, the purpose of the academic theological studies is evangelical and apologetic, and to confirm what has been settled upon in the holy Church, and

is not to make a new discovery nor theological addition no one has reached before us. We must keep the course of academic scientific research within its [proper] weight and place with regards to theological studies.

9. From a positive constructive point, I recommend the following:
    a. Dealing with theological issues rather than disputing in conferences for youth and servants.
    b. Releasing brief publications to explain the upright faith, to deal with the complicated ideological and theological issues.
    c. Prompting those in charge of producing curricula for Church education, for the different age groups, to include in the curricula the sound concepts of the faith.
    d. Inaugurating an official Facebook page for the Coptic Church, specific for responding to the stirred faith-related issues, [managed] by specialized fathers of the Church.
    e. Producing a directory of the faith, which explains all the details of the faith of the Coptic Orthodox Church, for reference to face those in opposition, so that it may be a guide for whoever desires to know the faith of the Church, on [the condition] that the Holy Synod adopts releasing this directory, so as not to be biased to the thought of individuals or groups, rather, so as to express the immovable[872] faith of the Church.

[872] Or: stable.

Bibliography

A Collection of Letters of Severus of Antioch, From Numerous Syriac Manuscripts, E.W. Brooks, trans. (Paris: Firmin-Didot, 1920).

Al-Kitab Al-Mukadas, Al-Ahd Al-Jadeed, Tarjamah Mutraniat Baghdad Wa Al-Kuwait Wa Tawabi'aha Lil-Roum Al-Orthodox [The Holy Bible: New Testament, Translation of the Roman Orthodox Diocese of Baghdad, Kuwait and its Affiliates]. (Baghdad: Roman Orthodox Diocese of Baghdad, Kuwait and its Affiliates, 2006).

Al-Kitab Al-Mukadas, Al-Tarjamah Al-Yaso'iah, Tarjamah Al-Rahbaniah Al-Yaso'iah [Holy Bible: Jesuit Translation. Translation of the Jesuit Monasticism]. (Beirut, Lebanon: House of the Holy Bible in the Middle East, 1992).

Al-Kitab Al-Mukadas, Al-Tarjamah Al-Yaso'iah, Tarjamah Al-Rahbaniah Al-Yaso'iah [Holy Bible: Jesuit Translation. Translation of the Jesuit Monasticism]. (Beirut, Lebanon: Dar El-Mashrik, 1994).

Ambrose *On the Belief in the Resurrection*. In *Nicene and Post-Nicene Fathers: Second Series* 10, P. Schaff, ed. (Peabody, MA: Hendrickson Publishers, 2012).

Ambrose, St., *On the Mysteries and the Treatise on the Sacraments by an Unknown Author*, T. Thompson, trans. (New York, NY: The Macmillan Company, 1919).

"Analysis of Peshitta," *Dukhrana*, http://dukhrana.com/peshitta/analyze_verse.php?verse=romans%205%3A12&-font=Estrangelo%20Edessa&fbclid=IwAR1blkm_A3gslQUC7qTOEPg-T_uUym3_3UZagoAJsAf5f_JIhDBmM2n_QII. Last accessed on 7 April 2023.

A Patristic Greek Lexicon, G.W.H. Lampe, ed. (Oxford, ENG: At The Clarendon Press, 1961).

A Pocket Lexicon to the Greek New Testament, A. Souter. (Oxford, ENG: Clarendon Press, 1917).

Archbishop Eleutherius, *On Redemption*, Paris, 1937 p. 47 (in Russian) (retrieved from Moss, Against Romanides, 39–40).

Archbishop Theophan, "The Patristic Teaching on Original Sin," *Russkoe Pravoslavie*, № 3.20 (2000).

Athanasius, *Against the Arians*. In *Patrologia graeca* 26.34c, J.-P. Migne, ed. (Paris, 1857–1886).

Athanasius *Defense of the Nicene Definition*. In *Nicene and Post-Nicene Fathers: Second Series* 4, P. Schaff, ed. (Peabody, MA: Hendrickson Publishers, 2012).

Athanasius, *Expositions on the Psalms*. In *Patrologia graeca* 27.241a, J.-P. Migne, ed. (Paris, 1857–1886).

Athanasius *Four Discourses Against the Arians*. In *Nicene and Post-Nicene Fathers: Second Series* 4, P. Schaff, ed. (Peabody, MA: Hendrickson Publishers, 2012).

Athanasius of Alexandria, *Athanasius: The Life of Antony and the Letter to Marcellinus*, R.C. Gregg, trans. (Mahwah, NJ: Paulist Press, 1980).

Athanasius, *On the Incarnation*. In *Patrologia graeca* 25.132a, J.-P. Migne, ed. (Paris, 1857–1886).

Athanasius, Saint, *On the Incarnation*, J. Behr, trans. (Yonkers, NY: SVS Press, 2011).

Athanasius of St. Macarius, Fr., *Al-Agpeya Ai Salawat Al-Sawa'i* [The Agpeya, That is, the Prayers of the Hours]. (Shobra, Egypt: Dar Nobar Press, 2006).

Athanasius the Apostolic, *Al-Rasa'il Aan Al-Rouh Al-Kudos* [Letters on the Holy Spirit], M. Tawadros and N. Abdel Shaheed, trans. (Egypt: The Orthodox Center for Patristic Studies, 2018).

Athanasius the Apostolic, Saint, *Izzah Hawl Alam Al-Rab Wa Salibaho* [A Homily on the Lord's Suffering and His Cross], S.H. Jacob, trans. (Egypt: The Orthodox Center for Patristic Studies, 2019).

Athanasius the Apostolic, Saint, *Tafseer Sifr Al-Mazameer Al-Joz' Al-Thalith* [Exegesis on the Book of Psalms Vol. 3], G.M. Andrawis, trans. (Egypt: St. Anthony Press–The Orthodox Center for Patristic Studies in Cairo, 2021).

Athanasius the Great and Didymus the Blind, *Works on the Spirit*, DelCogliano, A. Radde-Gallwitz, and L. Ayres, trans. (Yonkers, NY: SVS Press, 2011).

Augustine, Saint, *Against Julian*, M.A. Schumacher, trans. (New York, NY: Fathers of the Church Inc., 1957).

Augustine, *Against Two Letters of the Pelagians*. In *Nicene and Post-Nicene Fathers: First Series* 10, P. Schaff, ed. (Peabody, MA: Hendrickson Publishers, 2012).

Augustine of Hippo, *Four Anti-Pelagian Writings*, T.P. Halton, ed.; J.A. Mourant and W.J. Collinge, trans. (Washington, DC: The Catholic University of America Press, 1992).

Augustine of Hippo, *Letters 1*–29**, T.P. Halton, ed.; R.B. Eno, trans. (Washington, DC: The Catholic University of America Press, 1989).

Augustine of Hippo, *Tractates on the Gospel of John 1–10*, J.W. Rettig, trans. (Washington, DC: The Catholic University of America Press, 1988).

Basil, *Homilia dicta tempore famis et siccitatis*. In *Patrologia graeca* 31.324c, J.-P. Migne, ed. (Paris, 1857–1886).

Basil of Caesarea, *On Social Justice*, C.P. Schroeder, trans. (New York: SVS Press, 2009).

Basil the Great, Saint, *On the Human Condition*, J. Behr and A. Casiday, eds.; N.V. Harrison, trans. (Yonkers, NY: SVS Press, 2005).

Basil, St., quoted in Demetrios Tzami, *I Protologia tou M. Vasileiou, Thessaloniki*, 1970, p. 135 (retrieved from Moss, Against Romanides, 29).

Bibawy, G.H., *Mawt Al-Maseeh Ala Al-Saleeb* [The Death of Christ on the Cross]. (Egypt: Center of Coptic and Orthodox Studies, 2006).

"Bible translations into Bulgarian," *Wikipedia*, 20 June 2022, https://en.wikipedia.org/wiki/Bible_translations_into_Bulgarian.

Bishop Bulus Al-Bushi, Homilies on the Divine Feasts, A Homily on the Life-giving Annunciation. Articles of Abba Bulus Al-Bushi, Bishop of Egypt, of the thirteenth century scholars are introduced with revision and classification by Priest Mankarius Awad-Allah, pp. 9–10.

Bishop Epiphanius, Bishop and Abbot of St. Macarius Monastery, *Kholaji Al-Der Al-Abiad Tarjama An Al-Kobtia Wa Dirasa* [Liturgy Book of the White Monastery Translated from Coptic, with a Study]. (Egypt: School of Alexandria, 2014).

Bishop Gregorius, *Mawsouat Al-Lahout Al-Akeadi – Sirai Al-Tajasod Wa Al-Fidah Al-Joz' Althani* [Encyclopedia of Doctrinal Theology 7: The Mysteries of Incarnation and Redemption Part 2]. (Egypt: *Maktabat Al-Motana'ih Anba Gregorius* [The Library of the Late Abba Gregorius], 2004).

Brannan, R., *The Lexham Analytical Lexicon to the Greek New Testament.* (Logos Bible Software, Lexham Press, 2011).

Briere, M., *Les Homiliae Cathedrales de Severe d'Antioche: Homelies LXX a LXXVI.* (Paris: Firmin-Didot, 1915).

"Bulgarian Orthodox Bible (BOB)," *Bible Gateway*, 2016, https://www.biblegateway.com/passage/?search=romans+5%3A12&version=BOB.

Cabasilas, N., *The Life in Christ.* (Crestwood, NY: SVS Press, 1974).

The Canons of the Two Hundred Holy and Blessed Fathers Who Met at Ephesus. In *Nicene and Post-Nicene Fathers: Second Series* 14, P. Schaff, ed. (Peabody, MA: Hendrickson Publishers, 2012).

Clement of Alexandria, *Christ the Educator*, P.S. Wood, trans. (Washington, DC: The Catholic University of America Press, 1954).

Cyprian of Carthage, *Letters 1–81*, H. Dressler, ed.; R.B. Donna, trans. (Washington, D.C.: The Catholic University of America Press, 1964).

"Cyril and Methodius," *Wikipedia*, 29 March 2023, https://en.wikipedia.org/wiki/Cyril_and_Methodius.

Cyril of Alexandria, *A Commentary upon the Gospel According to S. Luke* 1, R.P. Smith, trans. (Oxford, ENG: Oxford Press, 1859).

Cyril of Alexandria, *A Commentary upon the Gospel According to S. Luke* 2, R.P. Smith, trans. (Oxford, ENG: At the University Press, 1859).

Cyril of Alexandria, *Commentary of Isaiah.* In *Patrologia graeca* 71.12A, J.-P. Migne, ed. (Paris, 1857–1886).

Cyril of Alexandria, *Commentary on Isaiah* 1, R.C. Hill, trans. (Brookline, MA: Holy Cross Orthodox Press, 2008).

Cyril of Alexandria, *Commentary on Romans.* In *Patrologia graeca* 74, J.-P. Migne, ed. (Paris, 1857–1886).

Cyril of Alexandria, *Commentaries on Romans, 1-2 Corinthians, and Hebrews*, J.C. Elowsky, G.L. Bray, M. Glerup, and T.C. Oden, eds.; D.R. Maxwell, trans. (Downers Grove, IL: IVP Academic, 2022).

Cyril of Alexandria, *Commentary on John* 1, J.C. Elowsky, T.C. Oden, and G.L. Bray, eds.; D.R. Maxwell, trans. (Downers Grove, IL: IVP Academic, 2015).

Cyril of Alexandria, *Commentary on John* 2, J.C. Elowsky, T.C. Oden, and G.L. Bray, eds.; D.R. Maxwell, trans. (Downers Grove, IL: IVP Academic, 2015).

Cyril of Alexandria, *Commentary on the Gospel according to S. John* 1. (Oxford, ENG: J. Parker, 1874).

Cyril of Alexandria, *Commentary on the Gospel according to S. John* 2. (London, ENG: Walter Smith, 1885).

Cyril of Alexandria, *Five Tomes Against Nestorius; Scholia on the Incarnation; Christ Is One; Fragments Against Diodore of Tarsus, Theodore of Mopsuestia, the Synousiasts.* (Oxford, ENG: James Parker and Co., 1881).

Cyril of Alexandria, St., *Letters 1-50*, J.I. McEnerney, trans. (Washington, D.C.: The Catholic University of America Press, 1987).

Cyril of Alexandria, St., *Letters 51–110*, J.I. McEnerney, trans. (Washington, D.C.: The Catholic University of America Press, 1987).

Cyril the Great, *Al-Sojoud Wa Al-Ibada Bi-Al Rouh Wa Al-Hak* [Worshipping and Serving in Spirit and in Truth], G.A. Ibrahim, trans. (Egypt: The Orthodox Center for Patristic Studies, 2017).

Dratsellas, C., *Questions of the Soteriological Teaching of the Greek Fathers: with Special Reference to St. Cyril of Alexandria.* (Athens: Journal θεολογια, 1969).

Eskander, I.M., *Tadbeer Mil' Al-Azminah* [The Economy of the Fullness of Times]. (Egypt: Panarion Press, 2019).

The Faith of the Early Fathers 2, W.A. Jurgens, trans. (Collegeville, MN: The Liturgical Press, 1970–1979).

Gregory of Nazianzus, St., *Festal Orations*, J. Behr, ed., N.V. Harrison, Trans. (Crestwood, NY: SVS Press, 2008).

Gregory Nazianzen *Oration XXXIII. Against The Arians, and Concerning Himself.* In *Nicene and Post-Nicene Fathers: Second Series* 7, P. Schaff, ed. (Peabody, MA: Hendrickson Publishers, 2012).

Gregory Nazianzen *Oration XLV. The Second Oration on Easter*. In *Nicene and Post-Nicene Fathers: Second Series* 7, P. Schaff, ed. (Peabody, MA: Hendrickson Publishers, 2012).

Gregory Nazianzus, Oratio XLV. *In sanctum pascha.* In *Patrologia graeca* 36.640c, J.-P. Migne, ed. (Paris, 1857–1886).

Gregory Nazianzus, *Select Orations*, T.P. Halton, ed.; M. Vinson, trans. (Washington, D.C.: The Catholic University of America Press, 2003).

Gregory of Nyssa *On the Baptism of Christ.* In *Nicene and Post-Nicene Fathers: Second Series* 5, P. Schaff, ed. (Peabody, MA: Hendrickson Publishers, 2012).

Gregory of Nyssa *On the Making of Man.* In *Nicene and Post-Nicene Fathers: Second Series* 5, P. Schaff, ed. (Peabody, MA: Hendrickson Publishers, 2012).

Gregory of Nyssa, *St. Gregory of Nyssa: The Lord's Prayer, The Beatitudes*, J. Quasten and J.C. Plumpe, eds.; H.C. Graef, trans. (Paulist Press, 1954).

Gregory of Nyssa, *The Life of Moses*, R.J. Payne, ed.; A.J. Malherbe and E. Ferguson, trans. (Mahwah, NJ: Paulist Press, 1978).

Hefele, C.J., *A History of the Councils of the Church* 2, H.N. Oxenham, trans. (Edinburgh: T&T Clark, 38 George Street, 1896).

Hefele, C.J., *A History of the Councils of the Church* 3. (Edinburgh: T&T Clark, 38 George Street, 1883).

Hilary of Poitiers *Book X*. In *Nicene and Post-Nicene Fathers: Second Series* 9, P. Schaff, ed. (Peabody, MA: Hendrickson Publishers, 2012).

"History of Eastern Orthodox Theology in the 20th Century," https://en.wikipedia.org/wiki/History_of_Eastern_Orthodox_theology_in_the_20th_century. Accessed in June 2022.

Horujy, S.S., "The Concept of Neopatristic Synthesis at a New Stage," *Russian Studies in Philosophy*, 57.1 (2019).

Irenaeus *Against Heresies*. In *Ante-Nicene Fathers* 1, P. Schaff, ed. (Peabody, MA: Hendrickson Publishers, 2012).

Jacob of Serug, *Mokhtarat Min Kasa'id Mar Yakob Oskof Sirouj* [A Selection of the Poems of Mar Jacob Bishop of Serug], Metropolitan Malatios Barnaba, trans. (Aleppo, Syria: Dar El-Raha,1993).

Jacobs, A., *Original Sin: A Cultural History*. (New York, NY: HarperOne, 2008).

John Chrysostom, Saint, *Homilies on Genesis 18-45*, R.C. Hill, trans. (Washington, D.C.: The Catholic Church of America Press, 1990).

John Chrysostom *Homilies on St. John*. In *Nicene and Post-Nicene Fathers: First Series* 14, P. Schaff, ed. (Peabody, MA: Hendrickson Publishers, 2012).

John Chrysostom *Homilies on the Epistle of St. Paul the Apostle to the Romans*. In *Nicene and Post-Nicene Fathers: First Series* 11, P. Schaff, ed. (Peabody, MA: Hendrickson Publishers, 2012).

Letter of the Synod to Pope Celestine. In *Nicene and Post-Nicene Fathers: Second Series* 14, P. Schaff, ed. (Peabody, MA: Hendrickson Publishers, 2012).

The Letters of Saint Antony the Great, Derwas J. Chitty, trans. (Oxford, UK: SLG Press, 2005).

Malaty, T., *On the Book of Psalms, A Patristic Commentary*. (Alexandria, Egypt: St. George Coptic Orthodox Church Sporting, 1991).

Mathetes *The Epistle to Diognetus*. In *Ante-Nicene Fathers* 1, P. Schaff, ed. (Peabody, MA: Hendrickson Publishers, 2012).

McCallum, N., "Original Sin and Ephesus: Carthage's Influence on the East." *Orthodox West Blog*, 4 Jan. 2019, https://journal.orthodoxwestblogs.com/2019/01/04/original-sin-and-ephesus-carthages-influence-on-the-east/.

Moss, V., *Against Romanides: A Critical Examination of the Theology of Fr. John Romanides*. (E-book: Vladimir Moss, 2018). (Retrieved in June 2022 from https://www.orthodoxchristianbooks.com/downloads/718_AGAINST_ROMANIDES.pdf).

Moss, V., "The Greek Neo-Soteriology," *Orthodox Christian Books*, 2011, https://www.orthodoxchristianbooks.com/articles/804/-new-soteriology/ The Greek Neo-Soteriologists.

Origen, *Commentary on the Epistle to the Romans, Book 1–5*, T.P. Halton, ed.; T.P. Scheck, trans. (Washington, D.C.: The Catholic University of America Press, 2001).

Origen, *Commentary on the Epistle to the Romans, Book 6–10*, T.P. Halton, ed.; T. P. Scheck, trans. (Washington, D.C.: The Catholic University of America Press, 2002).

Origen, *Homilies of Leviticus 1–16*, G.W. Barkley, trans. (Washington, D.C.: The Catholic University of America Press, 1990).

Origen, *Homilies of Luke and Fragments on Luke*, T.P. Halton, ed.; J.T. Lienhard, trans. (Washington, D.C.: The Catholic University of America Press, 2009).

"Orthodox Church History," *Las Vegas Orthodox*, 30 Dec. 2016, https://lasvegasorthodox.com/orthodox-library/orthodox-church-history/.

Palamas, G., *The Homilies of Saint Gregory Palamas* 1, C. Veniamin, ed. (South Canaan, PA: Saint Tikhon's Seminary Press, 2002).

Proclus of Constantinople and the Cult of the Virgin in Late Antiquity: Homilies 1-5, Texts and Translations, N. Constas, trans. (Boston, MA: Brill Publishers, 2003).

Pseudo-Macarius: The Fifty Homilies and the Great Letter, G.A. Maloney, trans. (Mahwah, NJ: Paulist Press, 1992).

Romanides, in Metropolitan Hierotheos (Vlachos), *Empeiriki Dogmatiki tis Orthodoxou Katholikis Ekklesias kata tis Proforikes Paradoseis tou p. Ioannou Romanidi* 2 [The Empirical Theology of the Orthodox Catholic Church according to the Oral Traditions of Fr. John Romanides Vol. 2]. (Levadeia: Monastery of the Nativity of the Theotokos, 2011).

Romanides, *The Ancestral Sin*. (Ridgewood, NJ: Zephyr, 2002).

Romanides, "The Ecclesiology of St. Ignatius of Antioch." (Atlanta, 1956).

"Russian Synodal Version," *Bible Gateway*, https://www.biblegateway.com/versions/Russian-Synodal-Version-RUSV/. Last accessed on July 2022.

Septuagint with Morphology. (Stuttgart: Deutsche Bibelgesellschaft, 1979). https://www.academic-bible.com/en/online-bibles/septuagint-lxx/.

Severus of Antioch, Saint, *Mariam Walidat Al-Illah Izzatan Lil-Kidees Sawaros Al-Antaki* [Two Homilies on Mary the Mother of God by Saint Severus of Antioch], Monk-Priest George of St. Anthony Monastery and the late Joseph Habib, trans. (Egypt: School of Alexandria, 2018).

Severus of Antioch, *Serat Wa Makalat Al-Kidees Sawirus Al-Antaki* [The Biography and Treatises of St. Severus of Antioch], Joseph Habib, trans. (Egypt: Baramous Monastery, 2017).

Sophocles, E.A., *Greek Lexicon of the Roman and Byzantine Periods (From B. C. 146 to A. D. 1100)*. (New York, NY: Charles Scribner's Sons, 1900).

The Sunday Sermons of the Great Fathers 2, M.F. Toal, trans. (Chicago: Henry Regnery Company, 1964).

St. Symeon, *Homily* 37, 3 (retrieved from Moss, Against Romanides, 25).

Syriac New Testament, Syriac-Arabic Interlinear Translation, Center for Oriental Studies and Researches, University of Münster, Germany, Antonian University, 2010.

Taft, R., *The Liturgy of the Hours in East and West*. (Collegeville, MN: Liturgical Press, 1985).

Tawadros, M., *Al-Khatiah Al-Asliah Wa Al-Khata'iah Al-Fih'liah* [Original Sin and Actually-Committed Sins]. (Egypt: St. John the Beloved Press, 1994).

The Teaching of Saint Gregory: An Early Armenian Catechism. R.W. Thomson, trans. (Cambridge, MA: Harvard University Press, 1970).

Thayer, J.H., *Greek-English Lexicon of the New Testament*. (Edinburgh: T. and T. Clark, 1901).

The Third World Council 1, J. Chrystal, trans. (Jersey City, NJ: James Chrystal, 1895).

The Third World Council 2, J. Chrystal, trans. (Jersey City, NJ: James Chrystal, 1904).

Velimirovich, *Missionary Letters of Saint Nikolai Velimirovich* 2, Milorad Loncar, ed. (Grayslake, IL: New Gracanica Monastery, 2009).

Wolf, D., "Unknown Athonite Monk: 'Concerning Noetic Prayer, Prayer of the Heart, and Watchful Prayer,'" *First Thoughts of God*, 16 Jan. 2017, https://firstthoughtsofgod.com/2017/01/16/unknown-athonite-monk-concerning-noetic-prayer-prayer-of-the-heart-and-watchful-prayer/.

The writings of Gregory Thaumaturgus, Dionysius of Alexandria, and Archelaus. In *Ante-Nicene Christian Library* 20. A. Roberts and J. Donaldson, eds. (Edinburgh: T. & T. Clark, 1871).

The writings of Pope Theophilus the Alexandrian preserved in Syriac. It was translated from Syriac and introduced by Fr. Zakka Faiz Labib, a lecturer in the theological school in Cairo, who has a certificate in Syriac Studies from Mar Ephraim the Syrian Theological College. [Translated from Arabic text].

www.ingramcontent.com/pod-product-compliance
Lightning Source LLC
LaVergne TN
LVHW091032080826
845145LV00002B/459

* 9 7 8 1 9 3 9 9 7 2 7 3 6 *